Wyndham Lewis: A Revaluation

Wyndham Lewis: A Revaluation

NEW ESSAYS

edited by

JEFFREY MEYERS

McGill–Queen's University Press
Montreal

Published in Great Britain by
The Athlone Press

Published simultaneously in Canada by
McGill–Queen's University Press
1020 Pine Avenue West
Montreal, Quebec
H3A 1A2

© Athlone Press 1980

ISBN 0–7735–0516–4

Legal deposit 2nd quarter 1980
Bibliothèque Nationale du Québec

Printed in Great Britain

For Rachel

Contents

Introduction

Though T. S. Eliot called Wyndham Lewis 'the most fascinating personality of our time' and 'the only one among my contemporaries to create a new, an original, prose style', Lewis is surely the most neglected and underrated major author of this century. The recent appearance, however, of Lewis's *Unlucky for Pringle*, *The Roaring Queen*, *Enemy Salvoes*, *Mrs. Dukes' Million*, the reissue of *The Revenge for Love*, the three critical studies and two bibliographies, the impressive exhibition at the Hayward Gallery and Cork's monumental study of Vorticism have provided a great deal of new material and created a strong Lewis revival. His books are in great demand; and an increasing number of graduate students and critics have become attracted to Lewis as the model for an independent, intelligent and courageous artist as well as perhaps the liveliest and most stimulating intellectual force in modern English literature.

The approach of Lewis's centenary year (1982) and the publication of his biography provide an appropriate occasion to revaluate his career and suggest his importance as a vital and versatile novelist, philosopher, poet, critic and editor. (His complementary role as an artist is scarcely touched on in this book and could well be the subject of another volume.) The contributors to this collection of original essays include close friends of Lewis (Tomlin, McLuhan, Bridson); perceptive critics of his work (Kenner, Holloway, Pritchard, Fox, Chapman, Materer, Smith, Munton, Lafourcade); and writers who have recently become interested in his books and have written dissertations on Lewis or on Pound, Eliot and Joyce: the 'Men of 1914' (Chace, Davies, Edwards, Flory, Parker).

This book intends to stimulate critical appreciation of the depth and diversity of Lewis's fifty years of creative life. It begins with five general essays that examine the relation of his verbal and visual images, his autobiographical writings, his philosophical influences, his friendship with Augustus John, W. B.

Yeats and Sturge Moore, and his prose style. The remainder of the essays provide authoritative readings of his brilliantly titled major works, in order of composition: his short stories, *The Wild Body*; his revealing mystery, *Mrs. Dukes' Million*; his play, *Enemy of the Stars*; his Nietzschean novel, *Tarr*; his fantasy, *The Childermass*; his satire, *The Apes of God*; his controversial political tracts of the 1930s; his travel book, *Filibusters in Barbary*; his picaresque novel, *Snooty Baronet*; his literary criticism: *Men Without Art* and *The Writer and the Absolute*; his fictional treatment of women, especially in *The Revenge for Love*; and his late masterpieces, *Self Condemned* and *The Human Age*. These essays show the progressive development of a major literary figure and, as Saul Bellow has noted, a 'brilliant, thoughtful and original observer' of contemporary society.

Jeffrey Meyers

Machine and Puppet: A Comparative View

JOHN HOLLOWAY

In connection with Lewis's portraits of the early 1920s, Walter Michel quotes from the second number of *The Tyro*: 'In a great deal of art you find its motive in the assertion of beauty and significance of the human as opposed to the mechanical; a virtuoso display of its opposite' (viz., of the human).[1] Undoubtedly this conception of what is distinctively best in the human manifestation was of crucial importance for Lewis; not only in his visual art but in his writing also. At the same time, it is barely possible to see those words as adequately diagnosing even the portraits of the early 'twenties taken in isolation. Lewis's attitudes, his creative drives, are more densely and variously intricated than that. Alongside the words quoted by Michel one should set, perhaps, what Lewis said in 1919 in *The Caliph's Design*: 'Machinery should be regarded as a new pictorial resource, as with a new mineral or oil, there to be exploited';[2] and also, later in the same work, 'Life ... however vivid and tangible, is too material to be anything but a mechanism, and the seagull is not far removed from the hydroplane. Whether a stone flies and copulates, or remains respectfully in its place ... is little matter.'[3] Fifteen years later, in a lecture given at Oxford, Lewis was to emphasize how this same awareness extended for him to mankind: 'An animal, in every respect on the same footing as a rat or an antelope ... except for what the Behaviourist terms his word-habit ... man is *that* and no more'[4] (italics Lewis's).

Lewis's examples from the animal kingdom were doubtless chosen advisedly. *Man approaches to animal approaches to*

machine, the formula (or call it vision) embodied in the several
remarks already quoted, enabled Lewis's sense of human beauty
to interplay with his social satire and with his sense, if you like,
of the precariousness of the human—its balanced imbalance
away from the animal-mechanical. The antelope, in fact, is
almost a favourite, and certainly a recurrent, model for those
early-twenties portraits. Lewis had a great sense of conventional
upper-class masculinity and good looks, 1920s model. Over and
over, he renders this dubious ideal with a kind of glossy and
dashing swish which, through its quality and superlatively
professional finish, passes facilely enough as a compliment to
the sitter. But look again, and the curious square-jaw languor of
the John Rodker (1923), the blankly skinny sensuousness of the
Violet Tschiffely (1923), or the unfocused intentness of the
Sacheverell Sitwell (1922) tell another tale also. So does the wide,
empty, antelope-like stare of the 1923 'Seated Woman Wearing
a Pendant'.[5] In fact, there is something a little deer-like about all
four of those drawings.

The same is true of some or the later portraits: like the aphasic-
seeming elegance of Mrs Desmond Harmsworth, or the repel-
lently dainty, cover-boy masculinity of the Henry John or Rev.
M. C. D'Arcy sketches[6] (my remarks, of course, relate exclusively
to what is presented in these particular works). No one can see
these as in other than a partly ironic light. Some of the portraits
of those years are of course different in quality. The two almost
owlish-looking self-portraits of 1927 and 1932 are ironical in
more surface terms:[7] the final impression of personality that they
leave is quite different, and here the bird-analogy would work
very differently. In these two drawings the modelling of the face
is detailed and subtle, and the irises (so often—and one knows,
deliberately—almost non-existent elsewhere) are deeply shaded.
In the 1927 drawing they are entirely lustreless, and give a
powerfully inward and pensive tenderness to the whole. Something similar is true of the mouth in these drawings, and eyes
and mouth are both treated similarly in the occasional quite
unsatirical drawing like that (probably) of Fanny Wadsworth
(1922–3). Here too, subtle though economical modelling, and a
depth in the treatment of the eyes, give a luminous humanity
to the result which calls the phrase 'a *speaking* likeness' to mind

(and stands in deadly contrast to the diagrammatized stag-at-bay treatment of Fanny's husband).[8]

But those two self-portraits, and the drawings which are like them, are the exceptions; and this relates to the fact that one of the most interesting literary problems about Lewis is how his relatively infrequent passages of humanity and tenderness emerge out of the general tissue of his fictional satire. For the novels are like the graphic works collectively taken, they are of course in the first place a satirical *oeuvre*, though also other and more. To pass from the one body of work to the other, and back again, is to find extended continuities and to be reminded again of the equation: *human → animal → mechanical*. For example, Victor Stamp's partner in *The Revenge for Love*, Margaret,[9] begins her role in the book rather as one of Lewis's mindless antelope-women; and, of course, in his fiction Lewis can show at length how the 'word-habit' the Behaviourist relied on to make his crucial distinction can only too easily degenerate to that machine-level from which, properly, it is a differential. Here is how she first appears in the book, and I think it strongly calls the shapely inanity of the almost contemporaneous 'Study of a Young Woman' (1936)[10] to mind:

> Her eyes were charged with the same painful uncertainty as was betrayed in her hesitation to get up ... There was something in her dully beating heart that sent out waves of apprehension from one end to the other of her halted body, awaiting the order to march ... she had learnt to disregard its invitation—to refrain, or on the other hand to execute, under the compulsion of some mechanical superstition...
> ... she had the head of a small wistful seabird ... arched downward on its neck to observe Lord Victor ...[11]

The handsome Victor, on the other hand, is strongly reminiscent of those glossily masculine portraits—and conspicuously a mechanism, and an animal, in his turn. Here is the account of him as he wakes up and embraces Margaret:

> Victor rolled in one movement, banging upon the box-springs with his revolving body; and flinging his arm out, behind Margaret's shoulder, drew her down so that her face got hidden at once under his granite chin ... they lay there

without moving, Victor glaring up . . . like a picture of an
Orang defending its young.

One should not, I think, relate Victor's 'granite chin' to the
extraordinary figure of the pugilist in 'Boxing at Juan-les-Pins'
(1929); but rather to the heavily doltish masculinity of the seeming kit-portrait of Mosley.[12] The novel itself obligingly records
that Margaret herself saw a '*distant* resemblance' between Victor
and the tame Blackshirt who had been frequenting O'Hara's
parties.[13] The point could be pursued, but of course it is not
isolated; and it is not such isolated and particular resemblances
between what is in the fiction and in the visual art that are of
greatest significance; rather, those places where resemblances are
in approach, and so have the informativeness of the generic with
regard to Lewis's mode of vision as a whole. Margaret herself, in
fact, offers further opportunity to pursue the human-animal-
mechanical equation through analogues in the visual art. Admittedly, her case is far indeed from the most obvious one in *The
Revenge for Love*; but it is of quite special interest precisely
because of how far that is from the truth, and the discussion
must revert to her.

But when, in the concluding Part VII of the novel, she comes
in for the irony of the old French hard-liner Communist Mateu,
it is in precisely the terms of Lewis's own satire of fashionable
beau-monde women (subdued in detail, of course, to the exi-
gencies of characterization) that we are invited to see her
for the moment: 'The English . . . No, all! Their *rabbit-toothed*
women are jokes as women . . . She is rabbit-toothed . . .' Where
in Lewis's visual art does satire most exploit that particular
defect? The answer is obvious: the 'Cept', the 'Brombroosh' and
the other 'Tyro' figures of 1921:[14]

> A tyro is a new type of human animal . . . into which one
> can translate . . . satirical observations . . .
> Teeth and laughter . . . are the Tyro's two prominent features,
> and I will explain why. Do you remember the remark of a
> celebrated Frenchman on all Englishwomen? 'They have such
> handsome teeth', he said, 'that they are all like death masks'
> . . . The Tyro, too . . . his vitality is immense, but purposeless
> . . . he is an animated, but artificial *puppet* (italics mine).[15]

No one can miss how Mateu's remark bears on Lewis's own remarks, just quoted, as they appeared in the *Daily Express*; Mateu, that is to say, is being made to satirize Margaret as if she were a female 'Tyro'. Another part of Mateu's sarcasm is to the point as well. A 1922 sketch by Lewis for the *Evening Standard* of a 'young suburban married woman' also has teeth of Tyro-like prominence. When, however, Mateu spoke of Margaret as a 'Petit Bourgeois, high-hatting, goose-stepping and grinning—', it is the companion *Evening Standard* sketch, 'Suitable walking dress for flapper', that comes to mind.[16] The textual details of the novel come very close indeed to this drawing of the over-dressed, respectably tartish figure, tightly corseted over its posterior, that begins in its more stylish aspects to be reminiscent of Lewis's more mechanical and stylized, indeed more abstract, figures in general.[17]

Needless to say, Margaret appears in this light through Mateu's hostile portrait, not from Lewis direct; by this point in the novel, indeed, Lewis has developed her character far beyond what she appeared like at first. Agnes Irons, however (see *The Revenge for Love*, VI.1), is a very complete example of Lewis displaying a Tyro through the verbal medium. 'For five or ten minutes after her entrance Agnes made no remark whatever without an obbligato of deafening laughter ... upon some principle of jolly-good-sortishness.' It is a memorable scene in the novel, crackling with vitality, blood-curdlingly hideous, hideously true (alas) to life. The type must have been familiar to Lewis for many years before he wrote the novel. 'The Laughing Woman' of 1911 is convincing as a representation of Agnes Irons, and 'Smiling Woman Ascending a Stair' of the same year a more ghoulish counterpart to it.

Perhaps at this point it is desirable to recall how the subject of this present discussion differs from the method by which that subject is being pursued. The method is to inter-relate certain selected parts of Lewis's fiction and his visual art, in order to cast light on the subject, which is his sense of the mechanical within the human. So far, this has been pursued mainly at the level of content; but attention to some of the less obviously representational of the paintings and drawings enables one to be somewhat more inward than that; because, obviously enough, the less straightforwardly representational the work, the more completely does its meaning reside in its formal nature, its design and texture and so on. Pursuing this point will enable us to identify a comparatively fundamental distinction between two variants of the 'mechanical' in Lewis's writing.

Consider, first, three similar passages, respectively from *Tarr* (1918), *The Revenge for Love* (1937) and *Self Condemned* (1954); and along with them, three examples of Lewis's visual art that happen, successively, to have been done more or less contemporaneously with the three novels. First, the culmination of the 'duel' fiasco in *Tarr*:

Soltyk became white and red by turns: the will was released in a muffled explosion, it tore within at its obstructions, he writhed upright, a statue's bronze softening, suddenly, with blood. His blood, one heavy mass, hurtled about in him, up and down, like a sturgeon in a narrow tank. . . . His hands were electrified . . . and the hands become claws, flew at Kreisler's throat. His nails made six holes in the flesh and cut into the tendons beneath: his enemy was hurled about to left and right, he was pumped backwards and forwards. Otto's hands... gripped along the coat sleeves, connecting him with the engine he had just overcharged with fuel . . .

. . . At this Bitzenko had rapped [Khudin] smartly upon the cheek. Khudin, who spent his mornings sparring with a negro pugilist, gave him a blow between the eyes, which laid him out insensible upon the field of honour. But Bitzenko's russian colleague, interfering when he noticed this, seized Khudin round the waist and after a sharp bout, threw him, falling on top of him . . . The field was filled with cries, smacks, harsh movements and the shrill voice of Jan exclaiming 'Gentlemen! Gentlemen!'[18]

In 1919 Lewis executed a pen drawing entitled 'Study'. It depicts, in the left-centre foreground, a figure with his back to us, melodramatically fainting, it would seem, into the arms of two straddling hussars or the like; the background repeats and varies this *motif* several times, in a space detached, with a deliberate awkwardness, from the foreground, and receding into ever-increasing congestedness.[19]

In *The Revenge for Love*. there is a fight between Jack Cruze and Percy Hardcaster.

> Old Jack's fighting glands were all in good order, thank you . . . Grasping his crutch-sticks firmly at his sides, Percy again advanced . . . Jack was upon him, his fists springing out from his sides, returning, and darting forward again, like deadly hammers of gum-elastic . . . his bowler-hat had been on all the while, bobbing about, and giving him the air of a puppet.[20]

This passage may be set beside the 1937 'Anti-War Design':[21] the two grinning, snarling figures, locked in a struggle, their daggers raised high, are clear enough. But the main features of the drawing are its aggressive black-and-white, and the conspicuously swirling curves, especially of the headdress, shoulders, tunics and feet, which convey that the embattled figures are locked in an endless vapid gyration. This is what makes their performance a sarcastic caricature and a work of anti-war art. At the same time, it is these elements of design purely, not content, that make the drawing a comment upon the shape of the Nazi swastika, set to twiddle aimlessly among the gladiators' flashy footwork. This piece may in fact be seen as a 'vortex' drawing in a very literal sense. 'In Vorticism the direct and hot impressions of life are mated with Abstraction. . .'.[22]

The scene in *Self Condemned* where René is battered in the drinking saloon by the draft-dodger is comparatively well-known, perhaps, but quotation is sharply to the point:

> he focused something of an entirely different character to anything else in this phantasmagoria. It was much more integrated and purposeful. A crouched, medium-sized figure was dancing in front of him. There was . . . hardly any face at all. It was an engine rather than a man . . .[23]

I find this description (the scene as a whole needs to be called to mind) reminiscent of both the content and the organization of the drawing 'Lebensraum II: the Empty Tunic', done in 1941–2, the very years when Lewis was undergoing the experiences depicted and distanced in the novel. In this piece there is indeed a tortured, distorted face, staring hideously out from what seems like the underside of a tunic tossed over an impossibly contorted body; but again, the dominant quality is the harsh black-and-white, and swirling intensity, of the design. 'By Vorticism we mean ... *Activity* as opposed to the tasteful *Passivity* of Picasso ... *Essential Movement* and *Activity* (such as the energy of a mind) as opposed to ... imitative cinematography.'[24]

In all these cases, the 'essential ... activity' is of course that of the creating artist, releasing violence, as timed and controlled by himself, into novels that had variously been providing a contrary posturing formality or futile inertness or enervating stasis, contributing to form, not content merely, by writing that is 'electric with a more mastered, vivid vitality, which is the conception of their mission held by most of the Vorticists'.[25]

By now, and with the help of those three examples to set alongside the earlier ones, it is possible to see that Lewis's fiction employs two rather distinct models of the non-human or the sub-human. On the one hand there is that of the engine: active producer of the mechanical. On the other, that of the puppet, mere product of the mechanical. The svelte, slight, but glossy portrait drawings of the early 1920s (Nancy Cunard, etc.),[26] or the 1930s (Mosley's neurotically posturing countenance of 1937—this is quite another drawing from that noted earlier on)[27] are among the puppets. So are most of the Bright Young Things at Sean O'Hara's party, and so is Starr the 'fairy-man', the 'leprechaun', in *Self Condemned*.[28] The same may be said with regard to that book of the slow-moving Mrs Glanz, or Mr Cedric Furber. On the other hand, the dance-encounter between Kreisler and Mrs Bevelage in *Tarr*: 'He took her twice, with ever-increasing velocity, round the large hall, and at the third round, at breakneck speed, spun her in the direction of the front door'[29] —this is a scene between a machine and a puppet; and the opening scene between Victor Stamp and Margaret (this was quoted from and discussed above) could at least in a preliminary way be seen in like terms.

This same distinction seems also to manifest itself in the visual art; and perhaps that part of Lewis's work makes it the easier to suggest—certainly it is no more than a suggestion—what may be for him the underlying realities of the distinction. Somewhat to my own surprise, I find myself desiring to put forward the view that there is something of the machine in the celebrated lost portrait of Pound done in 1919.[30] The sharply off-centre pose creates the sense of a tensed spring, and this impression of massive potential energy is reinforced by the swirling angular curves of the hair and clothes, the ubiquitous chiaroscuro, and the aggressive modelling. There is an interesting contrast: the male figure in the drawing entitled 'At the Seaside' (1913).[31] In this piece there is even a hint of the same facial expression as in the Pound; and it cannot be denied that the height, broad shoulders and general massiveness convey a clear idea of masculinity. But the insistent absence of relief, the stylized static gesture (and the strong contrast with the electrically vital figure in the foreground) leave their own impression as the dominant one: that this holiday *paterfamilias* is not an engine but a puppet.

The same sort of distinction shows in the war drawings. 'Drag-ropes', 'Shell-humping', and 'The Attack'[32] all display the tensed, frozen power and concentrated potential energies of the machine; as does the celebrated 'The Number 2',[33] where the brilliant illumination from the neighbouring gun, which has just fired, enacts at one level what the great trajectory-line in the upper half of the piece does at another, and the dehumanized recording-plus-leverage figure of the gunner himself, at a third. One of the war drawings, however, stands out curiously from the others. It is 'The Rum Ration' (1918).[34] The lieutenant leans (or seems rather to have been propped) against the wall, his legs splayed stiffly out. The NCO dispensing the rum-ration is hunched up high in the picture, his awkward and almost formless body looking as if it were stuffed with straw. Clearly, these two figures are two of Lewis's puppets; and in fact the soft shading and gently and informally curving lines of the picture are of a piece with Lewis's style for the more puppet-like of his portraits, discussed already. The point may be taken a stage further. This contrast between a bold, harsh style in line, relief and composition, and on the other hand an uninsistent lightness and softness of tone and design, runs clearly also through Lewis's more or less abstract art: as one may see briefly by comparing, say, 'Composition' (1913), or 'Red Duet' (1914), with the flowing lines and large light spaces of 'Still-life: in the Belly of the Bird' (1942) or 'Dragon's Teeth' (1941) or the earlier 'Creation-Myth' of 1927.[35]

The titles of these last three (the dragon's teeth are of course those that came to Cadmus) are particularly significant. In itself, a distinction between machine and puppet cannot be wholly adequate in respect of Lewis's visual art, nor can it of his fiction either. There is sure to be something of a continuous gradation —or more precisely, of a discontinuous one—and those who are interested will be able to call to mind the cases. But it seems reasonable to argue that, whether or not this is so, the distinction represents more than a mere factitious contrast that one may erect within the continuity of Lewis's work. It seems rather more than that: a genuine polarity; two fundamental movements whose nature, for Lewis, was to diverge.

It seems, that is to say, as if there may be something of a basic asymmetry in Lewis's work taken as a whole. This is not to fault it in any positive sense, merely to notice what it does and what it leaves undone. Those three light-style abstracts or near-abstracts selected just now were all, at bottom, studies in *fecundity*: in creation itself, how men might be born merely out of the ground, how the winged thing will emerge from the bald egg. Parallel to this is what occasionally happens—nearly always for *women*—among the light-style portraits. Among the elegant doll-pieces of the early 1940s we suddenly find, and in very much the same style graphically speaking, thoughtful, gently humane studies like 'Catnap' (1942: contrast the hands with those in 'Corinne' or 'Pauline Bondy'), or 'Portrait' (1944).[36] Likewise, among the earlier drawings the eye is caught, at quite another level, by the intensely realized 'Virginia Woolf' of 1921, or the poignant 'L'Ingénue' sketch of 1919.[37] The culmination of this trend is doubtless in some of the major portraits: 'Pensive Woman' of 1938 (the artist's wife, as were a considerable number of the same kind), or 'Naomi Mitchison' (1939).[38]

The style I have associated with machine-effects or engine-effects seems almost never to issue into suddenly moving and convincing humanity. There is something, for Lewis, in a puppet that is beyond a machine: it can come to life. The only exception that I can find is the richly meditative, I-Thou 'Portrait of the Artist' in oils, 1920–1.[39] Apart from that, what emerges are works (I do not impugn their power, only seek to diagnose their kind) like the ponderously hieratic automatisms of 'Praxitella'

(1920–1: the artist himself as Raphael),[40] the grim, Kreisler-like ink self-portraits of c. 1920, and the Tyros. Nor do such facts follow naturally, from the innate tendency of this one of Lewis's styles. That a broad, emphatic style and a hard line can issue in profound humanity in art we have not only the whole Orthodox Pantocrator tradition to witness, but also much of the work of Beckmann, Rouault, and perhaps especially Emil Nolde—all of them Lewis's close contemporaries. Their marvellous icons of profoundly questioning and questing humanity shows us potentialities that Lewis did not pursue.

What most interested Lewis, in these matters, seems to have been two not parallel, but contrary movements: that of humanity *into* machine, and that of the puppet who, wonderfully, re-animates into humanity. In a single painting, such movements have to be entirely *in posse*; they have to be in the egg, in 'the Belly of the Bird'. But fiction can have their registration as its characteristic task. *Tarr* is a novel peopled (if that is the word) by engines and puppets; but when Bertha (she has shown something of such potentialities before, earlier in the book) says 'Yes, I am *enceinte*', she establishes herself in a new dimension, and Tarr's response is to say 'Poor *Mensch*!'. Humanity has arrived in this world of 'violent puppets'. Victor Stamp's case, in *The Revenge for Love*, is a complex one; but Margaret is clearly a character who enjoys an anastasis from puppetry into humanity. It is she who, at Sean O'Hara's party, is the one to detect the symbolic false walls and hidden doors in that super-brombroosh's flat. It is in the last section of the book, however, that she for the first time achieves full stature, as she takes over the initiative of the action in an effort to save Victor from the consequences of his having, at least in one respect, become the puppet of others. 'It is *she* who is the trouble', says Hardcaster (the name is eloquent: he is the other kind), as he brushes Victor aside; and it is she whose 'tender' and human voice cries out to him, after her death, from the depth of Hardcaster's own memory and just possibly conscience.

The same two patterns are present, and more fully, in *Self Condemned*. 'I am not violent myself, because I am a civilized man', René says at Robert Kerridge's dinner party (Chap. 8). It is, at that time, a just remark. At the beginning of the novel he is the rational man in another society of puppets: violent, absurd or (like his wife) insignificant. By the end of the book, all is transformed: '... the body of his friend, *which had become an automaton*', McKenzie registers (Chap. 34). The vicissitudes through which René passes, and the processes of psychic induration that they induce ('digging himself in with concrete and steel'—not for nothing is René's surname *Harding*), leave him as a 'shell' of his former self. Hester on the other hand (she is often called 'Essie' in the book, and this I think is meant to call up the Latin word *esse*, simple Being) begins as one of Lewis's frivolous sex-kitten nonentities, an *esse* which is *non esse*, like so many of the drawings of women. What she then develops in the course of the book is not simply her deep desire to return home, but also a maturing and almost maternal love, deep and self-effacing, for her husband, that leaves her as the only fully human creation in the whole of this far-reaching satire. She cannot deal adequately with her situation, but for all that she it is who establishes herself within what Lewis himself was to call *The Human Age*. *Ess*, her last, clipped letter is signed. The manner of her death is that of Anna Karenina herself, and one cannot believe that Lewis did not mean his readers to pick up this clue to her stature. Lewis has enacted a Creation Myth of his own, here in the Belly of the Book, and his puppet, at the core of herself, has become an entire woman.

2

Letters and Autobiographies
ROBERT CHAPMAN

'I am always regretting that I was not born in a volcanic land;
in the matter of art anyhow: the sort of place where the aesthetic
structures have a slight shake-up every day and are periodically
swallowed up altogether.'[1] Written at the time of *Blast*, this
letter defines not only Lewis's attitudes during The Great English
Vortex, but also suggests those volcanic energies everywhere
apparent in his life and in his art. If Lewis's letters record the
immediacy of tremors at the epicentre, then the autobiographies
present the completed seismic patterns during whole periods of
his life. Trailing his coat at Philistia, shoring up the defences of
Western Man in a world without art—the essential Lewis is in
the letters. There are also some characteristically Lewisian stories
and insights in *Blasting and Bombardiering* and *Rude Assignment*, but these books too often reveal the strains of hasty composition for them to be considered as Lewis at his best. 'A page of
a novel', admits Lewis, 'takes me as long to write as twenty
pages of a *Blasting and Bombardiering*.'[2] In the latter, the effort
to sustain a matey tone, to keep it 'plainsailing', vitiates a narrative which is marvellously amusing in parts. *Rude Assignment*
is a more sober, bitter, uneven work containing Lewis's finest
critiques of his own writing combined with an uneasy mixture of
cultural criticism, politics and memoirs. Whatever their flaws
qua autobiography, these two books, like the letters, are central
to an understanding of the man, his works and his age.

Not one for the bib and the bottle—'How many novels are
intolerable', he asks, 'that begin with the hero in his cradle?'[3]—
Lewis never mentions his childhood in either autobiography.
A long series of letters to his mother sketches in some details.
There is a close, trusting maternal relationship and an amused
tolerance of his estranged, wayward father. The extended family

of mother, grandmother and Tomkins, the faithful retainer, provides a firm base after the 1890s when 'Pops' is mainly important for providing—somewhat erratically—an allowance for both mother and son. 'I think we might get something out of C.E.L. by a vigorous letter',[4] he writes from Paris in 1903. Four years later he is going through the same motions: 'I didn't certainly think that the Parent over the Water would respond to my amiable letter: he's an old rip. I dreamt of a fire the other night. Mrs. John tells me it's the luckiest thing in the world: praps he's posting me £50 in this minute.'[5] The young Lewis clearly did not wish to bite the hand that supplied the stipend, but C.E.L. was more to his son than provider of the jack that paid the fees. There is a genuine affection in references to 'the Old Rip' which is echoed in 'The Do-Nothing Mode' written in 1940 about this 'odd-man-out in a society of go-getters'.[6] There is, too, a detached, almost a connoisseur's interest in the 'fox-hunting, brigantine-owning, essay-writing bum',[7] the one-time captain in the New York Dragoons who rode with Sheridan in the Civil War. Captain Lewis made unrelenting efforts to persuade his son to enter Cornell, but the vaster alma maters of Paris and Munich claimed and transformed him: 'Gradually the bad effects of English education wore off, or were deliberately discarded.'[8]

The letters to his mother during his *Wanderjahre* in Europe are remarkable for their candour. Characterized by a lightness of touch and an openness rarely seen again, they relate those experiences which, recollected in tranquillity, became *Tarr*. First mention of romantic entanglement comes in Lewis's early twenties; the reductive Keatsian archaisms define his detachment: 'being exiled from the "fair", I have taken certain opportunities to bestow a kiss upon her blanched brow, and may perhaps have stroked her bosom.'[9] The situation develops like an early fiction: Mama makes Dickensian remarks about dowry, Papa about marriage, 'at which I scream with laughter. . . There is of course no cause whatever for alarm; but when unpleasantness sets in, like the winter winds, I, the swallow, flee away.'[10] These letters demonstrate that Lewis's early fiction is a species of *Erlebnisdichtung*: heavily disguised by irony, the fictional *personae* articulate and explore attitudes and positions close to their creator.

This incident, a prelude to the long drawn-out affair with Ida (Bertha of *Tarr*) presents the lodger as victim, an unwitting catalyst in a situation which almost engulfs him. Intimately involved, he is also able to distance himself from his self and appreciate stylistic anomalies and absurdities. The affair with Ida is presented like a French farce which has become tiresome by the second act. It begins with an Apache dance in which Lewis is not an altogether unwilling protagonist: 'to my unquenchable amazement she asked me to kiss her, and threw herself into my arms and kissed me with unabated vigour for three hours: well I'm very glad, since—*ça marche*: it saves me a lot of trouble and expense to have a very beautiful and nicely bred mistress.'[11] As the relationship sours, and drags on, the letters reveal just how much of the dialectical design of *Tarr* had its origins in experience. Out of the relationship with Ida comes 'a real desire to meet some day a woman I can take seriously'[12]: in the surrogate world of fiction—if not in life—Anastasya realized that desire.

These agonized affairs were the object of Augustus John's scorn. Five years his junior, Lewis had been an admirer since the Slade and John's portrait of Lewis in 1903 is of a fresh-faced, clean-cut youth, gazing pensively into the future. Lewis was obviously uneasy in the shadow of the master. 'Near John I can never paint', he grumbled to his mother in 1906, 'his artistic personality is too strong, and he is much more developed, naturally, and this frustrates any effort.'[13] However unstinting Lewis's praise of John's painting, his admiration for the man remained this side of idolatry. There is a sharp cutting-edge to his letter of 1910 which ostensibly expresses feelings of obligation to the older man for helping him through a rough time. The final implications are veiled in a reticence which is soon to disappear from Lewis's writing:

I believe with a Calvinistic uncompromisingness that one cannot be too hard on the stupidities of one's neighbours; and I thank you quite unaffectedly for having knocked a good deal of nonsense out of me, and am only sorry that I was not able (owing to my tender years and extravagant susceptibilities) to have rendered you a similar service.[14]

At some point between 1903 and 1907 the clean-shaven, ex-public schoolboy transformed himself into the hirsute bohemian. 'To show how changed I am, Everett, who met me in the street yesterday, talked to me for 10 minutes and left me without recognising me',[15] Lewis tells his mother. 'I let my hair down underneath the hat: the effect is astonishing.'[16] He includes two sketches to demonstrate the astonishing transformation. This is the figure, with his hat plucked about his ears, who emerged from the conspiratorial shadows to confront Ford with a story for *The English Review*. This, too, according to Ford, was the man who raged with Ezra and the young lions, terrorizing literary London. Looking back, in *Rude Assignment*, on these days of prelapsarian innocence before the War, Lewis writes:

My views regarding politics were those of a young alligator . . . I drifted into this relaxed and relaxing atmosphere and there was nothing at first to prick me into wakefulness . . . Everything was easy: I was healthy: the mind slept like a healthy infant, in the sunlit smithy in which World War I was being hammered into shape.[17]

This precisely catches the tone of much of Lewis's early writing: the amazed enjoyment, beyond good or evil, of the wild body in performance, and wonder at the underlying comedy of the human condition. The world-view which interprets life in terms of burlesque patterns, which is *never* serious about anything, which comprehends the totality of the absurd, is as prevalent in his correspondence as in the fiction. The characters Lewis parades in a letter to Sturge Moore could be residents at '*Beau Sejour*':

I am bringing some spaniards over with me; one to buy six suits of clothes,—another to have his pimples cured;—a third is coming because he dare not let the man with the pimples out of his sight, as he is his only means of support,—having lived with him and on him for several years now; he is grown very jealous of his benefactor's pimples, and when the latter grows despondent, or broods on some vague plan of curing once and for all his disfigurement, he who is his shadow sees ruin staring him in the face. I will bring my troupe to the Vienna [café] one of these days.[18]

Between 1909—when he finally settled in London—and the outbreak of the War, Lewis became one of the stars of the avant-garde. The underlying seriousness of what he and 'the men of 1914' were attempting—'manufacturing fresh eyes for people, and fresh souls to go with the eyes'[19]—went hand in hand with an obvious relish for shocking the bourgeoisie. The young lion who wished to 'Kill John Bull with Art' was flexing his muscles. This was sport, and Lewis was enjoying it. 'And John and Mrs. Bull leapt for joy, in a cynical convulsion. For they felt as safe as houses. So did I.'[20] Murals for Stulik's Eiffel Tower, the raw meat curtain for Frida Strindberg's Cave of the Golden Calf and the black 'Cubist Room' for Lady Drogheda; the Camden Town Group; the London Group; *The English Review*; *The New Age*; *The Egoist*; with Hulme in Frith Street, Pound in Kensington, Ford on Campden Hill, Fry at the Omega Workshops. The risorgimento was on.

If the Ideal Home Rumpus had not occurred, Lewis would have had to invent it. His relationship with the Omega—that 'arty-crafty conception, with a "post-impressionist" veneer'[21]—was never good, and the very public row which blew up because of the misplaced commission was finely stage-managed by Lewis. The Round Robin sent to the press and interested parties was a show-stopper:

As to its tendencies in Art, they alone would be sufficient to make it very difficult for any vigorous art-instinct to long remain under that roof. The Idol is still Prettiness, with its mid-Victorian languish of the neck, and its skin is 'greenery-yallery', despite the Post-What-Not fashionableness of its draperies. This family party of strayed and Dissenting Aesthetes, however, were compelled to call in as much modern talent as they could find, to do the rough and masculine work without which they knew their efforts would not rise above the level of a pleasant tea-party, or command more attention . . .

This enterprise seemed to promise, in the opportunities afforded it by support from the most intellectual quarters, emancipation from the middleman-shark. But a new form of fish in the troubled waters of Art has been revealed in the meantime, the Pecksniff-shark, a timid but voracious journalistic monster, unscrupulous, smooth-tongued and, owing chiefly to its weakness, mischievous.[22]

The private version of this encyclical plays with the Pecksniff notion, modifying it for a new audience (as often happens with a good idea in Lewis's correspondence). This piece of pitiable chicanery, he writes to Clive Bell, is 'worthy, in its inception and execution, of a bastard of Pecksniff by some half-cracked scullery-maid'. He has no wish, he continues, 'to remain longer in the vicinity of a bad shit'.[23]

The culmination of Lewis's involvement in the 'big bloodless brawl, prior to the Great Bloodletting'[24] was, of course, *Blast*. 'We were hefty guys in them days', wrote Pound from Rapallo, recalling 'the great MAGENTA cover'd opusculus.'[25] The genesis of 'The Great London Vortex' is memorably evoked in *Blasting and Bombardiering* and the letters add some unofficial footnotes to more orthodox histories. 'Eliot has sent me Bullshit and the Ballad for Big Louise', Lewis writes to Pound. 'I am trying to print them in *Blast*; but stick to my naif determination to have no "words ending in—Uck,—Unt, and—Ugger." '[26] Lewis's censoriousness, though wise, was not vigilant enough: Pound's relatively innocuous 'Fratres Minores' was emasculated and rendered meaningless by a more officious blue pencil.

Looking back on his *Blast* days, Lewis seems always intent to demythologize the Titans. Pound, Joyce, Weaver, Hulme, Ford, those 'exotic flowers of a culture that has passed',[27] are taken down from their pedestals in the literary museum and submitted to Lewis's reductive humour. In *Blasting and Bombardiering* especially, there is much tyronizing. Ford, for instance, is reduced to a cartoon which parodies and burlesques the reality. Belonging to an earlier generation, Ford never ran with the pack, and in *Blasting and Bombardiering* he blinks comatosely in the Kleig light of Lewis's ridicule:

Ford sneered very faintly and inoffensively ... He was being omniscient, bored, sleepy Ford, sunk in his tank of sloth. From his prolonged sleep he was staring out at us with his fish-blue eyes—kind, wise, but bored. Or some such idea. His mask was only just touched with derision at our childishness.[28]

More animate, but no less ridiculous, in *Rude Assignment* Ford is transformed into a Broombroosh:

Hueffer was a flabby lemon and pink giant, who hung his mouth open as though he were an animal at the Zoo inviting buns—especially when ladies were present. Over the gaping mouth damply depended the ragged ends of a pale lemon moustache.[29]

Lewis's Vorticist cohorts, too, take their place in this 'protracted comedy' of the past. Star billing goes to Ezra Pound, singing cowboy turned prickly mandarin: 'he was never satisfied until everything was *organised* . . . He had a streak of Baden Powell in him, had Ezra . . . He never got us under canvas it is true—we were not the most promising material for Ezra's boyscoutery.'[30] The sympathetic irony which deflates the 'Trotsky of the written word' is extended to Joyce, the Stage Irishman. The tale of the old brown shoes, sent by Pound to Joyce by way of Eliot and Lewis—a story which is too good to précis—embodies the latter's claim that in all reality there is a strain of Groucho Marx.

Groucho also gets in on the act in Lewis's war experiences. 'Writing about war may be the best way to shake the accursed thing off by putting it in its place, as an unseemly joke.'[31] But it was no joke to endure, and Lewis's letters from the Front include the fine details of mayhem. 'Do not be unduly anxious', he reassures his mother, 'many more people are wounded than killed.'[32] Twenty years on, the Grand Guignol has become a Crazy Gang turn of automata fouling up the war machine. Lewis's experience with a West Indian sergeant epitomizes the absurdity of this mud epic: the sergeant ignores '*a word of command*':

Whereupon I gave him a violent push. This propelled him through space for a short distance, but he immediately returned to where he had stood before. I gave him a second push—as if made of india-rubber, he once more reintegrated the spot he had just left. After this I accepted him as part of the landscape, and the shells had to be rolled round him, since they could not be rolled *through* him.[33]

In this plain tale of surface events, the pale cast of thought occasionally slows down the narrative as Lewis takes stock. 'I started the war a different man to what I ended it',[34] he writes: but the fruits of the political education that was the war are not part of this book. 'Always very serious, I have yet always been light-hearted.'[35] In *Blasting and Bombardiering* the levity is that of Socrates on his deathbed.

There died a myriad. The war robbed Lewis of close friends and colleagues; and in terms of his career, 'I had to some extent to begin all over again'.[36] The *enfant terrible* who had grabbed the headlines and become a star, now went underground. Eschewing the boiled shirt games of Mayfair, like Timon—Diogenes even—Lewis withdrew to a more austere vantage point from where he cast a cold eye on life and 'got through an unspeakable amount of work'.[37] The letters of this time suggest a man who is very quick to take offence—even with friends—and who has no compunction about voicing his indignation. Like William Bland Burn, his *persona* in the *Imaginary Letters*, it seems to have been 'a physical discomfort not to show, after a time, [his] feelings'.[38] Paul Nash gave as good as he got and Pound, 'candidly and cordially yours', snorts back in fine Ezraic style. But it is in public that the most memorable flyting occurs, where contumely is part of the argument. The putting-down of Clive Bell in *The Athenaeum* exemplifies this rhetoric of abuse reminiscent of *Blast*:

> It must be admitted at once, however, that beneath the parade of dishonesty and effrontery, Mr. Bell is really a sincere, if hallucinated, soul. For he regards Paris with something of the awe-struck glee and relish of a provincial urchin at the sight of a Cockney guttersnipe. Is there anything that almost any artist with a little prestige in Paris might not tell him that he would not swallow unhesitatingly? He is almost, you might say deliberately, the comic 'Anglais' of French caricature. He is a grinning, effusive and rather servile Islander, out on his adventure among French intelligences.[39]

T. E. Hulme 'was a very rude and truculent man', Lewis once wrote in praise of his friend. 'He needed to be.'[40] The iconoclastic scurrility, the philosophizing with a hammer, the muscular polemics, all are crucial to Lewis's role as public Enemy, the man outside the law. 'I have made it my habit never to go to law, but to shoot back when shot at', he writes in *Rude Assignment*. Desperate situations require desperate remedies: 'Once upon a time, according to English law, it was the duty of any man, observing another rustling a horse, to apprehend him (if he could) and to hang him (if he had a rope) to the nearest tree (if there was one thereabouts).'[41] In *The Athenaeum* Bell was subjected to a citizen's arrest and—if not a public lynching—a public pillorying.

The Tyro and the Enemy had many running battles with the Zeitgeist: some were calcified into fiction, but the Old Bailey, Lord Osmund, Samuel Shodbutt and their ilk were too insistent to remain at an aesthetic distance. In private and in public, Lewis baited and flayed the apes of an era. Arnold Bennett expressed no little distaste for Lewis's critical eviscerations: 'One of his minor purposes is to disembowel his enemies, who are numerous, for the simple reason that he wants them to be numerous. He would be less tiresome if he were more urbane.'[42] Urbanity, however, is not one of the masks of the Enemy. He was 'abashed' and 'compromised', he wrote to Julian Symons, by the Lewis number of *Twentieth Century Verse*: 'I have perused these articles rather in the way a notorious bandit would a shower of *many-happy-returns* and other obliging messages, at his birthday breakfast-table in his hide-out, from the local constabulary.'[43]

Lewis *chose* to be the Enemy; but was not that choice, asks Kathleen Raine, 'imposed by an integrity from which he never swerved?'[44] The letters only go part of the way towards answering that question. Lewis always stressed the distance between 'Mr. W. L. the writer and my own easy-going, anything but contentious, self'.[45] But just how far is that real self refracted through the fictional Lewismen and the social selves he created? 'Man is least himself', says Wilde, 'when he talks in his own person. Give a man a mask and he will tell you the truth.'[46] The multiple masks (first suggested by that Zarathustran primer for survival, 'The Code of a Herdsman') do not cohere; like six authors in search of a character, they articulate and dramatize Lewis's dynamic attitudes to the changing Zeitgeist. The 'Code' is worth quoting here; for if the terrain suggests the mythic

geographies of *The Human Age*, its message is never other-
worldly:

> Cherish and develop, side by side, your six most constant
> indications of different personalities. You will then acquire the
> potentiality of six men ... *Never* fall into the vulgarity of
> being or assuming yourself to be one ego. Each trench must
> have another one behind it.[47]

The Herdsman is not Lewis; but there is a lot of Lewis in the
'Code'.

If the letters cannot finally solve the ontological problems of
the man and his masks, they do give insights into less contentious areas. Lewis was often very hard up, and his correspondence
vividly underlines the economic basis of the arts. For long
periods, he both depended upon and despised patronage; a letter
to Mrs Edward Wadsworth in 1924 catches these ambivalent
feelings.

> There is no good indulging in humbug; and no letter I could
> write you under the circumstances would be pleasant reading.
> I am taking the £13 (the fund has been 'reducing') you sent
> me this morning because I am so hard up that if the devil
> himself offered me anything from half a crown upwards I
> should have to accept it: and having got so far with my
> writing, I cannot jeopardize this last week or so by being
> squeamish.[48]

The unglamorous realities of the modernist at odds with Grub
Street are chronicled in the letters of a lifetime: 'grinding away
all day with as few breaks as a popular dentist'; worried about
food, rent, heating, lighting; budgeting for twenty cigarettes a
week and two pints of bitter on a Saturday. 'It is not poverty,
grit and moral rectitude that ensure the writing of a good book,
but a golden bullet with which to shoot the wolf at the door.'[49]
Illness, exigence and the need to subsidise that uncommercial
work for which he is now most esteemed, pushed Lewis into
hasty journalism and the painting of portraits 'which will sell
themselves as I am bringing them down to the gallery'.[50] The
Abyssinian maid of John's dream, remembered by Lewis thirty

years on, had indeed spoken presciently: 'Britannia's hard on the lions!'[51]

Golden bullets were in short supply in the years before the Lewises left for North America. 'A bloodvessel will burst in my big toe if economic tension does not terminate. Returning home this afternoon, I found a wolf at the door, his teeth bared; next week is going to be awkward.'[52] The New World wolves were no less persistent and Buffalo—where the Lewises first settled— he found to be 'an animal inaccessible to artistic stimulus'.[53] The purgatorial imagery in a letter to J. J. Sweeney suggests the dark night of the soul that Lewis endured. This was written from New York, but hell has no limits, nor is circumscribed in one self place: 'I feel as if I were in some stony desert, full of shadows, in human form. I have never imagined the likes of it, in my worst nightmares.'[54] This is the world, and the mood, of *Self Condemned*, the novel which contains Lewis's finest autobiographical writing.

The rancorous voice of the tyro bawling out an opponent is rarely heard in the North American letters, but they do become thersytical in descriptions of Toronto. The *ethos* of this 'sanctimonious ice-box' is so vividly caught that it takes on a personality. 'I feel that someone is sitting on my chest—having to start with gagged me—and singing Moody and Sankey all day long.'[55] His thesaurus of abuse covers most aspects of life in this 'ugly teetotal Baal',[56] but most often focuses on the grimness, the bleakness of a people who 'outdour the Scotch'. The Scottish connection is behind the 'asphyxiating godliness' of the city and its 'reign of terror for the toper and the whoremaster, which makes life curiously difficult for the person who likes a couple of mild cocktails a day'.[57] Lewis is trapped by fortress economics into a debilitating way of life; the tone of the letters moves between querulous boredom and despair. The hack work he is forced to undertake is a mirror-image of that in pre-war London: 'painting portraits of opulent methodists up in this ice-box'[58] and writing articles—for cash on the nail—about the Canadian 'renaissance'. 'I came here as a result of an economic miscalculation. I remain here under an economic compulsion. I mean I can't get away.'[59] As the throw-away lines for help become more overt, more agitated, so the early bravado about ending his days in a Toronto flop-house soon evaporates. In 1945, when Lewis writes to John with a financial precision none too finical, he is clearly at the end of his tether:

> To get from Ottawa to London (2 people and baggage) will cost approximately 725 dollars or 182 pounds sterling. There is no means, that I can see, at this end, of getting such a sum . . .
> What you can do is this. You can communicate these sickening and idiotic facts and figures to anybody who might be interested . . . there are plenty of people whose duty it is to see that I should not be stuck eternally upon this not over-hospitable continent.[60]

When the Lewises eventually returned from that 'small and backward country'[61] it was to the capital of a dying empire, 'not crashing down in flames and smoke', he assured Geoffrey Stone, 'but expiring in a peculiar muffled way'.[62] *Rotting Hill* is everywhere apparent in the world of Lewis's last letters. Everything is dried up, withered, rotted: the horrors of the peace are legion in the Crippsean ice-age. Lewis becomes obsessed with shortages and the cost of living; he has dreams and super-dreams of returning to the States, teaching at Cape Cod, living modestly 'but with plenty of eggs, bread, cauliflowers, bits of meat and Cuban Honey—cigarettes (2 packs a day) and a bottle of gin a week'.[63]

Once again on his home ground, Lewis takes up position 'as full-back, before the cultural goal'.[64] The Enemy is as aggressive as ever. Surrounded by hostile forces—every prominent position in the press 'is controlled or occupied by an enemy'—he still shoots back when shot at. He imperiously challenges editorial alterations to a *TLS* review: 'I would be glad to know', he demands of Pryce-Jones, 'what there is so crassly incompetent about my article that (except for the question of the first person singular here and there) makes it impossible to publish it without your intervention on every line?'[65] And, with heavy irony— 'I apologise for my intrusion'—he sets straight the world and *Partisan Review*.[66]

Smouldering throughout Lewis's last years, the campaign to 'get Grandpa out of the bughouse'[67] never caught light sufficiently to succeed. Frustrated by Pound's continuing interest in radical politics and his refusal to contemplate a free pardon, the old strategist was confounded. Lewis's letters just after the war had attempted to make light of the situation: 'I am told that you believe yourself to be Napoleon—or is it Mussolini? What a pity that you did not choose Buddha while you were about it, instead of a politician.'[68] As the years pass, the valedictory 'Best wishes for freedom in New Year'[69] sounds more like an acceptance of the inevitable. A note of exasperation underlies Lewis's later hectoring:

It wearies me you remaining where you are. To take up a strategic position in a lunatic asylum is idiotic. If I don't see you make an effort to get out *soon*, I shall conclude, either that your present residence has a snobbish appeal for you, or that you are timid with regard to fate.[70]

In 1951 Lewis announced his blindness. As the sea-mists of winter closed around him, he experienced the dysfunctions of the ageing wild body with undimmed intellectual clarity. Almost half a century earlier, Ker-Orr had observed himself in detached, cynical, amused fashion, exulting with the frenetic energy of youth; Lewis *vieux* has lost none of that awareness of the absurd. As early as 1941, he had been warned of the possibility of blindness. The grotesque irony of that, for 'Pierce-Eye the Lewis',[71] underlay his reactions at the time: 'if my eyes go I go too. Loathsome as the world is, I do like to *see* it. *That* sort of blackout I could not live in.'[72] Ten years later, his moving and amusing article in *The Listener*[73] is without a trace of self-pity:

Pushed into an unlighted room, the door banged and locked for ever, I shall have then to light a lamp of aggressive voltage in my mind to keep at bay the night.

New as I am to the land of blind-man's-buff I can only register the novel sensations, and not deny myself the enjoyment of this curious experience. It amuses me to collide with a walking belly; I quite enjoy being treated as a lay-figure, seized by the elbows and heaved up in the air as I approach a kerb, or flung into a car. I relish the absurdity of gossiping with somebody at the other side of the partition. And everyone is at the other side of the partition ... Well, Milton had his daughters, I have my dictaphone.[74]

If old age brought honours to the Enemy, it did nothing to diminish his fighting spirit. The last campaign was waged against William Roberts, an erstwhile comrade-in-arms from the days of the Vortex. All the classic elements were present: public controversy, invective and the drumfire of camouflaged gunners. The tumour which would finally cause his death robbed Lewis of vigour but not of spirit: he went down fighting, stamping on the 'venomous misunderstandings ... scattered abroad' by Roberts in his criticism of the Tate retrospective, 'Wyndham Lewis and Vorticism'. In a letter to the press, Lewis offers a few necessary facts 'to disinfect this booklet called 'Vorticism', written about me by a little mister X'.[75] But the campaign was to be completed by Enemy cohorts, not by Lewis: this last letter was never dispatched.

3

The Philosophical Influences

E. W. F. TOMLIN

(i)

'One of our greatest superstitions', wrote Lewis in an early story,[1] 'is that the plain man, being so "near to life", is a great "realist". In fact, he never gets close to reality at all, in the way, for instance, that a philosophic intelligence, or an imaginative artist, does.'

It was always with respect and veneration that Lewis spoke of the 'philosophic' intelligence, and it is clear that he was drawn to philosophy from an early age. Nevertheless, his philosophical reading differed from that of the few who shared his general interest in or passion for ideas. This was no doubt due to the fact that his education, after the years spent at Rugby and the Slade, was acquired largely on the continent, and in his own time and manner. Between 1902 and 1908 he spent long periods in France, Germany, Holland and Spain. When Lewis came to contemporary British philosophy, therefore, it was fresh from deep study of thinkers who, even though their names may be familiar, have failed to exert a significant influence on Anglo-Saxon thought. The work of Schopenhauer, Nietzsche and Sorel never sucessfully penetrated the academies; and the impact of the one exception, Bergson, was short-lived. To Lewis, no British philosopher of his time rivalled in stature the great Germans and some few Frenchmen, even though he might come to dissent from much of what they wrote. To discuss Lewis's early philosophical background is therefore to gauge the influence exerted over him chiefly by foreign thinkers. The study of the lesser men, among whom he grouped most British and American philosophers and their epigoni, was made in the light of his deep understanding of the continental giants.

In this essay, I propose to begin with an outline of the change in philosophical climate in Europe that took place in Lewis's formative years. I shall then dwell upon the English philosophical scene, with particular reference to the emergence of what Lewis called time-philosophers, as a prelude to a definition of the time-philosophy itself. Although Lewis's critique centred on Bergson, as the chief modern European exponent of that philosophy, he found in Schopenhauer and Nietzsche two powerful precursors whose work provided the first direct challenge to the values that had animated Western Man over many centuries. Even so, Nietzsche's nihilism and diabolism were a good deal less congenial to Lewis than the more serene pessimism of Schopenhauer. I then pass to a consideration of a young contemporary of Lewis —T. E. Hulme—whose examination of the presuppositions of modern humanism influenced Lewis more perhaps than he cared to acknowledge; and I also stress his discriminating respect for the French neo-scholastic philosophers—which leads me to perhaps the most controversial part of my argument, namely Lewis's attitude to religion. I conclude with his critique of twentieth-century historical and social thought, centring on the work of Spengler and Sorel.

The anti-metaphysical tendency of the members of the Vienna Circle, led by Schlick, Carnap and Neurath—whose exile at the time of the rise of Nazism caused their ideas to be spread over the Anglo-Saxon world (though they had already established through Wittgenstein a foothold in Cambridge, England)—was responsible for a slump in the reputation of what was called, in an increasingly pejorative sense, 'German metaphysics'. And in due course the 'great problems' of philosophy tended to be regarded as issuing not from real difficulties but from verbal confusion. Consequently, the major thinker, the sage, began to lose his authority. In philosophy, as in psychology, the analyst took his place.

Yet the need for a broader outlook continued to assert itself. As Herbert Read wrote: 'It is idle to think that any good can come of a specialization that is not linked to some wider ethos. . . . Only a universal mind . . . is capable of "creative thought".'[2] He expressed the view that universality, in this sense, could be ascribed not merely to Aristotle, Dante, Leibniz or Goethe, but to Lucian, Diderot, Ruskin, and Emily Brontë. And such universality did not imply the possession of all knowledge or necessarily of any knowledge at all; it implied rather a capacity to *receive* knowledge and experience with a certain dispassionateness.

To the list of those singled out by Herbert Read as possessing the universal mind, or at least universality, Lewis might be added, though whether Read, who knew Lewis but perhaps viewed him with some antipathy, would have approved the addition is another matter. A book such as *Time and Western Man* continues to be read, if only by the few, because, whatever its aberrations, it is at grips with problems that will always clamour for attention, whatever teachers of 'philosophy' (fortunately not all) may say. And, inevitably, a universal mind, if such a prodigy can be expected to recur with the frequency—or infrequency—of the past, is more likely to be one possessing a grasp of the 'great problems' than one capable only of extreme specialization. The specialist who thinks he is nothing but that, does not repudiate a *Weltanschauung*: he merely entertains a particularly narrow one.

What is it that justifies our attributing this kind of universality to Lewis, and not, for all his wide-ranging interests, to Pound? Apart from the capacity to entertain 'pairs of opposites', as Lewis did from *Blast* onwards, and apart from the capacity to 'receive' all knowledge—for no one can possess it all—the universal mind has a particular grasp of the human situation. If we wish, we can call it, with Unamuno, the Tragic Sense of Life. In his book *Del sentimiento trágico de la vida* (1913), Unamuno sought to demonstrate that spiritual doubt and anguish, if genuine and not an histrionic pose, could be a source of power and energy. It was Lewis's possession of energy of this order, in contrast to his own personal gentleness, which marked his work from *Tarr* to *Self Condemned*, and which distinguished him from so many of his contemporaries, perhaps from Pound most of all. For Pound, restless and turblent though he was by nature, never, it seems to me, achieved in the *Cantos*, and only just missed in the superb *Cathay*, that sense of the grim, intractable mystery of life which the greater writer could on occasion reflect. This may indeed explain why Pound's poem needed to be prolonged beyond its original limits, and, more sadly, why its author ended up by brooding in despair and in silence over an *œuvre* which he

realized was inadequate. That Lewis's percipience occurs only
fitfully must be admitted; but I have tried elsewhere to define
that particular luminousness which is found in *Enemy of the
Stars, Childermass,* and at moments in *Self Condemned.*[3] Why at
the end of his career, or from the middle to the end, Lewis halted
on the threshold of a deeper understanding may have been due to
his continued addiction to satire, which he identified with the
'external' view of things. This preoccupation gradually hardened
into a prevailing mood, forming the carapace of a sardonic Stoic
philosophy, which masked an inner sensitivity; for in an important passage in *Time and Western Man* he made the plea 'that
we should retain our objective hardness and not be constantly
melting and hotly overflowing, that we should find our salvation
in being what we are, without wishing to disintegrate and invade
the Infinite or the mind of the Deity'.[4] But, to echo a saying of
Eliot, only those who have a sense of the infinite know what
it is to refrain from trespassing upon that unconfined domain.
And only those who know who and what they are, are aware of
what they might be. Throughout the second and third part of
The Human Age (*Monstre Gai* and *Malign Fiesta*), there is a
tantalizing sense of the presence of the Infinite or the Absolute
subsisting at one remove; but Lewis never encroached on that
sphere, and, had he embarked upon the final part, provisionally
called *The Trial of Man,* it is more than doubtful whether even
there he would have made the transition. Indeed, it is doubtful
whether such a thing can be done, though the end of Part II of
The Pilgrim's Progress might suggest otherwise. As it is, Dante
in the *Paradiso* and Shakespeare in plays of the last period such
as *The Winter's Tale* and *The Tempest* made the only successful
attempts in verse. Goethe's vatic utterance at the end of *Faust*
—'the Eternal Feminine beckons us onward'—would not have
satisfied Lewis. No doubt it did so beckon, and that was just the
trouble.

(ii)

What, we may now ask, was the time-philosophy that Lewis set
out to attack? Admittedly, he was concerned chiefly with a
direction of thought, and one manifest in several spheres; but he

made a very powerful, if unsystematic, case for the view that speculative thought, social and aesthetic theory, and indeed everyday conduct, were influenced in their various ways by assumptions about the nature of time whereby modern culture was distinguished from that of the past and from the static Orient. The result was an altered view of the nature of man, Western man, himself—a secular change, and secular was a time-word. In expounding his thesis, Lewis was at his best in providing concrete examples, some of the most effective of which were to be found outside his principal Time book. In *The Lion and the Fox*, he spoke of the way in which the Elizabethan stage substituted *exterior* action for the *interior* stress of the Classical theatre of Greece, and he provided a striking instance of the tension which this could generate: 'Technically, Hamlet... is a *time*-phenomenon. He could be regarded as a Greek got on to the bustling, elizabethan stage, and acting as a brake on the action by maladjustment to the altered time-sense, or rather absence of time-sense, he finds.'[5] In modern art, too, there was tension, because the artistic imagination, like the philosophic intelligence, was devoted to the search for form—or rather, this was the ideal of classical art, which Lewis, the artist, had been striving to recapture.[6] To that extent, art, like the intellectual vision, was, as he argued in the 'Physics of the Not-Self', the metaphysical commentary which followed *Enemy of the Stars*, the 'traditional enemy of life' (a Nietzschean idea). Indeed, as the protagonist of *Tarr* declared, 'Art is identical with the idea of permanence. Art is continuity and not an individual spasm.... Anything living, quick and changing is bad art always.'[7] On the other hand, 'the living, quick and changing' had become in the eyes of a number of modern thinkers a value in itself, so that time *as a process*, rather than the products of time—the ephemeral rather than the permanent, the flux rather than the eternal—had become the object of a cult. From the capacious work of Samuel Alexander, *Space Time and Deity* (1920), Lewis selected a passage which has become a *locus classicus* (I quote the key sentences): 'The most important requirement... is to realize vividly the nature of time.... We are, as it were, to think ourselves into time. I call this taking time seriously.'
Alexander was an original thinker, and his book is full of

insights, even though its central thesis that God is an emergence of space-time—i.e. that the world is creating God rather than the other way round—is difficult to fathom; but the above passage implies some form of quasi-religious initiation: 'We are, as it were, to think ourselves into time.' And Lewis argued that the cult of the 'blind' will and of action for its own sake, with which much modern thought was permeated, was precisely an example of 'taking time seriously' in this almost mystical sense.

The most famous time-philosophy, however, and that providing the best example of what Lewis sought to counteract, was expounded by Bergson. Lewis had attended some of Bergson's lectures at the Collège de France, and he realized how powerful a spell Bergson had cast over his contemporaries.

According to Bergson, there were two kinds of time, but only one involved real change and development. The first, which he called mathematical time, made no essential difference to change: e.g., if plants moved or developed twice as fast as they do, they would follow the same course. But real time, or what Bergson called duration, brought about something genuinely new. This was identical with life itself. It was 'a gushing forth of novelties', an 'intensive manifold', an interpenetrative process which could be seized not by intellect but by the immediate faculty of intuition. Indeed, it seemed to be very much like that 'constantly melting and hotly overflowing' medium which Lewis had warned us against. For Bergson, intellect was a secondary faculty which 'spatialized' events, cut them up, folded them out flat, and thus led to a distorted or mechanistic view of life.

With his anti-intellectual bias, Bergson therefore was 'the great organizer of disintegration in the modern world', and he was responsible for that 'destruction of the things of the intellect, and the handing over to sensation of the privileges and heirlooms of the mind, and the enslaving of the intelligent to the affective nature',[8] which might be detected in so much modern 'thought'. He was the mental force *against which* all traditional philosophy and metaphysics had been pitted since man began systematically to use his reason for the control not merely of his environment but of himself.

In the light of this summary, it is clear that Bergson was a 'gift' so far as Lewis was concerned; but it is also true to say perhaps that Lewis tended to saddle Bergson with too great a share in our cultural decline. The attack on the intellect and its values had been launched much earlier and on a wider front. And in any case, Bergson ended up as a student of the Christian mystics, believing that Christianity was the completion of Judaism, and, but for a laudable desire to remain among his people under persecution, he would have joined the Church of Rome, as he made clear in his will. I have got into hot water, specially brought to the boil by Geoffrey Grigson among others, for saying that Lewis might have ended up there himself; but my assertion was based upon personal confidences not merely from Lewis but from his wife, whose death occurred almost as these words were written.

(iii)

Whatever he might say about Bergson, Lewis came to the conclusion after the powerful effect of their work had worn off, that Schopenhauer and Nietzsche were chief among the precursors of the modern diffused time-philosophy. Indeed, these two subverters of current values seemed to have awakened him from his dogmatic slumber, if, given his precocious mental development, he ever passed through such a phase. Like Hegel, Schopenhauer and Nietzsche took the 'great problems' for their province, and never conceived the philosophical quest otherwise than in this light. Among Lewis's most lucid pages were those devoted in *Time and Western Man* to Schopenhauer, a philosopher whose own lucidity no doubt exerted a particular attraction for him. Schopenhauer's conception of the Will as the principle in and behind all things, which objectified itself as the phenomenal universe, was to Lewis a signal example of the time-philosophy, above all on account of its 'blindness'. Indeed, except for its daemonic remorselessness which gave rise to Schopenhauer's famous pessimism, the blind Will was Bergson's duration, his *élan vital*. It too was a 'will to live' acting no less unconsciously and needing 'no documentation, no memory, or any of the intellectual machinery that we carry about'. Thus Schopenhauer's unconscious—the first modern unconscious, dated 1818

—dissolved all values in its own inexorable passage as 'a vast, undirected, purposeless impulse'. Since it was a Will 'to nothing', it was as purposeless as mechanism; and for that reason Lewis credited Schopenhauer with having set the scene for the mechanistic outlook of modern physical or positivistic science. Its god was the same. 'The name changes, only, from hypostasized Will to an hypostasized Time.'[9]

In fact, Schopenhauer was quite clear about the relationship between the two terms, and, reading Schopenhauer, one finds it not inconceivable that Lewis may have derived from him the initial impetus to write the study which eventually became *Time and Western Man.* 'Time', wrote Schopenhauer, 'is that by virtue of which everything becomes nothingness in our hands and loses all real value.' That after all is Lewis's thesis in a nutshell.

What may have drawn Lewis to Schopenhauer, apart from his obvious sincerity ('Bergson was not sincere, hence his optimism'), was his 'Hindu' solution to the problem of the eternal flux. This was to jump clear of its passage, to break the chain of rebirth (to use the Hindu-Buddhist terminology with which Schopenhauer had become familiar through a German translation of a Persian translation of the Sanskrit Upanishads), and to maintain a position of intellectual detachment. For with intellect, Schopenhauer declared, 'we are really stepping out of life so as to regard it from the outside, like spectators at a play'. In Lewis's case, this intellectual stance, apparently cold and impersonal, was due partly to his Stoic desire to 'seek our salvation in being what we are', though the 'being' of an intellectual was naturally on a level superior to that of the average sensual man. No figure was less typically Anglo-Saxon than that of the pure intellectual; and it was as such that Lewis described himself by name in *The Apes of God.* The consequent attitude of aloofness— 'The intellect works alone'[10]—did not endear Lewis to the public.

Despite Lewis's repudiation of the time element in his work, Schopenhauer may be regarded as the nineteenth-century thinker most closely resembling him, at least in general outlook. There is about much of Lewis's work an extreme diffidence, a sense of disillusion, and at the same time a veneration for timeless values

—sometimes subsumed under aesthetic categories—which call to mind the German thinker. It is the disillusioned side of Lewis which has apparently alienated so many readers: for although the age congratulates itself on its freedom from illusions, it flees from this freedom at the first touch of its cold embrace. In *The Lion and the Fox*, Lewis dwells on Shakespeare's own disillusion as mirrored in such a play as *Troilus and Cressida*. 'The matter of his art, or what he sees and thinks, when not drunken with the grand style, is the mental material of *Troilus and Cressida*. Nothing more disillusioned has ever been written about the traditional heroisms of the world than *Troilus and Cressida*. *This is the pure intellect's true account of life*' (my italics).[11]

Schopenhauer once said: 'Life is a disagreeable thing: I have determined to spend it by reflecting upon it.' This seems to be how Lewis conceived his own role as a writer and thinker. Despite immense psychic energy, he was no 'lover of life'; and this anti-life disposition aroused the antipathy of Leavis, whose criterion of a work of art or literature, Does it make for life?, applied to Lewis, registered a decided negative. In any case, Lewis had devoted some of his most telling pages in *Paleface* to a critical examination of D. H. Lawrence—the great life-enhancer—and although he was prepared to concede Lawrence's artistry, he found his 'lower mysticism' bogus. Naturally, Lawrence resented Lewis's criticism (initially in *The Enemy*), and Leavis repeated Lawrence's counterblast.

In temperament and character, too, Schopenhauer and Lewis would seem to have had something in common, not least in their attitude to women. Lewis was a male author *par excellence*; and perhaps that is why so few women have written about him. He spoke of the 'male chastity of thought';[12] and in the climate of the present he would no doubt have felt even more 'out of key with his time' than he did in his own day. From *The Art of Being Ruled* there is evidence that he was well acquainted with that extraordinary book *Sex and Character* by Otto Weininger (1906), the brilliant German who, two years after completing this anti-female tirade, committed suicide at the age of 23. Lewis did not go so far as to adopt Weininger's extreme misogyny—'the meaning of woman is to be meaningless', 'woman cannot be evil, she is merely non-moral', etc. (Lewis was at bottom a devotee of

Anglo-Saxon commonsense); but he did to some extent share Weininger's views on the female ethos. It is common knowledge that he exhibited to the world, until his last years, a mode of existence which suggested that he regarded women, even those nearest to him, as subordinate creatures, doomed to remain inferior. In *The Art of Being Ruled*, he protested that his book was not 'against women', but he added these curious words: 'Eventually, I believe, a considerable segregation of women and men must occur, *just as* a segregation of those who decide for the active, the intelligent life, and those who decide (without any stigma attaching to the choice) for the 'lower' or animal life, is likely to happen, *and is very much to be desired*' (my italics).[13] On the other hand, like Weininger, the lover of Frieda Lawrence, Lewis evidently at heart enjoyed the company of women, and he certainly knew in his final years what a happy marriage could be: whereas it would seem that Weininger's powerful sexual drive, along with his belief that women were a snare, combined with other factors to set up so violent a conflict in him that life became intolerable. Another woman-hater to enjoy an exuberant sexuality was of course Schopenhauer himself.

(iv)

The other 'male' thinker of the nineteenth century who captured Lewis's early attention and whose influence has proved in general even greater than that of Schopenhauer was Nietzsche, though Nietzsche acknowledged a great debt to his predecessor. This included misogyny; but, like some other misogynists and denunciators of effeminacy, Nietzsche spent much time attacking 'priestly asceticism', and advocating liberation from ethical taboos—and indeed from conventional ethics itself—which he identified with 'slave morality'. He sought to attain a position 'beyond value'; but, to his surprise, total spiritual liberation, or what he deemed to be such, proved empty and objectless, even though he struggled to argue to the contrary. In one of his last books, *The Genealogy of Morals* (1887), he made great play with the remark, ambiguous like a good many others originated by him, that 'man would sooner have the void for his purpose than be void of purpose': which, if it means anything coherent at all, suggests that Nietzsche, despite his exaltation of 'dionysiac' action and the will to power, found purposelessness a great deal more difficult to stomach than Schopenhauer did.

In Lewis's view, Nietzsche signally failed to live up to his self-imposed mission. 'Nietzsche had very little in his composition of the health, balance, measure and fine sense of the antique world . . . towards which he returned so often: he had much more of the frantic, intolerant fanaticism of a genevan reformer or an Old Testament prophet.'[14] Thus although he denounced pedantry and exalted laughter and robustness in his earlier book *The Joyful Wisdom* (1882)—which is more accurately (if today somewhat misleadingly) translated *The Gay Science*, and without which we should not, I believe, have had such Lewis titles as 'The Soldier of Humour' or 'Laughter and the Wild Body'—the teaching was at bottom dreary enough. Lewis was not in the end beguiled by the melancholy strains of *The Joyful Wisdom*. (Indeed, shortly after the appearance of his book, Nietzsche wrote to Lou Salomé that he had taken a huge dose of opium, 'from despair'.) Being English and empirical, Lewis believed that scepticism, however far we take it—and Hume, whom he quotes, took it almost to the limit—must not 'destroy all action, as well as speculation'. But both action and speculation, understood in the rational sense, are frustrated if we surrender to the lures of 'ecstatic propaganda, of plunges into cosmic streams of flux and time, of miraculous baptisms, of the ritual of time-gods, and of breathless transformations'.[15] Lewis declared that he had 'other views on the subject of attaining perfection'. Nevertheless, to find 'our salvation in being what we are'—'creatures of a certain kind, with no indication that a radical change is imminent'[16] —was to find a very imperfect, quarrelsome, largely unattractive creature: an 'angry ape'. And these were the creatures who inhabited not merely the novel appropriately entitled *The Apes of God*, but *The Human Age* too. But whereas the puppets of *The Apes of God* have neither past nor future, the proto-humans of *The Human Age* await judgement and possibly redemption: in short, they await their humanity. *The Human Age* is a work infused with a 'vision of judgement'; it is eschatological, or pre-occupied with the doctrine of the last things.

For all Nietzsche's eulogy of ruthless action and the will to power—'What do men who can command, who are born rulers, who evince power in act and deportment, have to do with contract?' he asked in *The Genealogy of Morals*—the result, namely the void, deprived his philosophy of any meaning, even a tragic meaning. At least Schopenhauer had preached 'tolerance, patience, forbearance and charity, which each of us needs and which each of us therefore owes', though how he derived these lofty virtues from the workings of a blind Will he never satisfactorily explained. At any rate, Lewis concluded that 'Schopenhauer probably was a wiser man, and came to better terms with life, than Nietzsche.'[17] Increasingly, Nietzsche's work showed a morbid interest in insanity and that 'diabolical principle' of romantic Satanism upon which Lewis was to write an essay (1931); and in the end, as we know, he was confined to a home, first public and then private. Lewis's final words on Nietzsche have that note of impishness which, as Lewis employs it, is the reverse of superficial: 'Nietzsche was a death-snob (as Whitman was a life-snob): and he was also a madness-snob. This is a very ancient form of snob; but formerly the madness-snob never dreamt of going mad himself in his enthusiasm.'[18]

Nevertheless, we must not underestimate Lewis's debt to Nietzsche. Some of the remarks in *Time and Western Man* on the process of artistic creation as a trance or dream-state remind one forcibly of the early pages of Nietzsche's *Birth of Tragedy* (1872); and that work would seem to have influenced the essay on 'The Dithyrambic Spectator', companion to 'The Diabolical Principle', possibly even suggesting its title, seeing that Nietzsche speaks so frequently of spectators and dithyrambs. It also contains an apt use of the word 'vortex', though Pound is supposed originally to have interested Lewis in that term.

(v)

Some of the threads of our survey, so far, may conveniently be gathered together by considering a figure who, though difficult to classify, was in many ways as precocious as Lewis, but who was killed in 1917 at the age of 34. T. E. Hulme had studied under Bergson and, as commonly happened, had started out an enthusiastic disciple. He was also the translator not merely of the master's *Introduction to Metaphysics* (1913) but of Sorel's *Réflexions sur la Violence*, a work much influenced by Nietzsche. But Hulme then went on to formulate a point of view of his own. He was therefore a transitional figure to whom Lewis, and even more Eliot, owed a great deal. Indeed, Lewis in a somewhat misleadingly lighthearted assessment called him 'one of the most promising intelligences produced by England since the Shaw-Wells-Bennett vintage'.[19] Hulme's ideas, together with his few poems, were assembled in a book entitled *Speculations*, published in 1924 and edited by Herbert Read. In launching an attack against the entire Humanist tradition, Hulme argued that all post-Renaissance philosophy rested on 'the same inability to realize the meaning of the dogma of original sin'. And he added: 'Our difficulty now, of course, is that we are really incapable of understanding how any other view but the humanistic could be seriously held by intelligent and emancipated men.' Nevertheless, it was a 'realization of the *tragic* significance of life which makes it legitimate to call all other attitudes shallow'. Finally, '*a man is essentially bad*, he can only accomplish anything of value by discipline—ethical and political. Order is not merely negative, but creative and liberating. Institutions are necessary' (*Speculations*, author's italics).

Lewis refers to Hulme at length in the chapter on 'The terms "Classical" and "Romantic"' in *Men without Art*, and in two amusing chapters (viii and ix) in *Blasting and Bombardiering*; he clearly found Hulme's ideas congenial. 'If . . . you regard man as the perfectly fixed and "static"—corrupt, evil, untidy, incomplete—animal, as I do, as Mr. Hulme did, it is pretty evident that a kindly, tolerant and humanitarian attitude is the last thing expected of us.'[20] Not merely is this avowal compatible with our earlier references to Lewis's view of man, but it helps to explain the respect in which he held another school of thinkers, namely the French Neo-Scholastics or Thomists. Jacques Maritain, the leader of the group, whose influence in Europe between the wars was considerable and controversial (he sided with the Republicans in the Spanish Civil War), was both an acute metaphysician and a writer on art and social affairs.

During the Second World War, Lewis met him in exile in Canada, and he alluded to this meeting, which was evidently a pleasant one, in *Rude Assignment*; but as early as *Paleface* he had declared his respect for the Neo-Scholastic passion for clear definition and its emphasis on absolute values. 'I range myself', he wrote, 'in some sense, with the modern scholastic teachers.'[21] And in *Time and Western Man* he acknowledged that 'constantly in our criticism we march with the "thomist"'.[22] It is true that Lewis qualified his admiration for Maritain, feeling, as did Eliot, that the former Bergsonian was 'still far too much tainted with the manners and the thought of his orginal master'. This applied particularly to his style. For he felt that some of the Neo-Thomists were infected by the time-doctrine if only by attaching a disproportionate importance to *one* time. A Catholic intellectual who exerted a powerful, if unobtrusive, influence over Lewis was the Jesuit philosopher, Father M. C. D'Arcy, a Thomist expert and a good friend over many years, who, in his book *The Nature of Belief*, cited *Time and Western Man* with approval at a period when such an allusion was somewhat daring.

    Although Lewis maintained that the dogma of original sin and some of the Neo-Scholastic principles could be entertained in the absence of religious faith, he committed himself in *Time and Western Man* to a statement of belief which, if in some ways Deistic and based upon an aesthetic analogy, cannot be ignored in assessing his philosophy of life, much as some of his admirers have tried to ignore it:

    As an epigraph to this book, I have used a passage from the *Metaphysics* of Aristotle. In it he says that if all we had to make up our idea of God with were what we possess in our experience (what we could take from the highest reaches of our contemplative states), then that God would be 'worthy of our admiration'. What we are suggesting here is that that is exactly all we have, indeed, with which to construct our God. . . . To at once be perfectly concrete, we can assert that a God that swam in such atmosphere as is produced by the music of a Bach fugue, or the stormy grandeur of the genii in the Sistine ceiling, or the scene of the Judgment of Signorelli

at Orvieto, who moved with the grace of Mozart . . . such a
God would be the highest we could imagine.[23]

(vi)

Enough has been said perhaps to show something of the originality but also the isolation of Lewis's intellectual position in
English letters, if indeed such isolation were not the result of
having an intellectual position at all. In the textbooks Lewis will
always be grouped with Eliot, Pound and Joyce, and this is
appropriate enough: the four men were well acquainted, and
they certainly exerted considerable influence over one another.
But Lewis remained the odd man out, and his intellectual
interests differed somewhat from those of the rest, and were
perhaps wider. This is not to underestimate Eliot's versatility,
such as his grasp of the oriental mind (though he never journeyed
east of Suez), or Joyce's close acquaintance with such a figure as
Vico. But The Art of Being Ruled is still regarded as forbidding,
no doubt because its authorities are drawn from a tradition of
which most readers have but the haziest knowledge.

Proudhon, Fourier, Leroy-Beaulieu, Péguy, Sorel, Spengler—
these names, with the possible exception of Spengler, were
familiar only to a restricted circle, chiefly perhaps because they
were overshadowed by the greater, if somewhat mythologized,
figure of Marx. It is only recently that men such as Fourier, with
his labour co-operatives or phalansteries, and Proudhon, for
whom property was 'theft'—both of whom Marx dismissed
contemptuously as Utopian socialists, ignoring the Utopian and
almost messianic element in his own thought—have been given
the attention they deserve. The same is true of that isolated
figure Péguy, poet, socialist and friend of Maritain, though not
formally a Catholic until a week or two before his death on the
battlefield, and even more so of Sorel, whom Lewis described as
'the key to all contemporary political thought'. In reading these
men without Marxist prejudices, Lewis was as usual much in
advance of his time.

Sorel made his début in England, as we have seen, through
Hulme's translation of his Réflexions sur la Violence (1908—

it is not easy to 'reflect' on violence, but Sorel did. Originally an engineer by profession, Sorel became a political force by combining, at the start of his public career, an intense belief in revolutionary change with something very like a 'tragic sense of life'. As a disciple of Nietzsche, he called it instead 'a heroic conception of life'; for this partisan of social transformation did not believe in progress—his *Illusions du Progrès* (1908) is a more convincing book than the *Réflexions*. In due course, the tragic and heroic conception gained ascendancy over the revolutionary one, and Sorel ended up within the fold of Action Française, the right-wing and monarchist group headed by that apostle of Classicism and 'non-croyant' Catholicism, Charles Maurras. No wonder Lewis described Sorel as 'a fabulous hybrid, attacking himself, biting his own tail, kicking his own heroical chest, contunding his own unsynthetic flesh, and showing his wounds with pride—self-inflicted, *self* in everything'.[24]

Nevertheless, it is sometimes from the extremist that we have most to learn, even if that is no justification of extremism. Sorel, who, like many another ideologist, was a myth-maker— he believed in his 'socialist' days that the General Strike was a myth necessary to galvanize the working classes to action, though he never thought such a thing likely to happen—held that something must take the place of traditional religion; and the chief difference between his early and his later outlook was that he came to believe that nothing, certainly no secular myth, *could* take its place, though one suspects that the Catholicism he finally embraced was of the 'unbelieving' kind of Maurras. Lewis may have sympathized with Sorel on this point—his attitude to religion was for long ambivalent; but he denounced Sorel most of all for his treason to the intellect. Indeed, he likened his 'vulgar frenzy' and his flirtation with 'spontaneous action' and the will to power (which the advocacy of violence amounts to) to the tirades of Nietzsche, whose influence he never succeeded in shedding.

(vii)

If one occasionally receives the impression that Lewis was apt to force some of his witnesses to disclose their part in the time-conspiracy—Whitehead, with his concept of Eternal Objects, was surely a great deal less guilty in this respect than Alexander —the fact remains that there were others who betrayed themselves out of their own mouths. Such a one was Oswald Spengler (1880–1936), author of the once best-selling *Decline of the West*, but now overshadowed by Toynbee. Spengler, to whom Lewis devoted a chapter of *Time and Western Man* (Part II, Chap. 2), was perhaps the most remarkable philosopher of history since Hegel. For him, as for Croce, history was time; but, more than that, we were history—for all history was of the present (Croce)— and therefore, to quote Spengler, '*we ourselves are time*' (his italics). This was to go one better than Alexander. The latter had enjoined us to 'take time seriously' and 'to think ourselves into time'; but Spengler maintained that we were already in it and constituted its essence, which was to take it seriously enough. And this idea that we were the 'focus' of temporality was as much as to say that we were identical with the Bergsonian Duration, the intensive manifold. Nor was it surprising, as Lewis pointed out, that the Spenglerian temporal process should be pronounced 'ineffable', to be grasped intuitively rather than intellectually. For Spengler spoke of two logics, corresponding to Bergson's two kinds of time: one was notional or intellectual and the other was 'an organic logic, an instinctive dream-sure logic'. Thus the world-as-history, which was the world-as-time, proceeded somnambulistically, with 'dream-sure logic', since it could not be sure in any other way. Now we seem to have heard of something like this before. Going back beyond Bergson, it is the world-as-'blind'-Will of Schopenhauer. So it all hung together.

Indeed, the more we examine Lewis's excursions into philosophical exegesis, the more we are struck by his capacity to observe interconnections, hidden links and common assumptions in what may at first appear to be disparate systems of thought, or ideas claiming independence which can be shown to be parasitic upon systems. *Time and Western Man* remains a stimulating book, not merely because it succeeds in making out its case, but because, to anyone who has continued to keep abreast with philosophical thought, it retains its relevance, and throws light upon what is happening now. Existentialism has come and gone; and although it never took firm root in Anglo-Saxon soil, Lewis devoted a short but forceful chapter to it in *The Writer and the Absolute* (Part III, Chap. 9), pointing out among much else that Sartre's master Heidegger wrote a book called *Being and Time* (1927). Moreover, J. P. Sartre's 'Il n'y a de réalité que dans l'action' is pure Nietzsche-Sorel-Bergson, just as the new physicalism is in many respects old behaviourism writ large. Much of what Lewis says about behaviourism and its erosion of the idea of personality and the self could apply equally well to modern neo-materialism. His knock-about handling of the Tester ('When the figure works slowly you call it "thought". When it works quickly, you call it "reflex" ') is relevant to Quine's 'neurology is the place for explanations ultimately', and to remarks of similar purport by Chomsky.

Nevertheless, professional philosophers continue to fight shy of Lewis, first perhaps because he treats their subject with less than customary seriousness, and secondly because of his concern with problems which, as more than one university syllabus insists, are no longer regarded as coming within the province of philosophy at all. To echo the early quotation from Herbert Read, however, no form of specialization can be effective unless it is associated with some wider ethos. To pursue specialization for its own sake is fruitless, except as affording incidental clarification; for, as Maritain put it in the subtitle of his major work, *Les Degrés de Savoir*, it is necessary to 'distinguer pour unir'. The universal mind is the unifying mind, whether that mind chooses to express itself in art or in speculative thought. And an outstanding intelligence is a condition of the pursuit of one goal as much as the other. It is by a kind of instinct that we know that the world's great poets, for instance, were persons of supreme intellect, even though their art was deployed in the realm of feeling. What I have said of Lewis must not be taken to imply that I place him among the supreme intelligences of mankind: at some point there was a failure of nerve, and the enormous promise of his early career was not maintained. But he stood 'in solitary schism' by the values of the intellect and of the philosophic intelligence; and the current recognition of his significance, however grudging it may be in some quarters, is surely very much overdue.

4

Lewis and the Patriarchs: Augustus John, W. B. Yeats, T. Sturge Moore

TIMOTHY MATERER

'What an entangled Absalom!', W. B. Yeats wrote to T. Sturge Moore after reading *Time and Western Man*. Yeats refers to Wyndham Lewis's rebellious spirit in that book rather than to the kind of arrogance Absalom showed in defying his father King David. Moore, however, may have sensed an adverse criticism because he replied defensively that Lewis's 'hair is dangerously long and he is too suspicious all round, but there is something of genius if only he could get and keep hold on it'.[1] We will see that Yeats actually admired *Time and Western Man* even more than Moore did. The immediately significant feature of Yeats's and Moore's exchange is the paternal tone they take toward Lewis, which Yeats's witty allusion to Absalom supports. The tone is appropriate because Yeats and especially Moore encouraged Lewis at crucial times in his career and were models of the artistic character to him. Other men encouraged Lewis's development, such as the architect William Stirling, who bought Lewis pastries and praised his poetry in his adolescent years, and William Rothenstein, who helped Lewis throughout his career as a painter.[2] But Moore and Yeats, as well as the younger artist Augustus John, were uniquely valuable to Lewis because they set for him the pattern of the artist's life.

No reader of Wyndham Lewis would accept a psychological argument that Lewis, a virtually fatherless child, searched all his life for a father figure. To use one of Lewis's own phrases, such a theory would seem too 'Freud-infected'. Yet one can see in Lewis's life at least a Joycean pattern in which he rejects his natural father and finds a spiritual one to foster the artist in him.

In the letters of Lewis's Paris years, his name for his father is 'The Old Rip', and his sole concern with him is how to 'extract' money from his 'Parent Over the Water'.³ His father's break from and then neglect of his family would not necessarily mean that Lewis's dependence on mature artists was any greater than it is for any artist. Lewis's relationship with Sturge Moore, for example, is paralleled by Ezra Pound's with Laurence Binyon.⁴ Nevertheless, the effort Lewis made in 1940 to interpret his father's life of outward idleness and irresponsibility as somehow noble suggests that the break with his father deeply affected him. Only a late-developing filial piety could explain why Lewis would plan to edit (but never complete) a collection of his father's 'War Sketches'. Although he admitted in a fragment called 'The Do-Nothing Mode' that his father was a 'fox-hunting, brigantine-owning, essay-writing *bum*', he also justified him as an 'odd-man-out in a society of go-getters'. Charles Edward Lewis is described as an 'eccentric' who 'became so perhaps in protest against the American uniformity of mercantile endeavour: he grew into a notable solitary, as well.' Lewis believes that his father could have been 'quite a good writer, had someone taken him in hand,' and he concludes sympathetically that his father's life was that of the 'confirmed romantic'.⁵ In the light of this ingenious interpretation, Lewis's father could have been a model for him. The potential artistic character in the father's life was realized in the son's.

But the young Lewis found models less remote than his Parent Over the Water. Augustus John was the first major one. Although John was only four years older than Lewis, Lewis's description of his meeting with him shows how well John filled a patriarchal role. Before he even reached John's flat, 'there was a noise of children, for this patriarch had already started upon his Biblical courses.'⁶ Lewis was prepared for John's biblical and mythological dimensions. When Lewis enrolled at the Slade School of Art, John's works were displayed in the halls as the nearest approach any student had made to the High Renaissance ideals that Professor Tonks upheld there. But John's visit to a drawing class upset the professor's regimen. Lewis describes this visit, the first time he ever saw John, in one of the liveliest passages in *Rude Assignment*:

One day the door of the life-class opened and a tall bearded figure, with an enormous black Paris hat, large gold ear-rings decorating his ears, with a carriage of the utmost arrogance, strode in and the whisper 'John' went round the class . . . with a ferocious glare at the model (a female) [he] began to draw with an indelible pencil. I joined the group behind this redoubtable personage. To my great surprise, a squat little figure began to emerge upon the paper. He had forsaken the 'grand manner' entirely, it seemed. . . . Needless to say everyone was tickled to death. They felt that the squalor of the Dutch, rather than the noble rhetoric of the cinquecento, was, and always had been, the thing. John left us as abruptly as he had arrived. We watched in silence this mythological figure depart.[7]

Lewis would copy John's mysterious entrance and exit and his Paris hat throughout his life, but his artistic style was never modelled on John's. The older artist's achievements were important, however, as a standard against which Lewis could measure himself. He recalled that Professor Tonks's life became 'a hell on earth' when Lewis and his fellow students were inspired by John's visit to rebel against the 'grand manner'. John's influence was eventually so powerful that Lewis was unable to paint. Lewis wrote to his mother in 1906: 'I want to do some painting very badly, and can't do so near John since his artistic personality is just too strong, and he is much more developed, naturally, and this frustrates any effort.'[8] Michael Holroyd thinks that this frustration was one reason that Lewis concentrated on his writing during this period. For his part, John did his best to encourage Lewis's art. He was one of the first to purchase a Lewis painting when he bought an oil called Port de Mer in about 1910.

Since John showed Lewis and the Slade students how to rebel against established canons of taste, it was only natural for Lewis to play Absalom to John's David and criticize his achievement. This Lewis did in Blast when he praised him as a 'great artist' but also detected a dated quality in him: 'it was John who inaugurated an era of imaginative art in England, and buried the mock naturalists and pseudo-impressionists. . . . It was his Rembrandtesque drawings of stumpy brown people . . . that

made him the legitimate successor to Beardsley and Wilde. . . .'
The 'era' John inaugurated was in fact only a decade before the
Vorticist revolution in 1914, and Lewis suggests that the very
power of John's gifts 'seemed to prematurely exhaust him'.[9]
This criticism hurt John deeply because he felt that it might be
true. The *Blast* article led to a public scene between the two
artists when John accused Lewis of being 'malignant', and
Lewis refrained from violence, he said, only because John was
with a lady. John apologized by letter, admitting that Lewis's
criticism was 'salutary' if not accurate and Lewis replied that the
'thought of scrapping with you causes me a feeling of shame, re-
ferrable to our long intimacy and my position at first of a cadet'.[10]
    Lewis's cadet days were not entirely over. There was some-
thing even a Vorticist could learn from John. Soon after the
Blast period, both Lewis and John were recording the war as
official war artists. Lewis said that his war experience showed
him the dangers of Vorticist extremism: 'when Mars with his
mailed finger showed me a shell crater and a skeleton, with a
couple of shivered tree stumps behind it, I was still in my
"abstract" element. And before I knew what I was doing I was
drawing with loving care a signaler corporal to plant upon the
lip of the shell crater.'[11] The intimacy between John and Lewis
was re-established as they travelled together near the war front,
where John would terrify the soldiers who thought that this tall,
bearded man was King George V. In later years, Lewis's reviews
of John's shows were always enthusiastic and revealed a new
affinity between the two men as artists. In one review Lewis
argues that John is really a classic and not, as generally believed,
a romantic painter: 'in his "Little Concert", for instance, reigns
an Augustan peace. . . . These are stylistic creatures of a world
forever sheltered from the intrusions of passion.'[12]
    This interpretation may sound too close to Lewis's artistic
ideals to seem a convincing interpretation of John's art. But
another review of John's work strengthens Lewis's case and
suggests what he could have learned from John. Lewis is here
praising a show of John's Jamaican pictures:

Mr. John opens his large blue eyes, and a dusky head bursts
into them. . . . His large blue eyes hold fast the dusky object

while his brushes stamp out on the canvas a replica of what he
sees. . . . Nature is for him like a tremendous carnival. . . .
And it is only because he enjoys it so tremendously that he is
moved to report upon it—in a fever of optical emotion, before
the object selected passes on and is lost in the crowd.[13]

Lewis's key terms are all here: the eye fixed on the object
selected from the crowd of objects within Nature. Although
Lewis may be verbally recreating John in his own image as an
'eye-man', in much the same way that he made his father into a
potential artist, the passage shows that John was still serving as
a model for Lewis. John helped him in what Lewis called his
'escape' from the abstract style of his *Blast* period: 'what
I was headed for, obviously, was to fly away from the world of
men, of pigs, of chickens and alligators, and to go to live in the
unwatered moon, only a moon sawed up into square blocks, in
the most alarming way. What an escape I had!'[14] This statement
is from *The Demon of Progress in the Arts*, in which Lewis
complains that the current extremism of the visual arts makes it
impossible for a traditionalist like Augustus John to be recognized for his pre-eminence in art, as a composer like Benjamin
Britten is in music. The unfortunate result of this extremism is
that painting lacks the standards of professionalism that com-
posing enjoys. If John were acknowledged as the master he is,
Lewis argues, both traditional and non-traditional achievements
could be better understood.

To Lewis's charge of 'extremism' in the arts, Lewis's critics
retorted with a charge of 'reaction'. But Lewis's defence of
representational painters in *The Demon of Progress* has been
vindicated by the success of painters such as Francis Bacon,
David Hockney, and Lucian Freud. Lewis's attachment to external, visual reality was never reactionary because it was never
simplistic. It was the complexity of Lewis's attitude toward the
reality of the physical world which so impressed W. B. Yeats.
When Yeats began to read formal philosophy in the twenties, he
was looking for what Richard Ellmann calls 'an interpretation of
the external world which gives the mind autonomy, while at the
same time insisting that no one's mind is isolated'. The essential
quality in a philosophy for Yeats is 'its adaptability to poetry and

its power to free the mind from abstractions'.[15] Lewis wanted a philosophical outlook which would have the same practical benefit for the painter.

Lewis aided Yeats's quest for a philosophy by helping to unmask abstract systems of thought such as those of Bertrand Russell and the scientific 'realists'. Replying to Moore's defence of Lewis's 'something of genius' quality, Yeats explains that he in fact agrees with Moore's high opinion of Lewis and even defies his doctor's orders by reading *The Art of Being Ruled* and *Time and Western Man*: 'henceforth I need not say splenetic things for all is said. [Lewis] mixes metaphors in the most preposterous way but he can write; he has intellectual passion.... I do not always hate what he hates and yet I am always glad that he hates.' To Olivia Shakespear, Yeats wrote that he was reading *Time and Western Man* with 'ever growing admiration and envy —what energy!—and I am driven back to my reed-pipe'.[16] Lewis put Yeats's admiration to good use when he quoted the eminent poet's letter in praise of *The Apes of God* in *Satire and Fiction* and his letter in praise of *Tarr* in *Rude Assignment*. Lewis's letters to T. Sturge Moore show how encouraged he was by Yeats's admiration for a work such as *The Childermass*. The image of Yeats as a benevolent patriarch must be dropped, however, as we examine the philosophical ideas that Yeats discovered in Lewis. In this area, as Yeats wrote to Mrs Shakespear, 'I am in all essentials [Lewis's] most humble and admiring disciple. I like some of the people he dislikes but I accept all the dogma of the faith'.[17]

The 'faith' was an entirely negative one—a matter of hatred or, better, destructive energy. Lewis states the thesis of *Time and Western Man* when attacking the 'realist' Alfred North Whitehead. He explains that Whitehead's reality is that of primary objects, such as colour and form, which cannot be sensuously apprehended. In *Science and the Modern World*, Whitehead says that his doctrine of 'organic mechanism' is that 'the whole concept of materialism only applies to very abstract entities, the products of logical discernment'.[18] Lewis comments on this passage:

The only kind of thing that can be described as 'matter', then, is such a thing as his 'eternal' entity colour. A colour is eternal. 'It haunts time like a spirit.' Is it not strange that the only sort of 'material' thing that Professor Whitehead will allow should remind him of a *spirit*? Yet it does; and that use of words is not without significance, nor a slip of a pen.[19]

This criticism of Whitehead leads Lewis to the 'fundamental issue' of his book: 'the problem of the "abstract" versus the "concrete" at the base of the various world-pictures to be discussed. For what I have called the time-school, time and change are the ultimate reality. They are the *abstract school*, it could be said.'[20] Time enters these world-pictures because the 'objects' that the 'realists' believe exist independently of the mind are conditioned by it. In *Our Knowledge of the External World*, Bertrand Russell writes that 'a thing may be defined as a certain series of appearances' that are constantly changing in time.[21] From this perspective, 'reality' is in time—not in the thing; or rather a space-time 'event' replaces the thing. Russell's own term for the basic units of reality, 'neutral entities', recalls Whitehead's 'abstract entities'. Lewis thus complains that the objects Russell holds 'up to us, as our mirrors or as pictures of *our* reality, are of [a] mixed, fluid and neutral character' that dissociates them from sense experience.[22]

Lewis's analysis of the weakness of modern thought confirmed Yeats's own intuitions. In his essay 'Bishop Berkeley' (1931), Yeats wrote that the philosophical 'mischief' began when John Locke 'separated the primary and secondary qualities; and from that day to this the conception of a physical world without colour, sound, taste, tangibility . . . has remained the assumption of science, the ground-work of every text-book.'[23] The results of this dissociation for the artist, according to Yeats, are works such as Joyce's *Anna Livia Plurabelle* and Pound's *Cantos*, in which the artist is 'helpless before the contents of his own mind'.[24] This intellectual disaster occurs because 'reality', as modern scientists and philosophers describe it, seems too abstract to be the material of art. Thus Yeats says that the artist must work with 'his active faculties in suspense, one finger beating time to a bell sounding and echoing in the depths of his own mind'.[25] This evocative if misleading description of writers like Pound and Joyce duplicates Lewis's view of these two artists as dire examples of the influence of 'abstract' philosophy. Indeed, Yeats told Lady Gregory that he intended to extend the criticism of Pound made in *Time and Western Man*, but he eventually abandoned the task as too difficult.[26]

Lewis and Yeats meet on the common ground of Bishop Berkeley's philosophy. According to both artists, Berkeley's greatest contribution to modern thought was his conviction that the mind is an active, creative force. Yeats writes that 'only where the mind partakes of a pure activity can art or life attain swiftness, volume, unity', and it attains this in Berkeley's philosophy.[27] For this reason, Berkeley is the inspiration for Lewis's attempt to state a philosophical position to replace the 'abstract school'. Although Berkeley took the extreme Idealist position that the existence of objects is dependent upon our perception of them, Lewis defends it as a valid attempt 'to destroy the myth of the superiority of the "abstract" over the immediate and individual'.[28] For Berkeley, there is no thing-in-itself, or any neutral or abstract entity which accounts for appearances. Berkeley's things are what they appear to be. In his *Commentaries*, Berkeley says that objects in his system retain 'Bulk, Solidity, and such like sensible qualitys'. The Conclusion to *Time and Western Man* refers to this paradox that Idealism provides a more sensuous, common-sense, 'real' world than scientific and philosophical 'realism':

> it is argued here that the entire physical world is strictly unreal; and the unrealist part of it we believe is that part or aspect supplied us by science. So with bridle and bit we ride the phantoms of sense, as though to the manner born. Or rather it would be more descriptive of our actual experience to say that, camped somnolently, in a relative repose of a god-like sort, upon the surface of this nihilism, we regard ourselves as at rest, with our droves of objects—trees, houses, hills—grouped around us.[29]

This passage suggests the complexity of Lewis's view of the external world. The world is appearances, but those appearances are real. The more we appreciate the illusory nature of the world, the more we will hold on—'with bridle and bit'—to its sensuous qualities.

How seriously is Lewis taking Berkeley's philosophy? His argument in *Time and Western Man* is the practical one that Berkeley's Idealism provides a better ground for literature than scientific Realism. He stops short of endorsing Idealism and freely admitted to Sturge Moore his limited competence in such matters. On the other hand, Lewis concludes his book with a promise to publish 'the particular beliefs that are explicit in my criticism', and the context seems to imply a future statement of Berkeleyan or Idealist beliefs. Yeats and Moore speculated on the direction Lewis would take as they continued their discussion of what Moore called 'Absalom's abundance'. Yeats claimed that Lewis 'considers that both "space and time are mere appearances", whereas his opponents think that time is real though space is a construction of the mind'.[30] Moore disagreed and said that Lewis's position could not be so simple: 'one cannot properly tell before he expounds his own position in the book he is now writing. I doubt if he really thinks Space and Time mere appearances, or if he does, I feel sure he is wrong. They are obviously modes of appearances, conditions of experience.'[31] Moore tells Yeats that Lewis 'always seemed to me to be a genius but most unfortunate, almost as horribly unfortunate as Baudelaire'.[32] To explain Moore's overstatement about Lewis, and to appreciate what is at stake in the Yeats–Moore debate over Lewis's Berkeleyism, we must know more about Moore's forty-year friendship with Lewis.

According to Victor Cassidy, who has edited a valuable selection of Lewis's correspondence with Moore, the two artists met in 1902. Lewis recalled their early meetings in a letter to Moore in 1941, only three years before Moore's death:

How calm those days were before the epoch of wars and social revolution, when you used to sit on one side of your work-table and I on the other, and we would talk—with trees and creepers of the placid Hampstead domesticity beyond the windows, and you used to grunt with a philosophic despondence I greatly enjoyed. It was the last days of the Victorian world of artificial peacefulness—of the R.S.P.C.A. and London

Bobbies, of 'slumming' and Buzzards cakes. As at that time I had never heard of anything else, it seemed to my young mind in the order of nature. You—I suppose—knew it was all like the stunt of an illusionist. You taught me many things. But you never taught me *that*.[33]

Lewis explains that it was his experience in World War I that taught him how illusory the pre-war appearances were. But he might have understood this truth on the basis of Moore's 'philosophic despondence' alone. It is fitting that this letter, one of the last Lewis wrote to Moore, should concern the reality of our perceptions of the world. This theme is central to both Lewis's and Moore's works.

By 1909 Lewis was identified as a protégé of Moore, who introduced him to the 'British Museum Circle' of William Rothenstein, R. A. Streatfield, and Laurence Binyon. In Canto 80 Ezra Pound recalls meeting Lewis in the Vienna Café, where this group would gather regularly:

> So it is to Mr Binyon that I owe, initially,
> Mr Lewis, Mr P. Wyndham Lewis, His bull-dog, me,
>   as it were against old Sturge M's bull-dog.[34]

In return for serving as Moore's 'bull-dog', Lewis received advice and encouragement from the maturer writer. Like Lewis, Moore was trained as an artist; but it was Lewis's prose writings that Moore encouraged. Lewis read his early sketches for *The Wild Body* to the Moore family, and his correspondence with Moore contains a valuable account of the development of *Tarr* through many early versions. Moore's advice even extended to the insistence that Lewis have the complete manuscript of *Tarr* typed, at Moore's own expense, so that it would make a better impression on a prospective publisher. Lewis acknowledged Moore's generosity when he wrote in 1926 of 'those times when by your generous kindness in putting your great gifts and maturer training at the service of my young idea your society was of such great benefit to me'.[35]

Moore's dedication of *A Sicilian Idyll* (1911) 'To Percy Wyndham Lewis Affectionately' shows that he recognized his paternal role. This long poem contrasts the lives of two passionate young

men. The narrator of most of the poem, an old man named
Damon, attempts to guide the life of the more intellectual young
man, Delphis. Delphis' mother tells Damon:

> well know I there is no end
> To Damon's kindness; my poor boy has proved it;
> Could but his father so have understood him![36]

I think that Moore meant Lewis to see something of his own
character in that of Delphis. Damon's analysis of this young
man may help to explain why Moore called Lewis a 'genius but
most unfortunate'.

Before the action of A Sicilian Idyll begins, Delphis has
squandered his great gifts as a 'town-wastrel' and in reaction to
this self-indulgence has begun a rustic life. When Damon meets
him again, Delphis' manner is no longer 'wicked with exceptions
to things honest'. But his rivalry with another young man who
is travelling with Damon brings new conflict into his life, and
soon Delphis is again 'Passionate, stormy, teeming with black
thought.' Now the 'rebel Delphis' again expresses 'anger and
contempt for gods,/Who he asserted were the dreams of men'.
In a later exchange with Damon, Delphis makes a proud boast
that Damon considers that of a 'madman':

> Free minds must bargain with each greedy moment
> And seize the most that lies to hand at once.
> Ye are too old to understand my words;
> I yet have youth enough, and can escape
> From that which sucks each individual man
> Into the common dream.[37]

If we read Moore's poem as in part a cautionary tale for Lewis,
its criticism of Delphis resembles Moore's criticism of the avant-
garde direction Lewis's art was taking. When Lewis complained
about the critical response to his drawings in a show of 1911, he
received no sympathy from Moore: 'I believe that you have put
your head in a pudding bag aesthetically speaking, and hope you
will take it out again before it is too late.' He admitted to being
impressed by Lewis's semi-abstract canvas Kermesse of 1912, but
added that 'it did not at all charm, allure or delight me'.
He implicitly criticized Lewis in his comments on the Second

Post-Impressionist show, in which Lewis exhibited his *Timon of Athens* series, as a 'reaction not an action' and a mere disowning of the past. Moore told Lewis that any kind of impressionism was 'suicidal' because artists of 'real temperament and genius like Manet Whistler and Gauguin fall to pieces dwindle disintegrate by the mere force of their conviction'. To Moore, the post-impressionist movement is a 'declivity with madness and death at the bottom'. This comment leads to a marvellous rejoinder from Lewis:

> madness and death are on all sides of any mountains worth the climbing. Though with a satisfactory set of guides and the latest appliances, one can be borne safely, no doubt, to any summit indicated. To be a poet is to have the courage of one's sensations, at least as far as lyricism goes.[38]

This is especially effective as a reply to a post-romantic poet like Moore, whose best lyrics are themselves explorations of his own sensations. But Moore thought that Lewis's scorn for conventional limits would lead to a Baudelairean self-destructiveness. The issue here concerns how far one explores.

In a letter to Yeats, Moore defined the temperamental differences that not only divided Moore from Yeats but also from the young Lewis: 'Your temperament inclines you to metaphysics and hypothetical systems. I have some leaning in that direction but my main anxiety is to remain central, not to lean very far towards any extreme.'[39] In the letter to Yeats in which he characterizes Lewis as being as unfortunate as Baudelaire, Moore states that 'it is no use pretending that what is not known is known because some body has got excited about the possibility that it might be known'.[40] Philosophical system-building seemed to Moore an evil seduction for the artist. He wrote to Yeats in 1928:

> Whether there is a supreme mystic experience may be doubted but at any rate no one that claims to have experienced it has been able to say anything significant about it. If it is, it surpasses language, just as philosophy is never equal to language, always being more clumsy than poetry and imagination.[41]

As the brother of G. E. Moore, the Cambridge philosopher whose attention to the meaning of words helped to deflate the claims of Idealist philosophy, Moore could speak with particular authority on this issue.

Moore should therefore have been glad that *Time and Western Man* was followed, not by an attempt to state a Berkeleyan or any other kind of philosophical system, but by a work of the imagination, *The Childermass*. Lewis was entering the most creative period of his career, and the warmth of the Lewis–Moore correspondence increases as Moore enthusiastically praises works such as *The Childermass*, *Snooty Baronet*, and *One-Way Song*. Although Lewis was by now a mature artist and a greater one than Moore, he still needed Moore's praise. In response to Moore's comments on *The Childermass*, Lewis wrote that 'Your approval is, as you know, one of the only things I covet.' When Moore praised *One-Way Song*, Lewis replied, 'When I burst into raucous song, you are one of the two or three people I think of with trepidation. But I remembered your encouragement, so precious to me, in the past, and that was I found the best specific against stage fright—or of such stage fright as a hardened ruffian of my type is capable!'[42] As a mature artist, Lewis had also come to accept the very terms Moore used in criticizing mere 'reaction' and the artists whose extremism prevents the full, patient development of their powers. The Moore of 1912 sounds very like the Lewis of *The Demon of Progress in the Arts*, who also believes in the necessity of limits:

> There are daring drivers who enjoy driving along the edge of the cliff, whenever opportunity offers. All I am saying is that there is such a thing as driving *too near* the edge of a cliff. There is no sense in shooting over it. It is quite simple; beyond a certain well-defined line—in the arts as in everything else—beyond that limit there is *nothing*. Nothing, zero, is what logically you reach past a line, of some kind, laid down by nature, everywhere.[43]

The image Lewis uses here recalls the fate of Victor Stamp in *The Revenge for Love*, a painter of some talent but of an extremist bent—in politics and philosophy as much as in art—who is literally a 'daring driver' and who indeed dies by falling over a cliff. After his initial flirtation with extremism, Lewis the spatialist was concerned with drawing the lines beyond which meaning and form were lost.

Recognition of limits and fidelity to human experience were basic to Sturge Moore's theory of art. The work by Moore that Lewis most valued was the study of Flaubert, in which Moore wrote in a section called 'Impersonal Art':

> Errors, illusions, dreams have in the past been rendered by beauty, often doubtless charged with detached or half-apprehended verities; now, with the experimental method and the historical sense added, modern artists have the opportunity of thus rendering the probable and the known. Solidarity of thought, feeling, and expression begets beauty. He who would use objective reality in art can never, as Flaubert said, have enough sympathy; for heart and soul, as well as mind, must be filled by the facts studied, or he will fail.[44]

It is Moore's impersonality and classical control that, in Yvor Winters's opinion, has limited Moore's reputation. Winters writes that Moore 'has received the neglect that is commonly the lot of a perfectly lucid mind'. His description of Moore's principal theme as a poet echoes the terms Moore used when warning Lewis of the dangers of post-impressionism. Winters believes that Moore's theme is 'his own relationship to the Romantic tradition, the tradition of rejuvenation through immersion in sensation. . . . Mr. Moore's immersion has actually led to rejuvenation, to an inexhaustibly fascinating freshness of perception: the immersion of other poets has too often led to disintegration'.[45] Moore never goes beyond the limit that marks rejuvenation from disintegration, or in Lewis's words, from 'nothing, zero'. Moore defines this limit in his lyric, 'To Silence', in which silence stands for the zone beyond the limits of words and meaning. As a Romantic, Moore enters this zone and is momentarily immersed in the destructive element, like a bather in the sea:

> Languidly drifted with thy tide,
> Appearing dead to those I passed,
> I lived in thee, and dreamed, and waked
> Twice what I had been. Now, I cast
> Me broken on thy buoyant deep
> And dreamless in thy calm would sleep.

Moore resists the temptation of this dreamless sleep. 'To Silence' speaks of those who ask too much from life (one can imagine Moore thinking of Baudelaire, Rimbaud, and the young Wyndham Lewis) until 'craving grew to be a pain'. Such artists flee to the oblivion of silence, but Moore's case is different:

> Yet I, who for all wisdom pine,
> Seek thee but as a bather swims
> To refresh and not dissolve his limbs.[46]

Moore's conception of silence is like Lewis's in 'The White Silence' chapter of *Self Condemned*. After Hester's death and his fall against the morgue slab, René is placed in a hospital 'Silent Ward' where his

> mind began to dream of white rivers which led nowhere, which developed laterally, until they ended in a limitless white expanse . . . at last consciousness ebbed quietly away, and Réne lay in a dreamless sleep, alone in this place dedicated to silence, totally removed from life.[47]

René's tragedy is that he cannot hold on to what he thinks of as the 'sanity of consciousness', which is rare in any period of history but particularly in the modern age. Lewis wrote in *Rude Assignment* in 1950, four years before the publication of *Self Condemned*, that 'Consciousness is privileged. The fashionable denigration of it is, like so much of that order, insincere. . . . For us the world has presented itself to our senses sharp and hard of outline. It is stamped with the objectivity of the rational.'[48] René loses this privilege: 'there was, from the moment of the blow, and the days spent in the white silence of the hospital, no chance that he could survive, at all intact'. His friend the Scottish philosopher McKenzie realizes that he must 'speak of [René's] decadence: of his *death*'.[49] Like Victor Stamp in *The Revenge*, René went beyond the human limit into decadence and death.

As much as Lewis, Moore insisted that the artist be fully conscious. In his satiric 'Response to Rimbaud's Later Manner', Moore contrasts the cow and the dryad, creatures who are wholly absorbed in nature, with his own fully conscious self: 'They, they, and not I,/Never ask why/The Cathedral Tower/Dreams like a flower.'[50] By remaining outside of nature, man can use his rational consciousness to form metaphors beyond the ken of merely natural creatures. Moore's attitude toward nature here resembles that of Margot, Victor Stamp's mistress in *The Revenge for Love*. Margot is reflecting on the French countryside:

> In London bed-sitting rooms she had trod the untrodden ways —surprised a violet by a mossy stone, half-hidden from the eye. But this was, in fact, the first occasion on which Margot had lain upon the banks of a pukka torrent . . . in the mountain air, among the uncivilized birds and bustling insects . . . without feeling a fish out of water, she nevertheless would not have wished to be a trout in this particular watercourse. She reserved her right to remain *outside* of nature, now it came to the point; not to participate in its sunny dream. . . . It was too artless. . . .[51]

Unfortunately, Margot's perception of the value of consciousness cannot halt Victor Stamp's drive toward its extreme limit.

In his poem 'Nature', Sturge Moore rejects Samuel Taylor Coleridge's statement in 'Ode: To Dejection' that 'we receive but what we give/And in our life alone does Nature live'. Moore does not try to refute Coleridge's belief on its own terms; he simply thinks that no one can possibly know enough to make such a statement. Moore writes that we must stay on the level of solid, human reality:

> We note, think, feel;
> The flesh we study is no whit less real.
> Say, our best joys be shadows cast by thought
> Beyond our bodily forms; would they be aught
> Did they no solids grace?[52]

Moore wanted to stay with the 'solids'; and so did Lewis, even in the Berkeleyan conclusion to *Time and Western Man* already quoted, when he says that we should 'regard ourselves as at rest, with our droves of objects—trees, houses, hills—grouped around us'. The difference between the two artists was that Lewis was more concerned with understanding the ultimate reality of the world's appearances, which Moore feared would lead Lewis, like the Delphis of *A Sicilian Idyll*, away from the full development of his genius.

Moore's worry that Lewis would exceed the limits of rational discourse or visual reality was of course unfounded. *Time and Western Man* did not lead Lewis away from the reality of the sensuous world anymore than *A Vision* limited the sensuality of Yeats's poetry. Like Yeats's speculations, Lewis's questionings of the reality of the external world only freshened his sense of its particularity, much as Moore's incursions into the zone of silence strengthened his dedication to what can be clearly known and expressed. Augustus John, Yeats, Moore and Lewis are in this sense all kindred artists. They all knew and reinforced in one another Oscar Wilde's belief that 'It is only shallow people who do not judge from appearances. The mystery of the world is the visible, not the invisible.'

5

Lewis's Prose Style

MARSHALL McLUHAN

Lewis was an *avant garde* by himself, the greatest pictorial draughtsman of his time, the most controversial prose stylist of our day. For readers who are accustomed to action in prose narrative Lewis is baffling. Especially his early novels provide passage after passage which are like nothing so much as a package of materials with directions for making a painting. As Dr Johnson said of Richardson's novels: 'If you were to read them for the story, Sir, you would hang yourself.' A good deal of work is left for the reader. But the result enables the reader to *see*. And the effect is finally more vivid than a ready-made painting. Lewis the painter turned to literature in an age of passive mechanical photography. As a writer he set out to educate the eye by means of deft organization of gestures. He translates what he sees into terms of painting, and translates this in turn into words which embody, in embryo, as it were, the same gestures. So that these translations issue as painter's instructions, as in this passage from *Enemy of the Stars*:

> Hanp and his master lie in a pool of bleak brown shadow, disturbed once by a rat's plunging head. It rattles forward yet appears to slide upon oiled planes. . . . Beyond the canal, brute-lands, shuttered with stony clouds, lie in heavy angles of black sand. They are squirted upon by twenty ragged streams; legions of quails hop parasitically within the miniature cliffs.[1]

Passages of this kind are not background to an action. They are not an aura for characters, but have to be mentally painted by the reader. Lewis's painter's eye having translated the situation into painter's terms and then back into words, the reader must approach the passage as he would a translation from Chinese, for instance.

The image is the primary pigment; and the syntax, the

painterly line and gesture by which Lewis directs the reader's hand and eye in a do-it-yourself exploration of the visible world with which the ordinary eye is quite unable to cope.

It was precisely this 'do-it-yourself' discovery of poets and painters some fifty years ago which outraged the conventional art consumer who had long been accustomed to swiftly moving conveyor belts of narrative action and imagery which arrived untouched by the human hand and ready for instant and effort-less consumption.

Mechanical photography released the painter from literal representation just as a little later the movie released poet and novelist from the business of backdrops, costumes and stage properties.

As the mechanical world became frantically activated the artist turned to a more severe form of contemplation than had been known in the Western world. Lewis's own words on this subject are apropos: 'But in the moment of passion, or the moment of action, there is no truth—And even the truth of passion . . . is an inferior truth: just as the man of action is an inferior man to the man of mind.' He continues, however, to explain why he repudiates his early fanaticism for the abstract in painting insisting on the painter's right to tell a story the simplest could understand saying: 'This he has as much right to do as the literary man, a Dickens, or a Tchekov, or a Stendhal'. Lewis tells how he was liberated from his early abstract passion by his ex-perience in the first war:

> Those miles of hideous desert known as 'the Line' in Flanders and France 'were a swift cure!' Had you at that time asked me to paint a milkmaid in a landscape of buttercups and daisies I should probably have knocked you down. But when Mars with his mailed finger showed me a shell-crater and a skeleton, with a couple of shivered tree stumps behind it, I was still in my 'abstract' element. . . . The coming of the war and the writing—at top speed—of a full-length novel ('Tarr') was the turning-point. Writing—literature—dragged me out of the abstractist cul-de-sac.[2]

In *Tarr*, Lewis describes Paris in the Spring with stereoscopic novelty:

The new summer heat drew the heavy pleasant ghosts out of the ground . . . spectres of energy, bulking the hot air with vigorous dreams. Or they entered into trees, in imitation of pagan gods, and nodded their delicate distant intoxication to him. Visions were released in the sap, with scented explosion. . . . The leaden brilliant green of spring foliage hung above . . . ticketing innumerably the trees. In the distance, volume behind volume, the vegetation was massed, poising sultry smoke-blocks from factories in fairy-land.[3]

The effect is like that of looking at an ordinary scene through an unusually intense medium. Lewis once said that all art is the expression of a colossal preference. An artist has an intense bias which he imposes on the senses of weaker or lazier men. But to see one's own casual world through an artist's intense sensibility is to awaken to the reality that is *there*. The nature of the ordinary observer is Art.

Ten years later in *The Childermass* Lewis used the medium of the talking picture before it had been invented. It is a talkie in full colour. A passage will provide a striking contrast with the prose from his later novel, *Self Condemned*. Lewis went blind in his last years with the result that his prose was much changed in the direction of colloquial, conversational narrative. But here is a do-it-yourself passage or package from his middle period. It concerns those in a state beyond life, as in Dante:

They stagger forward, two intoxicated silhouettes, at ten yards cut out red in the mist. . . . Only trunks and thighs of human figures are henceforth visible. There are torsos moving with bemused slowness on all sides. . . . In thin clockwork cadence the exhaused splash of the waves is a sound that is a cold ribbon just existing in the massive heat. The delicate surf falls with the abrupt clash of glass, section by section.[4]

This, of course, is an eerie contemporary equivalent of the vision of Timon of Athens: 'Come not to me again; but say to Athens: Timon hath made his everlasting mansion upon the beached verge of the salt flood who once a day with his embossed froth the turbulent surge shall cover.'

Lewis was well aware that it was, in the age of the new media, quite impossible for the serious artist also to be a crowd or a mass-artist like Shakespeare or Dickens. But this awareness led him to seize on the mass media of movie and B.B.C. to make of them instruments of art. In a way quite distinct from Eliot or Joyce, Lewis made the press and radio, movie and television modes of his vision. So that whereas Dante's world is built according to the scale of moral perfection, the world Lewis presents in his great trilogy *The Human Age* is scaled according to the audience ratings of the medium and the programme. 'Third City' in *The Human Age* is the B.B.C.'s Third Programme.

Lewis was a visionary for whom the most ordinary scenes became the means of intense seeing. The artist's personality at hostile grips with the environment is dramatically offered not for its pathos or anguish or as a moral evaluation, but as a means of clairvoyance.

6

The Taming of the Wild Body

BERNARD LAFOURCADE

(i)

Studies of Lewis's works have sadly neglected what ought to have formed the basis of their investigations—the early period. This is understandable in view of the scarcity of biographical details and the fact that Lewis's early works weave together a story which may easily pass unnoticed beneath the profusion of his output.

Certainly, the critics concur in stressing the importance of 'The Wild Body' (e.g. the texts published between 1909 and 1927), and thereby confirm the author's statement that 'what I started to do in Brittany, I have been developing ever since'.[1] Yet the leading critics generally devote only a few pages to these early works, and are content to compare the original and final versions of certain representative texts, or else to consider the transition of Lewis's technique from that of the travelogue to that of the short story.

These brief accounts, scattered through six or seven critical studies, are hardly sufficient to do justice to the considerable problems posed by 'The Wild Body'. For in its various stages we can trace—as with *Tarr*, in its successive versions, only here in an infinitely more supple and significant manner—the development of the author in the formative years between 1909 and 1927; or perhaps one should say 'between 1882 and 1927', since these early texts are directly linked with Lewis's early youth. And they may also tempt us to search even further back, and seek his forbears, for it is appropriate to recall here William Pritchard's formulation that 'In terms of Lewis's own fiction, his father was a "wild body".'[2]

It was not till he reached the age of 45 that Lewis at last put these early literary essays into their final form. Such extensive and continual reworking reflects immense problems in self-analysis. And the critics' relative unconcern has helped to impose the—admittedly gratifying, but naive and misleading—idea of a Lewis appearing out of the blue, a lover of secrecy and the enemy of all. We may be sure that things must have been both simpler and more complex. This might seem to refute the thesis of Hugh Kenner, that pioneer of Lewis criticism, whose fine study portrays Lewis as a being springing from nowhere. Nothing of the sort. Subscribing to a chthonic and eruptive phenomenology is justifiable in Lewis's case, but it must not prevent sounding out other depths. The fact that Lewis himself cultivated the image of a sudden melodramatic appearance (akin to Karl Jaspers') in no way means that he appeared from nowhere. It is precisely this story which 'The Wild Body' begins to relate.

(ii)

The first essential is to get a clear view of the corpus, with its eventual ramifications and the successive stages in its elaboration. Let us recall that not only is there no complete study of 'The Wild Body' in existence, but that certain texts are ignored by all the critics. Thus, there is no analysis of 'A Spanish Household'— a lightweight and somewhat peripheral work, but in certain respects significant. 'Brotcotnaz' has never been compared with its big brother of 1911, 'Brobdingnag', nor has anyone described the differences between the aggressive strategies of Bestre in the 1909 and 1922 versions. No one has pointed out that the poem 'Grignolles' belongs indisputably to 'The Wild Body'. Robert Chapman, whose study is the most complete, thinks that 'Unlucky for Pringle' stands on the periphery of 'The Wild Body', which is incorrect; and on the other hand he suggests that 'Cantleman's Spring-Mate' and the other war stories belong to 'The Wild Body', which is quite untenable, unless we are prepared to bring together under this heading all of Lewis's works up to The Red Priest. It is clear from this that we must attempt to distinguish between The Wild Body as a guiding concept, 'The Wild Body' as it developed between 1909 and 1927 and The Wild Body as it appeared in 1927. Even more vital perhaps, as it says a lot about Lewis's outlook, 'Our Wild Body', an essay published in 1910, has not been considered, though it contains the first seeds of the unifying theme which later enabled the author to organize in a coherent sequence texts which hitherto had been widely disparate. It is quite obvious that any in-depth appreciation of 'The Wild Body' calls for a clearer vision of how these myriad short texts assembled and reacted on each other.

It is now possible to draw up a reasonably precise schema. Chronologically we can distinguish four broad bands in the spectrum of 'The Wild Body', which is confirmed by Lewis, with considerable insight, in *Rude Assignment*: 'After two or three intermediate stages I reached ultimately an outlook that might be described as almost as formal as this earliest one was the reverse.'[3]

(1) The first avatar of 'The Wild Body' includes all Lewis's output from the years 1909 to 1911, that is to say all the early published texts, including, of course, those omitted from the 1927 collection. That 'Grignolles' and 'Unlucky for Pringle' do belong to this corpus was confirmed by Lewis's list of late 1916.[4] Similarly, although they do not figure in this hastily drawn-up list, the themes and recurrent ideas of 'A Breton Innkeeper' and 'A Spanish Household' show that they belong irrefutably to the corpus. We must add to these, 'Crossing the Frontier',[5] a passage of which is incorporated in 'A Spanish Household', and 'A Breton Journal',[6] which may be regarded as the embryo of 'The Wild Body', and which Lewis consulted forty years later when analysing the genesis of 'The Wild Body' in *Rude Assignment*. Lastly, as Lewis indicates in the 1927 version of 'Inferior Religions' (p. 232), the primary 'Wild Body' had had a 'Doppelgänger', a 'nautical set [which] never materialised'. We nevertheless get echoes of it in certain of the examples given in 'Inferior Religions', in 'Brobdingnag' and especially in the Breton Journal, as well as in certain drawings (Michel, nos. 13, 14 and 19).

It is worth noting that these texts were most probably written in the order in which they were published between 1909 and 1911. Those that the author retained appeared in exactly the same order in the 1927 collection. Lewis states in his preface that this order follows that of the narrator's experiences, with the exception of 'A Soldier of Humour', which illustrates 'a later stage of his comic technique' (p. vi). Thus in 1927, the author went over the various stages of what then appears to us as a repetition of an original, deeply felt experience. Psychologically, this seems to be extremely significant. The texts published in *The English Review* (without question the most remarkable), are probably those that Lewis had begun to work on in Brittany.[7] There follows several months' silence which indicates that the following texts—those published in *The New Age* and *The Tramp*—were not written in the immediate light of the Breton experience, though possibly based on notes, as they are more documentary and less intense. Last of all, 'Unlucky for Pringle', which has a London setting but is unquestionably part of the first 'Wild Body', must have been written two years after the first texts; in its use of humour this transitional story greatly resembles *Tarr*, which Lewis was then writing.

(2) During the second stage, which may be limited to the years 1916–17, Lewis realized that these early texts should be gathered into a collected edition. He had not previously been aware of the underlying unity of the texts, or at least had not looked on them as aspects of 'The Wild Body'. The title (*Our Wild Body*) which occurred to him when he drew up the 1916 list was clearly inspired by the 1910 essay (whose importance he stressed in this listing), but this relatively superficial apology for the body was in no sense a meditation on his Breton experience. When this idea of a collected edition was raised again a year later in *The Little Review* (in the 'Editor's Note' by Ezra Pound) the title given was no longer *Our Wild Body* but *Inferior Religions*. To be sure, it was Ezra Pound who announced this new title, but this reflected Lewis's own intentions, as he himself confirmed in an unpublished work of 1949, where he stated: 'Before I had published anything I started out to write a book to be called "inferior religions." I was living in Brittany at the time.'[8] Lewis is obviously compressing the chronology here, for it is inconceivable that he was already thinking in 1908 of the title 'Inferior Religions'. It is of vital importance to recognize that the concept of The Wild Body did not prevail from the start, and that Lewis most probably decided on the definitive title only in 1927.

The second problem is that of dating 'A Soldier of Humour'. Published at the end of 1917, but included in the 1916 listing, could this be a half-forgotten text from the period 1909–11? It would seem that Lewis did not return to Spain between 1909 and 1914, and the setting for the story is indeed that which the author had known in Vigo in the spring of 1908. An early sketch could well have been reworked, but the ambitious proportions of the text, so unlike those of the early texts, suggest that Lewis must have written this piece to make his collection more substantial. Moreover, a paragraph about the Germans (rather in the style of the preface to the 1918 *Tarr*, and likewise later abandoned) suggests that the text must have been written after the outbreak of hostilities, but probably not before the second issue of *Blast*, where Lewis could have included it. We may reasonably assume, therefore, that the period in question runs from the end of 1915 to the end of 1916.

The continuing concern with the events of 1908 seems all the more remarkable in view of this, though in 'A Soldier of Humour' the thematic structure, the style and especially the narrative technique have evolved enormously since the early texts. However the narrator, whose appearance has been much discussed, although described physically in the 1917 version, does not receive the name Ker-Orr until 1927, when he is also given a telling family background which we will consider later in more detail.

Finally, the 1916 listing confirms that the war-stories ('Cantleman's Spring-Mate', 'The French Poodle', etc.) were never regarded by Lewis as belonging to 'The Wild Body'. He reaffirmed this in the Foreword of 1927 ('with the exception of . . . a group of war-stories', p. v). This is an important point; though there are numerous similarities between these texts, Lewis always distinguished between The Wild Body as a whole and a particular 'Wild Body' which appeared to him in 1908.

(3) The next stage, which would appear to correspond to the years 1920–22, is chronologically and thematically the least straightforward of all. A salient feature is the publication of a heavily reworked version of 'Bestre' in *The Tyro* (March 1922), whose editorial states that the character is a 'Tyro' in the same

way as X and F, the protagonists of 'Tyronic Dialogues'. A year earlier, 'Note on Tyros' had made clear the nature of the graphic Tyros, associating them closely with the characters of 'The Wild Body'. This note also completed the analysis of laughter given in 'Inferior Religions' and clarified the originality of the short stories (with their parodic primitivism, freezing of the action and search for the grotesque):

These immense novices brandish their appetites in their faces . . . A laugh, like a sneeze, exposes the nature of the individual with an unexpectedness that is perhaps a little unreal . . . But most of them are, by the skill of the artist, seen basking in the sunshine of their own abominable nature . . . The action of a Tyro is necessarily very restricted, about that of a puppet worked by deft fingers, with a screaming voice underneath.

We are struck not only by the echoes of 'Inferior Religions' but also by an imagery similar to that used in *Rude Assignment*,[9] where Lewis relates his Breton experience.

It is therefore tempting to see in 'The Tyros' a new avatar of 'The Wild Body'. This seems particularly true in the case of the graphic 'Tyros': the 'Brombroosh' (Michel, no. 449), for example, could quite well be a satisfactory portrait of Bestre or Monsieur de Valmore, but we must face the fact that the style of 'The Tyros' is less well suited to the other characters of 1909–11. Once again (and here we recall the frolicsome Cro-Magnons of 1912 (Michel, plates 8 and 9)), we realize that in spite of obvious relationships, Lewis always avoided linking his works, be they literary or graphic. (It is astonishing that he did not illustrate his books, except for a few dust jackets and designs, see note 20). An attempt to integrate the literary 'Tyros' into 'The Wild Body' also runs into difficulties. Firstly, it does not appear that 'Bestre' was specially revised for *The Tyro*, as is suggested by a statement from the short story ('I realised as little as he did that I was patting and prodding a subject of these stories', p. 119), which shows that when Lewis began work on the text again, he still had in mind his collection of short stories rather than a separate publication in a magazine. Is it possible that 'Bestre' was revised much earlier? Certainly not. The introduction of the word 'libido' is conclusive (*The Tyro*, no. 2, p. 63): it was revised quite definitely some time after the end of the War. If we now turn to consider the other literary 'Tyros' specially written for the magazine (e.g. the inmates of 'Tyronic Dialogues' and the brief dialogue used as a caption in *The Tyro*, no. 1, p. 7) we cannot fail to see that even though 'The Wild Body' dwells at length on conflicts, the use of dialogue sets these two texts apart from all the texts of the corpus by virtue of their form. The fundamentally aphoristic nature of their content brings them closer to 'The Code of a Herdsman'. One cannot escape the conclusion that Lewis, having completed the graphic series, noticed a kinship with the world of 'The Wild Body'. Thus the undercurrent of his primal experience draws him on, with 'The Tyros' acting as a catalyst or filter when it comes to putting 'The Wild Body' into its definitive form. 'Bestre', as pointed out by Hugh Kenner,[10] was to prove the link between the primitives of yore and the future character of the Enemy.

This transitional phase poses yet another, and analogous problem, for it saw the publication of two texts which would finally appear in *The Wild Body*, but which were obviously not connected with the long-drawn-out reinterpreting of the summer in Brittany. These texts are 'Sigismund', published in late 1920, and 'Will Eccles', first part of the future 'You Broke My Dream', published in the first number of *The Tyro*. Lewis did not feel the need to link the latter with 'The Tyros' (as he would do for 'Bestre'), and the conclusion was not published in the following issue of *The Tyro*, which suggests that it was not necessary for an elucidation of the Tyro concept. It is clear that 'Sigismund' and 'You Broke My Dream' were only to be included in *The Wild Body* (and even then in a separate section, as an appendix) because the author later realized that they were independent illustrations of the final conclusions of 'The Meaning of the Wild Body'. Without them the collection would probably have seemed lightweight.

(4) The final stage is better known, but *The Wild Body* in its published form invites a few queries. Here again we may trust the author's statement in the Foreword that the texts he had retained had been reworked in the preceding months, that is to

say in early 1927. The important details added to 'A Soldier of
Humour' and the rather more superficial ones added to 'Bestre'
confirm that Lewis had indeed gone over all the texts at the same
time, inspired by a unifying vision and eager to define the
personality of a narrator who would strengthen the philosophic
message from within. This message is clearly stated in 'The
Meaning of The Wild Body', an essay written specially to serve
as a conclusion. Written in a far less incantatory style than
'Inferior Religions', it shows that Lewis was at least able to
clarify the meaning of the initial experience. This essay, which
justifies the title of the collection, marks the final return to the
concept of The Wild Body.

The saga of 'The Wild Body' ends on a note of irony which
completes the circle. 'The Death of the Ankou', the only story
from 1927 which had never previously appeared, is apparently
the first one the author wrote. At least this is what Lewis states
in *Beginnings*,[11] and it is true that although the style dates from
1927, the story is consistent with the initial experience. Why it
was not published in 1909, like the others, remains a mystery.

(iii)

Chronology is one thing, but we must now attempt to evaluate
the overall significance of this singularly tortuous development.
Critics concur in emphasizing how the structure of the short
story came to replace that of the travelogue, a fact that seems to
tally with the author's own analysis when he states that he
finally reached a vision 'almost as formal as this earliest one was
the reverse'. The problem lies in deciding exactly what is meant
by the words 'formal' and the 'reverse' of it.

We may agree with Robert Chapman's view that the early
texts have the air of documentaries, where the emphasis is placed
on sociological analysis, and that this aspect later tended to fade
into the background. The aesthetic (on the whole impressionistic)
of the fragmentary vision and the realistic detail, which together
are typical marks of the travelogue, gave way to a fictional,
dramatized concentration of effects characterized by the introduction of a narrator and dialogues. Thus 'Bestre' omitted the

sociological preamble of 'Some Innkeepers'. Similarly, 'A Breton Innkeeper' and 'A Spanish Household' were most certainly omitted in 1927 because they contained no seeds of a plot. 'Unlucky for Pringle' suffered the same fate, even though its structure came closer to that of fiction, because the personality of the narrator was incompatible with the all-encompassing role bestowed on Ker-Orr. This much does seem coherent.

Yet it would be a mistake to assume that all that lay behind the first versions of these texts was the mere desire for documentary realism. In 'A Spanish Household', which, as a series of sketches, seems to come closest to the basic definition of the travelogue, experience has none the less undergone a rationalization: in 'Crossing the Frontier' the motive for the young man's arrest remains obscure, while it is fully explained in the final paragraph of 'A Spanish Household'. This suggests firstly, that these texts, though apparently rough observations, may already be elaborated (and there is nothing to say that the 'raw material' has not already been distorted, rather as we find in Defoe), and secondly that what immediately strikes us in Lewis is a certain intractability on the part of reality. The apparently spontaneous awkwardness of 'Grignolles' may very well be a good example of this. Kenner indicated that this initial reality was peripheral and deliberately melodramatic in nature,[12] but in so doing he appeared to emphasize rather too exclusively a fascination more cultivated than genuinely experienced. What in fact happened was far more dialectical. The young Lewis's attitudinizing (cf. the famous visit to Ford Madox Ford, or later, the precepts of 'The Code of a Herdsman') both prolongs and compensates for a lack of certainty, a timidity, 'the awareness of a fissure in reality' (one is already tempted to speak of 'false bottoms') which Maurice-Jean Lefevre sees as the essence of fascination.[13] All that Lewis says in *Rude Assignment*[14] confirms that there was indeed fascination, that the early gesticulations of 'The Wild Body' were perceived in a state of semi-hypnosis. And it is probably with a view to restricting and taming this disturbing intractability that Lewis resorts to a Dickensian surreality (pointed out by Hugh Kenner) or to sociological generalizations (noted by Robert Chapman).

That Lewis was the slave of this fascination as much as the

master of it is confirmed by the fact that he kept on questioning himself about his characters' motivations, as if they had been handed to him by external reality rather than formed by his own imagination. Brobdingnag could only think of obliterating the marks left on his wife by a mysterious rival by covering them with his own; Brotcotnaz is stunned at the realization that henceforth he may not do away with an invalid woman with impunity. This is a surprising inversion: fascination has been reduced to mean calculation. In the same way, the first Bestre's eye-victory was never fully explained—it belonged to the realm of pure fascination. The final version of the text insinuates that, not being content with mere ogling, he must have resorted to some kind of sexual exhibitionism. If, over the years, fiction seems to have intruded more and more, this is not really to the detriment of reality, but rather in an increasingly subtle elucidation of a dialectic of the real and the unreal, firmly rooted in early experience.

Therefore, rather than contrasting an intrinsically paradoxical or unstable realism with the ultimate formalism of *The Wild Body*, it would be better to pay heed to the author once again when he states clearly in *Rude Assignment* that during the Breton period, he was 'militantly vitalist'. Such are the attitudes, the concept and the philosophy which are opposed to formalism, and it is no surprise that in this work Lewis should have decried this naive primitivism that he had to overcome: 'Deliberately to spend so much time in contact with the crudest life is, I believe, wasteful of life. It seems to involve the error that raw material is alone authentic life.'[15] Vitalism must be opposed to formalism— an opposition that holds true for Lewis's contemporaries, describing, for example, the gulf which separates the poetry of D. H. Lawrence from that of T. S. Eliot.[16] This vitalism is particularly apparent in the Breton Journal of 1908, which, in quivering romantic tones and the vocabulary of a somewhat fuliginous mysticism, revels in the basic, not to say base, aspects of life. All this was not lacking in depth, but we can well understand why Lewis subsequently defined this fascination in the face of an apparently impenetrable veil as 'Dummheit.'[17] However, without this fascination there would probably have been no continuous re-examination, and ultimately no 'Wild Body' at all. And Lewis preserved his Breton Journal (possibly just as Pascal preserved his *Memorial*).

Having clarified this point, we must also inquire what precisely lies hidden at the far end of the spectrum, behind this vision we have termed 'formalist'. What is the final product of this distilled rationalization? Nothing less than the absurd. With *The Wild Body* we are already in the full flood of this non-moral satire—non-moral and therefore fundamentally ontological and gratuitously violent—which *Men Without Art* will later consider. The development of the essays which accompany 'The Wild Body' clearly marks this groping towards the absurd. 'Our Wild Body' with its vitalist 'our', which must be contrasted with the formalist 'the' of *The Wild Body*, was vitalist and flatly so. Half way between the two, 'Inferior Religions' was vitalist by virtue of its lyricism but absurdist by the virtue of its strident imagery. Lastly, in 'The Meaning of the Wild Body', with its restrained style, the author perceived 'the chasm lying between being and non-being', harping on the key word 'absurd' (the word or its derivatives occur no less than nine times in seven pages, excluding the synonyms with which the text abounds). It was precisely the discovery of the word 'absurd' which marked the fulfilment of 'The Wild Body'. It was the absurd which brought about the 'reductio' of that fascinating veil of primitivism of which, one may suspect, Lewis was somewhat critical from the outset, since he was as much imbued with pre-surrealism as with post-romanticism. Let us not forget that according to Virginia Woolf, human nature changed in about 1910. Indeed in a period of upheaval, the absurd can prove to be a wonderfully universalizing instrument.

At any rate, it is the absurd which alone could have caused Lewis to include 'Sigismund' in the 1927 collection, for what other link conceivably exists between this short story and the world of 'The Wild Body'? A further proof of the impact this illuminating word must have had on Lewis's vision in 1927 is given in 'The Vita of Wyndham Lewis', where he states, with respect to the Breton experience: 'The subject was people obsessed, as it were religiously, with small, isolated (and therefore unreal) things, like a fishing boat, some athletic interest . . . It was the absurdity of their . . . ('existence,' probably, the page was torn here) that drew up my attention.' Thus twenty years later we find the same word recurring to describe the essence of what the author had once perceived. But one comment must be made here: the absurd being inseparable from a certain formalism (it takes a logical mind to perceive the absurd), it is quite clear that Lewis was doing some reconstruction when he claimed that the vitalist of 1908 could fully appreciate the absurd. Anyway the fundamental opposition between vitalism and formalism in no way implies the impossibility of a dialectic between fascination and absurdity, as is amply shown by all of Lewis's work. The summer in Brittany, whose fascination had an immediate impact, could not at the outset have been perceived as fundamentally absurd. This only came with time.

It must be stressed that in 1927 Lewis was breaking new ground, that his insistence on the concept of the absurd was an important literary conquest. Of course, absurdity was common currency long before 1927 (indeed from as far back as the Renaissance), and it is no exaggeration to say that the century wallows in absurdity, which is probably its motive force. But to the best of our knowledge, this is the first time—with the appearance of 'The Meaning of the Wild Body'—that it is promulgated so forcefully as a concept. And this long before the Existentialists, or 'The Theatre of the Absurd'. Henceforward it seems clear that the reversal of Bergson's analysis of laughter made in 'The Meaning of The Wild Body' may no longer be considered, as has only too often been said, as artificial. For sooner or later we must arrive at that commonplace of Lewis criticism. Substituting, as a source of laughter, 'the observations of a *thing* behaving like a person' (notice the pre-existentialist emphasis on the word 'thing') for 'du mécanique plaqué sur du vivant' perfectly illustrates the advent of absurdism. Bergson, like a good vitalist, strove to make his epoch come to terms with itself, and one has only to reread the few singularly inoffensive pages in *Le Rire* (chapter III, section 4) devoted to the absurd, or, more precisely, to 'comic absurdity' (which is likened to the nature of dreams) to appreciate the intentionally tranquillizing effect of Bergson's approach. Lewis was most certainly inspired by Bergson, but his black Cartesianism was at the opposite pole from Bergson's thinking. His absurd is all-embracing, his laughter anything but reconciliatory, and numerous scathing analyses of English humour occur through his work.

(iv)

Yet, as we have seen, the absurd offers the chance of a kind of reconciliation. To be truly absurd, the absurd must infect *everything*, and hence, even if this done derisively, it will end up making the whole world homogeneous. Yet, however universal this calling might be, the absurdists in fact only approach it from a biassed point of view, from the standpoint of some personal obsession, from some all-engulfing metaphor: rarefaction in Beckett or overabundance in Ionesco, to name but two antithetical examples. Thus, modern absurdity would be both universal and subjective. In Lewis's case, this bias—and here once again the gulf separating him from Bergson seems enormous—appears to have been the body itself. As we have seen, it is only gropingly that Lewis (the shy youngster, the lion etc.) realized that the common denominator of those totems which had haunted his summer in Brittany was the grotesque otherness of a Wild Body, which was to fascinate him until he could identify himself with it. At the outset, what Lewis had sensed was that 'The Wild Body' was not simply that parade of primitive puppets submitted to his scrutiny, but also the voyeur, whom he had not identified as himself. Rather than a sentimental 'search for identity', this seems to be a question of a 'search for otherness' (in other words, an alienation effect). This sense of alienation, which causes a fissure to appear in reality, is probably the source of Lewis's fascination. The fact remains that the transparent author of 1909 gives way in 1917 to 'a barbarian clown' with a body 'large, white and savage', but anonymous. It is not till 1927 that this 'bastard' is given a name, which Lewis solemnly bestows in the Foreword (p. v), handing over no less solemnly the ownership of the texts he has just revised: ' [They] now form a series belonging to an imaginary story-Teller, whom I have named Ker-Orr.' Not all that imaginary, since he is obviously far more than a simple mouthpiece for the author. For Lewis invents a family background for him (pp. 4–5), which is loosely based on his own:

My father is a family doctor on the Clyde. The Ker-Orrs have been doctors usually. I have not seen him for some time: my mother, who is separated from him, lives with a noted Hungarian physician. She gives me the money she gets from the physician, and it is she I recognize as my principal parent. It is owing to this conjunction of circumstances that I am able to move about so much, and to feed the beast of humour that is within me with such a variety of dishes.

Is it not significant that humour, wandering and wildness—the very substance of 'The Wild Body'—are thus linked with the separation of the author's parents and made possible precisely because of that separation? We know that the author's parents separated when he was about ten, and that the father, who was later to start a new life in the United States, gradually disappeared from the son's view. Not only during his childhood, but long after adolescence, the author was to find his mother an attentive, affectionate and critical confidante as well as a source of cash which he used and abused in order to finance his interminable European holidays. It is therefore reasonable to assume that the break-up of the family unit, creating a polarization which upset the world, could both have contributed to the young man's opting for exile, and for the sort of inertia which the years spent in France (a case comparable to Synge's) seem to illustrate. Lewis was later to see in this period the effect of a 'cryptic immaturity' prolonged 'beyond the usual period',[18] a diagnosis confirmed by Augustus John's memoirs.[19] Is it then not likely that the reworking of 'The Wild Body' was simply the inevitable prolongation of this early uncertainty? 'The Wild Body' took shape, 'emerged' for the first time during that crucial summer of 1908, when Lewis realized that he had to return to London, yet could not bring himself to leave Brittany.

This scenario is confirmed by a singular and highly important phenomenon that has not been sufficiently stressed. It is not only 'The Wild Body', but all his important early work which is repeated and reformulated over the twenty years leading up to The Wild Body. Not only Tarr (a Bildungsroman, by the way), but also 'Enemy of the Stars' and 'Cantleman's Spring-Mate' (aped by 'The War Baby', not to speak of all the abortive texts of 'The Crowd-Master'). What a vortex! Everything that takes place suggests that Lewis was mimicking, parodying and exorcising that initial separation. And it is not inconceivable that it is as a direct result of this separation, and by the same dialectic, that Lewis's two-fold genius came into being.[20] It is therefore more understandable that the great works of his mature period could not be put into their final form before the question of the early works had been settled once and for all. The impossible, gargantuan *The Man of the World*, whose absurdist globalism probably reflects the inhibitions born in the Breton summer of 1908, would only disintegrate around 1925 to be ultimately reused in those manageable fragments *The Art of Being Ruled*, *The Lion and the Fox*, *The Childermass*, and, perhaps, *The Apes of God*. After all, The Wild Body (which is basically childless) had been procreative.

When 'The Wild Body's' time was come, everything appears to indicate that Lewis achieved a sort of self-analysis, which, accurate or not (it matters little) brought him face to face with the absurd. Finally, Lewis confesses that in the past he had indulged in shallow posturing, but that writing the book had helped to free him from this habit. The case of Lewis bears a singular resemblance to that of Sartre, as examined by Francis Jeanson in his well-known study.[21] At a distance of twenty years, the two writers reveal similar attitudes towards psychoanalysis as a result of their self-analysis. But let them speak for themselves:

We maintain that, in so far as the psychoanalyst uses the mind to interpret consciousness, we might as well face the fact that the explanation for what takes place in our consciousness can only be found in consciousness itself. (Sartre: *Esquisse d'une Théorie des Emotions*)

So it is that *the Subject* is not gently reasoned out of, but violently hounded from, every cell of the organism: until at last (arguing that 'independent,' individual life is not worth while, nor the game worth the candle) he plunges into the *Unconscious*, where Dr. Freud, like a sort of mephistophelian Dr. Caligari, is waiting for him. 'Consciousness' is perhaps

the best hated 'substance' of all ... (*Time and Western Man*.
Book II, part 2, chap. 3)

Sartre's bastard and Lewis's enemy are certainly close relatives. And here we may ask ourselves out of what timorous
superciliousness the critics have refused to contemplate the
appropriateness of applying Freudian analysis to a notoriously
complex, secretive and aggressive author, while feeling quite
free to toy indolently, a little naively or quite maliciously with
the theory of an extreme persecution mania.

The fact remains that it is certainly the recent discovery of
Freud which must have started Lewis on the path of a more or
less liberating self-analysis. Indeed we may note here a typical
ambivalence. On the one hand, the 1927 Ker-Orr proclaims:
'In these accounts of my adventures, there is no sex interest at
all,' ' "Sex" makes me yawn my head off' (p. 6). But we have
already remarked on the occurrence of the word 'libido' in the
1922 'Bestre', which firmly places the accent on the character's
sexuality. This is nothing new, since 'Brobdingnag' and the very
Sartrian 'Unlucky for Pringle' had already dwelt on such fantasies. In short Freud irritates him, and this is why Lewis finally
comes out with this spendidly liberating formula: 'Freud explains
everything by *sex*: I explain everything by *laughter*' (p. 6). Here
again, Lewis uses mimicry to underline his point, as he had done
before with Bergson.

Must we see here a victory for laughter over his initial uncertainty? Very probably. Both his parents had recently died,
his mother in 1919, his father soon after. But no exorcism of
such a situation can be complete, and *The Wild Body* perpetuates
his original themes. The situations and metaphors of the 'family
novel', in the sense in which Freud meant it, had prevailed from
the outset.[22] As Lewis points out in 'Note on Tyros', the deeds of
his characters do not lead to action in the normal sense of the
word, but to parodies of action marked by a sort of impotence,
and finally, because of an overwhelming, intrusive style, to a
veritable set of gestures in words, which provide a sort of veneer
on the wavering reality of his characters.[23]

Confronted with this insecurity of the self in time, the early
setting and geography display a remarkable stability, to which

all of Lewis's work will remain faithful. From the time of the very first texts, 'The Wild Body' uses out-of-the-way settings to illustrate the alienation of the family unit (a complex alienation when one recalls that not only were his parents separated, but his mother was English and his father American). The atmosphere of those hotels, boarding-houses, cafés and other public places where the author-narrator tries to fit in. Domestic infernos contrasting with that complementary obsession, the wide open spaces of tramps afflicted with delirium, histrionics or blindness. The narrator, seeking his place, examines different father-figures, often lonely and humiliated, sometimes grotesquely triumphant, or else he wheedles his way into some family. Everywhere the empty universe of the vagabond is confronted with closely guarded doors, and all these stories speak ultimately of trespass and eviction. In an extreme form, made possible by the archetypes of the popular novel which give free rein to obsessive metaphors, it is this fragmented universe which recurs in the same period in *Mrs. Dukes' Million*: Lewis's first novel, a rapidly-written pot-boiler, is all the more revealing.

We can now see why Lewis's eruptive emergence cannot be separated from the constant revisions of these early works. Looking on 'The Wild Body', which he could see struggling in the depths of some platonic obscurity, Lewis was to exclaim, parodying Sartre this time, just as he had parodied Bergson and Freud (the mimicking distortion here lies in the 'as if'): 'From the start, I behave *as if I were free*,'[24] He could only be liberated from time, that extension of an initial spatial dichotomy, by a burst of laughter which recognized the fundamental absurdity of abysmal life, and turned the 'enfant sauvage' into an enemy.

7

Mrs. Dukes' Million:
The Stunt of an Illusionist

HUGH KENNER

Mumming, miming, masquing, identities commingled; simulacra indistinguishable from what they simulate; Milton's Satan's remote descendant the Byronic picaro unsettling authorized order (Dr Jekyll) or restoring it (Sherlock Holmes); *The Wrong Box, A rebours, The Prisoner of Zenda*; Dickens' lifeless hand dropping the pen midway through a novel of crime; Wilde carrying Art into the prisoner's dock, forcing public officials into supporting roles in a tragedy he could enact but never write; the world of *Dorian Gray* and *The Man Who Was Thursday*: such was the world in which the young Wyndham Lewis slowly came into possession of his powers, a world to which there seemed a secret which decades later he accused Sturge Moore of having withheld from him. Moore never told him, Lewis wrote from Canada, that 'it was all like the stunt of an illusionist'.

The lines that precede this good-natured accusation are as nearly nostalgic as any Lewis ever permitted himself. They have already been quoted in this volume but justify repetition.

How calm those days were before the epoch of wars and social revolution, when you used to sit on one side of your work-table and I on the other, and we would talk—with trees and creepers of the placid Hampstead domesticity beyond the windows, and you used to grunt with a philosophic despondence I greatly enjoyed. It was the last days of the Victorian world of artificial peacefulness—of the R.S.P.C.A. and London Bobbies, of 'slumming' and Buzzards cakes. As at that time I had never heard of anything else, it seemed to my young mind in the order of nature. You—I suppose—knew it was all like

the stunt of an illusionist. You taught me many things. But
you never taught me *that*. I first discovered about it in 1914—
with growing surprise and disgust. (*Letters*, 293)

What Lewis discovered in and after 1914 was the substance of
his postwar novels: the false bottoms of *The Revenge for Love*,
the pervasive counterfeiting of *The Vulgar Streak*, the 'cemetery
of shells' that culminates *Self Condemned*.

> Civilization is hooped together, brought
> Under a rule, under the semblance of peace
> By manifold illusion—

so another friend of Sturge Moore's, W. B. Yeats, summarized
in 1934 a perception quite as bleak; also (1915):

> What portion in the world can the artist have
> Who has awakened from the common dream
> But dissipation and despair?

Those were things one could learn in the time of the breaking of
nations, and see confirmed in the decades of General Strike, of
economic collapse, and Hitler's hooked cross.

   Still, semblance and manifold illusion were thoroughly familiar
to Wyndham Lewis well before 1914. They inhered alike in
The Yellow Book and in the light fiction whose consumers
thought *The Yellow Book* a moral peril. And they were highly
congenial to the temperament of the young Lewis, who perhaps
as early as 1908 had found 'the stunt of an illusionist' sufficiently
entertaining to spin 518 pages of typescript around it: *Mrs.
Dukes' Million*, a so-called 'miserable pot-boiler' meant to get
money for the leisure in which to write *Tarr*. It is the earliest of
several Lewisian efforts to solve financial problems by writing a
book that would sell, a purpose it encompassed so unsuccessfully
that it was not even published. The celebrated agent J. B. Pinker
thought it 'not marketable', and the typescript vanished into
England's Sargasso Sea of discarded papers, to surface after nearly
five decades in a London junkshop.

   Later efforts to write a best-seller—*The Roaring Queen*, *The
Red Priest*, *Twentieth Century Palette*—were doomed by excessive contrivance. Only one of these books was tested in the

market-place, not successfully; the first was withdrawn amid threats of prosecution, the third left in unfinished draft at Lewis's death. None, though, had much chance. Mixing sensation, sex and an 'inside story' in proportions Lewis judged the book-buying herd would respond to, they reject a cardinal motif of best-sellerdom, empathy: a sequence of small unfakeable indications that a good time is being made available for us all to share, that the writer in some fundamental important way enjoys the world he is presenting. Lewis by the 1930s had acquired the satirist's habit, which is to disapprove. That was what he had learned in 1914: not that the illusionist, the virtuoso of semiotics, commanded the time's imagination—he knew that already; rather that this being's activities were dangerous.

In *Mrs. Dukes' Million*, though, he is unsuspicious, to the point of having nothing but fun. None of the book's illegal goings-on, save perhaps the triple murder of the brothers Passion, incurs the story-teller's disapprobation in the least. As it twists and turns like a merrily epileptic snake, his plot achieves scene after scene of pure farce. Into the offices of Truman and Hatchett, Attorneys, workmen haul an enormous safe, which appears to be *snoring*. Mr Hatchett jnr. 'with a fearless gesture' unlocks it. And into the purview of four amazed and very proper lawyers springs their sexagenarian client, Mrs Dukes, eccentrically dressed as always, 'adjusting her bonnet, but as cool as a cucumber', a coolness compatible with non-stop vociferation: ''E came back when you'd gone, Mr 'atchett, and was in such a tearin' passion as you never saw. I 'ad to get into that'—she pointed to the safe—'to get out of 'is stormin' truklent way. . . .' It would make a capital film.

This is not, moreover, actually Mrs Dukes. This is an actor named Evan Royal, impersonating Mrs Dukes, whom none of the Trumans and Hatchetts has ever actually seen. There is also a backup impersonator, Hercules Fane, who has studied his part from Royal's impersonation, which Royal had studied from Mrs Dukes herself, before she was translated to America to get her out of the way. This, and much more, has been contrived to keep Mrs Dukes from learning that she has inherited over a million pounds, and to put the impersonators in the way of collecting it.

As two decades later Lewis would make his Apes of God dance to the tune of an invisible Pierpoint, so the troupe of actors who animate *Mrs. Dukes' Million* enacts the designs of an eastern illusionist named Serandur Khan. Readers of *The Apes* or *The Human Age* will recognize a familiar neo-Platonic hierarchy, the real origin of power always one level beyond the level we can see at the moment, which we must in consequence understand to be diluted by the unreal. Khan, had Lewis contrived him twenty years later, would have been the focus of many remarks about the hierarchies that descend from the remote down to the immediate, where all is sham and the stunts of illusionists bemuse us. The Lord Sammael in *Malign Fiesta* is more real, more *serious*, than his functionary the Bailiff of *Monstre Gai*; Sammael in turn commences to turn meretricious as *Malign Fiesta* winds up, anticipating our encounter with God; and God, in the only fragment of *The Trial of Man* Lewis completed, is 'the old magician of the cloudy wastes of heaven': the ultimate illusionist, albeit benign. But in 1908 the man at the top of the hierarchy does not interest Lewis especially. Khan personifies the conventional Mysterious East of escapist fiction, and the scenes he is meant to dominate are among the most sketchily realized in the novel.

The man who does interest Lewis is the actor Evan Royal, whose names tell us that he is both kingly and Welsh, and whose unfailing resourcefulness tends to suggest that he is the young novelist's daydream. Royal performs in the Khan troupe for fun, not money, and contrives in the final chapters to outwit his employers, escaping with two friends and a slice of the boodle sufficient to support a lifetime's escapades. He doesn't, this Lewisian dream fulfilled, write *Tarr*; no, in the last pages, playboy of fashionable France, he is indulging in the gay new sport, aviation, and within reach of a great fortune from a plane of his own design. He has, we are told, 'the conscience, in common with many other attributes, of a Napoleon or an Eastern conqueror'. This remark receives no amplification; embedded in a perfunctory last paragraph, it serves only to explain why the story of Mrs Dukes' Million can end here, Royal feeling no need to make restitution to Mrs Dukes.

Much earlier in the book (Chap. 13) we find something else on which the Lewis of later years would have conferred much more significance. An emissary of Khan's is recruiting Royal's understudy, Fane, for the troupe.

This is the prime difference between our theatre, which has the whole world for its stage, and the theatre that you are used to. We improvise. No pieces are written for us. The actors act the part as they go along. That is what I myself always wished to do when I was acting. . . . I wanted to see actors no longer bound by the 'piece' they had to play, but to *act* and *live* at the same time. . . . [For us] the play goes on sometimes in several places at the same time. One of the present players in my company is playing his part six thousand miles away from here, without audience, but none the worse for that.

There would come a time when Lewis the moralist would reprobate any blurring of boundaries between art and life. But Lewis the novelist did not always listen to Lewis the moralist. Nor did Lewis the private man, whose zestful connoisseurship of the spurious salted his friendship with the amateur forger and con-man A. J. A. Symons (from whom he learned the method of forging signatures expounded in *The Revenge for Love*) and his sponsorship of the bogus poet David Kahma (who amused him by forging Ezratical Cantos; it is one of Kahma's typescripts that is spread out before T. S. Eliot in the 1949 portrait [Michel, P124]). And in 1908, before the moralist had coagulated, art could interpenetrate life with playful gaiety, not as in *The Caliph's Design* to upbraid its slackness of contour, but solely in the cause of entertainment.

For the criminal enterprise of Khan and Company is meant to entertain and not indoctrinate. So, we may hazard, is what Lewis may have turned his hand to immediately afterward, the Kreisler stratum of *Tarr*. *Tarr* feels like two novels conflated, one, the Kreisler part, drafted in a spirit of play, the other, the Tarr part, in the service of ideas the author had not yet worked out. The result is a transitional work, and one use of *Mrs. Dukes* is to help us see what it makes a transition from. For the war gave Kreisler, that alarming German, an unanticipated portentousness, disguising the high spirits in which he was conceived. And from the war emerged Wyndham Lewis, didact, with no thought of salvaging *Mrs. Dukes' Million* ever. He had always, he would have us believe, been serious. So Wyndham Lewis, the Novelist of Ideas, was somewhat ambiguously launched.

The earlier Lewis, creator of Mrs Dukes, was working a lode to which he had easy access, so much more congenial to him were the best-sellers of 1908 than the sort he would try to imitate in the 1930s. Thus from the time we first hear of Wyndham Lewis, he was sharing with Evan Royal the habit of being continuously on stage. His very speech was studied. Rugby had marked him with a public-school accent he deemed inappropriate for bohemia —like the name 'Percy'—and accordingly got rid of, achieving in reverse the metamorphosis Penhale accomplishes in *The Vulgar Streak*. Consequently for months every utterance, and especially the most trivial, entailed premeditation, deliberation, self-appraisal. He was turning P. W. Lewis into 'Wyndham Lewis', who would later turn into The Enemy. Extending this central role, he would play the game of turning up in cafés in what he imagined to be disguise, having first defied acquaintances to recognize him. (The late Iris Tree once assured me that they always could.) What he was playing at, we may guess, was being a character in the sort of fiction *Mrs. Dukes' Million* derives from: a tale by Stevenson or Chesterton, of intrigue, romance and jolly disguise. That was one form fin-de-siècle aestheticism took. Art in the blood, Sherlock Holmes said, may manifest itself in strange ways, and there was no more consummate master of impersonation than Holmes.

So *Mrs. Dukes' Million* came easily, the more so as Lewis hadn't yet discerned the possibilities, and the burdens, of an arresting prose. Writing, in those years, wasn't something he took trouble over, but the recreation of a painter on holiday. A painter watches people, and Lewis had only to imagine himself learning to imitate one of the models he was accustomed to scrutinize so closely. And the eye of a painter that would soon specialize in X-ray geometries was the eye that divined the possibility of trap-doors and secret passages in complacently solid chunks of Victorian architecture, and conceived the bizarre place on Inchbeck Road in Liverpool—Liverpool! Apotheosis of the humdrum!—where Royal plays dangerous hide-and-seek with Khan's men.

That house, Wyndham Lewis would gradually decide, was the

House of Fiction itself, and even more: was the House that Jack Built where nothing is as it seems, in fact *Haus Europa*. False Bottoms would be fun no longer, but metaphors for a lethal public duplicity capable of making bombs rain from the skies. Mrs Dukes would one day return as Mrs Harradson (*Self Condemned*) and, chillingly, as the Bailiff's mother ('A Very Sinister Old Lady') in *The Human Age*. Evan Royal would return as Victor Stamp, still a minor painter but entrapped into deadly schemes that were no fun for anyone. The Communist, always on stage, would attract the satirist's indignant eye. The Wyndham Lewis Repertory Company had a busy future ahead of it in which to enact savage morality plays. And the book in which the Company was first assembled would be published only in 1977, after two world wars, in a world containing hardly anybody left alive who could remember those innocent years of 'artificial peacefulness', years long since vanished in an unfixable instant when the drunken mind of Europe had changed its theme.

8

Enemy of the Stars

WENDY STALLARD FLORY

Enemy of the Stars was clearly important to Lewis. We can see this in the most graphic way from the page of his copy of *Blast I* —covered with his handwritten revisions—which Omar Pound and Philip Grover reproduce in facsimile in their bibliography.[1] Every line of the text has been changed with minor deletions and extensive additions, and when we compare the rest of the 1914 version to the one published in 1932 we see that Lewis has worked through the whole text in the same painstaking way. Most significantly, we find that his changes do not correct the earlier version so much as amplify it, making clear that after eighteen years his concern was not to modify or qualify what he originally wrote, but to present the same characters and the same basic ideas as forcefully, dramatically and accessibly as possible.

If his extensive revision shows, as I believe, a desire to express his meaning as effectively as he could, his purpose would seem so far to have been thwarted. *Enemy of the Stars* has not been taken as seriously as he hoped it would—as seriously as it deserves. Arghol clearly foreshadows Lewis's archetypal 'Enemy' persona and Hanp is so obviously his antithesis that it is possible to dismiss the work as a rather simplistic dramatization of some of the author's strongly-held opinions about the inevitable antipathy between the true artist-intellectual and the rest of society. If we read this primarily as a play about the fate of Arghol, it is likely that we will find it unsatisfactory—the action too predictable and the characters too artificially stylized and obviously symbolical. Yet once we realize that Lewis's presentation of the agon of these two characters is a means to an end, rather than an end in itself, we can see *Enemy of the Stars* for what it is: a serious, eloquent and complex piece of self-analysis in which the power and grandeur of the style is commensurate with the intensity of the author's personal involvement with his subject. Lewis's 1932 revisions make the play more accessible and also more immediate. The additions spell out more explicitly points that had been made elliptically before, and the speakers are now identified clearly. The staccato effect of the earlier version was so mannered and obtrusive that it focused attention on the writer, whereas the more discursive style of the revision, together with the change from past to present tense, shifts the focus away from Lewis as stylist and on to the hero. Arghol's awareness now seems both more complex and more tentative, showing how Lewis, articulating his own dilemma through his hero's, is still in the process of extending his analysis and pursuing the ramifications of his insights.

Enemy of the Stars is not, strictly speaking, written as a play but as a description of a play being shown, far in the future, to 'the cream of Posterity, assembled in silent ranks, generation behind generation'.² Nor is the action and its outcome the major point of the play, as we see from the way in which Lewis announces at the beginning what the ending will be. All the action here is ineffectual, circular and predetermined, and merely contributes to the main effect of claustrophobia:

... Posterity slowly sinks into the hypnotic trance of art; then the arena is transformed into the necessary scene.

THE RED WALLS OF THE UNIVERSE NOW SHUT THEM IN, WITH THIS FOREDOOMED PROME-THEUS. THEY BREATHE IN CLOSE ATMOSPHERE OF TERROR AND NECESSITY, UNTIL THE EXECU-TION IS OVER AND THE RED WALLS RECEDE— THE DESTINY OF ARGHOL CONSUMMATED, THE UNIVERSE SATISFIED!

[*THE BOX OFFICE RECEIPTS HAVE BEEN ENOR-MOUS.*] (p. 5)

Lewis's main object is to create this 'close atmosphere of terror and necessity', to explore for himself and create for his reader the harrowing state of mind that is not only Arghol's but ultimately, and much more urgently, that of the author himself. Acutely aware of the constant struggle between his own interior 'Arghol' and 'Hanp', Lewis on the first page of the play reminds his readers, 'It is our "agon" too. Remember that it is our destiny!'

Lewis's style is most striking in the descriptive set-pieces, and although there might be a temptation to see these as somewhat separable *tours de force*, we discover that the grandiose perspectives of these descriptions are directly related to the state of mind of the protagonist—that the vast scale of these perspectives is correlative to the urgency and devastating effect of Arghol's meditations. The claustrophobic situation of Arghol—locked into a stifling and painful relationship from which he can never free himself—except by death—is projected in cosmic dimensions as the narrator describes the forces that Arghol is aware of as he lies in the moonlight looking up at the stars. These forces are the subject of that impressive early section of the play called 'The Night'. (In the following passage I have italicized those sections which constituted the original version as a convenient way of showing how much more explicit the revised version is.)

Arghol meditates, his head out of the mist-patch. *The ice-fields of the sky sweep and crash silently* overhead. *Blowing wild organism* out of the mouth of nothing *into the hard splendid clouds, some Will casts* down *its glare, as well, over him.* He lies dazzled and still in the silent illuminations.

... now *the stars shine madly in the archaic blank wilderness of the Universe, machines of prey. Mastodons, placid in electric atmosphere—they are white rivers of power. They stand* fixed, *in eternal black sunlight.* They stand up and sing, louder than the morning, shriller than the firstcomers of the twilight, more profoundly than the foghorn of the sun.

Tigers are beautiful imperfect brutes. The animal beauty of the star-stamped intoxicating heavens is greater than tigers' (for all the head-lights of the killer, muscles of quicksilver)—it is imperfection much more of the splendour of gods. At the steadfast lightning of this dark storm of worlds the eyes of Arghol wink starwise in sympathy with the effects of a far-offness of long light years.

Throats iron eternities (drinking heavy radiance)—limbs towers of blatant light—the stars poise, stupendously remote.

Metal-sided [Blast: 'immensely distant, with their metal sides'] meteoritic, they are the pantheistic machines fashioned by the astronomer.³

Arghol has no power to change his circumstances or his fate, yet he is able to increase his understanding of his predicament. Lewis makes it clear that at this point his protagonist does not fully understand what his relationship with the stars is: 'Imprisoned in a messed socket of existence, his place in the panorama of power is obscure.' He realizes that their power is immense and impersonal, but as yet they seem to him 'stupendously remote', and when his eyes 'wink starwise in sympathy with the effects of a far-offness of long light years', it is clear that he does not realize how directly and fatally they threaten him. He seems more exhilarated than threatened at the emptying of the heavens of gods and Blakean angels.

The ending of this section forewarns us that Arghol will not be able to preserve his aloofness for much longer: 'But so far the violences of all things have left him intact. He is whole as a stone, the core of erosions.' He can only maintain a 'stone-like' invulnerability by being sure that he is ruled entirely by the intellect and by suppressing the physical, the emotional and the mystical. He may manufacture visions inside his own head, but he must not believe that mystical experiences come to him from a point outside of himself. He has committed himself to trying to purge himself of the common human tendency to idealize the human condition. Explaining to Hanp why he must stay with his uncle and suffer the daily beatings, he describes himself as:

A visionary tree. Not migratory. Visions from within . . .
A man with a headache lies in deliberate leaden inanimation
—he isolates his body, floods it with phlegm, sucks numbness up into his brain. So it should be with the spirit, maybe. Soul is a good sodden word, of the old verbal dough. Use that— say soul. A soul, that is the wettest dough, the doughtiest plumber's stock-in-trade. It is the perfect bullet. To drop down Eternity like a plummet—accumulate in myself, day after day, a dense concentration of pig life! Nothing spent, stored rather in strong stagnation, till rid at last of the evaporation and lightness characteristic of men! Thus to burst Death's

membrane through—slog beyond—not float in appalling distances! (p. 22)

He believes that it is necessary to resist what he considers to be the dishonest and egocentric desire to discover 'among the stars' evidence of the workings of a divine power well-disposed toward humanity—to rid himself of this particular kind of 'evaporation and lightness'. His meditations on the stars energize his intellect, but he is not receiving from them any revelation of transcendent truth:

> Energy has been fastened upon me from nowhere—heavy, astonished, resigned, I accept it. It is without meaning I agree —or at least if it have a meaning I cannot discern it. However, I will use it, as prisoner his sheet or bedding for escape. Not as a means of idle humiliation. Why should I not make use of these senseless gifts? (p. 22)

Later in this long conversation with Hanp he explains this further:

> Anything I possess is drunk up here upon the world's brink, by big stars, and returned me in the shape of thought, ponderous as a meteorite. The stone of the stars will serve for my seal and emblem. I practise with it a monotonous 'putting', so that I may hit Death when he comes. (p. 26)

These thoughts prove to be his anxieties about mortality which are like 'stones', both in 'weighing him down' with depression and in being intractable.

Arghol is the 'Enemy of the Stars' because they stand for 'Time', but 'Time' is the enemy only because it brings death. The stars, 'light years away', are constant reminders of the inevitability of extinction. Enemy of the Stars shows that the fear of mortality lies at the heart of all Arghol's problems and this play provides us with a crucial insight into Lewis's own thinking that helps us to understand the nature of the satire in his other works. The most outstanding characteristic of his satire is its reiteration of the physical repulsiveness of his characters. The intensity of his revulsion argues against the kind of dispassionate observation of surfaces that he claims to be engaged in, yet it is clearly not warranted by the usually trivial or innocuous stupidities or pretensions that the characters display. We see that his revulsion is aroused by the simple fact of their physicality alone which is such an outrage to him because it is a constant reminder of the corruptibility of the body, of his own as well as theirs. We see this very clearly at the beginning and end of *The Apes of God* where Lady Fredigonde is presented as loathsome because she is old and decrepit and about to die. As a *memento mori* she is an object of fear to Lewis, yet, rather than confronting and presenting this fear directly, he masks it with revulsion which he then displaces on to her.

Lewis's categorical rejection of all possibilities of transcendence inevitably locks him into a painfully claustrophobic state of mind and he dramatizes this powerfully in his presentation of Arghol's predicament. Arghol knows that the fact of death should only be reacted to intellectually; that an emotional reaction such as anger is certainly pointless and possibly dangerous, but he tells how, at first, he could not accept this: 'One night Death left his card. I was not familiar with the name he chose, but the black mourning edge was deep. I flung it back. A thousand awakenings of violence visited me then. I was ready to act' (p. 22). He quickly learns that action is useless. He hides a jack-knife in his sleeve, ready to murder his uncle, but is cut himself before he can draw it out as his uncle's first kick 'brought [him] to his senses'. After this he lies passively, ready to be kicked, in what Lewis describes as a 'female gesture to facilitate aggression' (p. 7).

The regular kickings administered by Arghol's uncle are partly equivalent to the painful reminders of mortality which constantly assault Lewis and partly equivalent to the hostile reactions of other people to his satire and depressing philosophy. Lewis sees both of these as equally inescapable. Arghol insists —and tries to convince Hanp—that it is his destiny to be abused by his uncle, that it is no use to resist because nothing can change his situation: 'Change is an illusion' (p. 15). He wants to believe that each beating is an accident, but Hanp, reminding him that they happen at the same time each day, is naturally enough not convinced. Arghol first attempts to explain his uncle's animus toward him by suggesting that it is the envious anger of someone who is conventional toward anyone who thinks as an individual:

> Self, sacred act of violence, is like murder on my face and hands. The stain will not come out. . . .
> That is the one piece of property all communities have agreed it is illegal to possess. The sweetest-tempered person, once he discovers that you are that sort of criminal, changes his tune—looks askance at you, is upon his guard . . . As between Personality and the Group, it is forever a question of dog and cat. These two are diametrically opposed species. Self is the ancient race, the rest are the new one. Self is the race that lost. But Mankind still suspects Egotistic plots, and hunts Pretenders! (p. 14)

But 'murder' suggests an offence more dangerous than individualism and we realize that the 'sacred act of violence' that leaves a stain 'like murder' on Arghol is Lewis's philosophy, his contention that human existence is sordid and pointless and that any attempt to be optimistic about human nature or to find a divine plan in the course of human affairs or in the workings of the universe is escapist idealism.

Arghol makes no attempt to conceal his contempt for 'the Group':

> Existence. Loud feeble sunset—blaring like lumpish, savage clown, alive with rigid tinsel, tricked out in louse-infected pantaloons . . . upon the trestled balcony of a marquee, announcing events in a stable programme of a thousand breakneck sports . . . a showman who bellows down to penniless herds, their eyes red with stupidity, crowding beneath him clutching their sixpences.

But no matter how pointless, tawdry and demeaning life is, we cling to it anyway because the alternative is extinction.

> And after that? . . . To leave violently this slow monotonous life; that is, to take header into the boiling starry cold. . . . Hell of those Heavens uncovered, whirling pit, every evening! You cling to any object, dig your nails into the galloping terra firma beneath you, not to drop into it. (pp. 18–19)

This is only one of many instances throughout the play when Arghol articulates the basic tenets of Lewis's philosophy for him, but in case the reader should still be in any doubt about these points, Lewis appends to the 1932 edition an essay, 'Physics of the Not-Self', which begins: 'This essay is in the nature of a metaphysical commentary upon the ideas suggested by the action of *Enemy of the Stars*. Briefly, it is intended to show the human mind in its traditional rôle of the enemy of life, as an oddity outside the machine.' The 'machine' is, of course, the 'wild body' and the mind is the enemy of life because it knows about death. The knowledge of death as extinction is what Lewis calls the '*Not-self*', which, 'established in the centre of the intellect betrays at every moment its transient human associate'. 'Scientific' or objective truth, the concern of the true philosopher, acknowledges the presence of the *Not-self*, but, Lewis claims, most people find this too frightening and choose a more optimistic view of life, 'discovering' the kind of reassuring 'truth' that they want to find. Unlike the true philosopher, the 'wise man' tries to deny the presence of the '*Not-self*' and 'keeps it locked up, a skeleton in a cupboard, or an abnormal offspring that it would be disastrous to exhibit' (p. 51). People who refer in public to this 'unfortunate by-product of the human state... this intellectual abortion or death's-head', 'convict themselves on the spot of being *no gentleman*, or, at the best, an enemy' (p. 52). Hence the stain 'like murder' on Arghol's face and hands.

In his presentation of Arghol's plight, Lewis is examining the fact that he habitually provokes hostile reactions from other people and clearly wants to satisfy himself that this is the result of something more honorable than wilful masochism. His immediate justification is that he is simply more honest than other people—a 'philosopher' rather than a 'wise man'—and that they are outraged because, seeing the truth as it is, he refuses to falsify it to make it more palatable. Yet there is still room for wilfulness. To have seen the truth does not mean that one must constantly thrust it in people's faces when they so obviously want to close their eyes to it. This is clearly an invitation to hostility and seems to be what Lewis has in mind when he has Hanp accuse Arghol of having forced his uncle to assault him, of having 'Mounted the whole bag of tricks from top to bottom

—made the bed you were to lie on with your eyes open' (p. 25). Arghol reacts as though there is an element of truth in this as he 'draws away from Hanp, his eyes somewhat dilated, as if in an absent-minded fit of half-suppressed alarm' (p. 26). When Hanp asks whether what he has said is not true, Arghol concedes: 'It is your view of me. It is how you interpret this. But if what you said were true, it would still be my fate, as you wish us to call it' (p. 26). Lewis wants to believe that he is bound to elicit hostility, simply because he is able to treat the painful truth about the human condition as fundamentally an intellectual matter, but Hanp's challenge shows that Lewis is aware of the possibility of a more emotional involvement. Arghol claims that he cannot escape his unpleasant destiny and when Hanp asks why, he confesses his own confusion:

I am in the dark as much as you! I simply cannot understand it. When I look round, I am sometimes dumbfounded at the oddness, more than you! I am disgusted too. I am disgusted with myself for being guilty of such a destiny—and such a décor! I am ashamed of absolutely everything—to be per-fectly frank. (p. 25)

Lewis sees the intellect as, by instinct and desire, outside the province of time and yet, because it is yoked to the body, doomed to be dragged down into obliteration. Hence Arghol's 'exotic headpiece . . . heavy and bird-like, weighted with a ballast of pig-iron to strike with—living enchained upon his mobile body —ungainly red atlantic wave!' (p. 20). At first Arghol describes the unruly power of the body, but, as the play progresses, this is no longer an idea articulated, but a suffocating experience to be lived out. Early in the play Arghol confidently explains its supremacy to Hanp not realizing the implications for himself of what he is saying. He claims that 'the wild machine—that is the animal—alone is normal', and that the 'red badge of our pre-datory category' is covered with nothing more durable than 'lily pollen of Ideal', a 'nap of sentiment' which can easily be scraped down or worn off (pp. 16, 18).

Later Arghol expresses his feelings about the 'wild body' at much greater length, but this is still comfortably theoretical as Lewis wants us to notice when he tells us that his hero is indulging in a 'diatribe' of 'egotistic self-castigation'. Arghol admits as much himself. Hanp has hinted that his master is not as secure behind his mask of enlightened and stoic aloofness as he pretends to be and says: 'All the talking you do does not seem to bear out your pretensions. For what you pretend you are, you talk too much' (p. 29). Arghol goes on to give what amounts to a lecture on the subject:

> Again let me do a lot of extraordinary talking ... As to the use of my tongue, that is a purgative ... Men possess a repulsive deformity, it is generally referred to as 'Myself.' This is a disfiguring disease. Promiscuous rubbing against their fellows is responsible for it ... Only one operation can cure it—the classical stoic operation, namely—emptying an artery into the bath. But Self is enormous—the thing is like a snuffling parasite, far more bulky than the louse or flea. I have smashed it against me. Still, however, the creature writhes, a turbulent mess. I have shrunk it in frosty climates, and attempted to starve it out. But it has filtered filth into me, until my most hermetic solitude is impure as the water of a public washing-brook. (p. 30)

The dilemma Arghol describes here is certainly claustrophobic, yet we are hearing how his intellect perceives it more than seeing, as we will shortly, how his body suffers it. Up until now he has been able to survive by stoically accepting his painful destiny, but he feels the need not only to understand his position but to spell out his insights for Hanp and this proves to be his undoing. Lewis's own situation is not basically different from his hero's because, even though he understands clearly the relationship between his own interior 'Hanp' and 'Arghol', this does not help him to cope with their irreconcilability. Also, Arghol's problem of 'talking too much' is equivalent to the fact that Lewis, as a writer, is constantly putting his views into words, which means dwelling upon troubling matters, and also frequently provoking hostile reactions from his readers. Arghol describes his perpetual talking to Hanp as partly from carelessness, partly inevitable, partly a release of tension and partly almost masochistic:

It was because you were nobody and nothing . . . But it is a physical matter too—simply to make use of one's mouth and stretch one's tongue. My thoughts to walk abroad—not for ever to be stuffed up in my head—ideas to banjo this big sounding-box—to pipe with this big windbag of a body. That is one reason among several . . . I am a great extraordinary talking man, who only stops to sleep—my relatives assault me because I will not hold my tongue. I can go on . . . I can talk off a *dog's* hind leg! (pp. 31–2)

By revealing his limitations to Hanp, Arghol ensures his final death at Hanp's hands, but it is clear that he could not anyway have stopped himself from talking. His most serious mistake is his failure to fully understand the relationship between Hanp and himself. He can see part of the truth. After expatiating upon the loathesomeness of Hanp—'a poop fired off by Mother-Nature in derision, a bad smell'—he says 'My constant discovery is that you are me . . . We are improperly separate. You grow in me' (p. 32). In the course of talking to Hanp he discovers more about their relationship. He had thought that he could be the master and could remain detached from the 'wild body' and admits to Hanp: 'I find I wished to make of you a yapping Poodle-parasite, a sort of mechanical bow-wow, to fetch and carry for my inferior nature—to be The Animal to me!' He now realizes that Hanp has more power than he and is not his servant but his pimp: 'The fact is I shall be a prostitute always' (p. 33). Given this insight into his situation, his next move is irrational and proves ultimately to be fatal. He tries to order Hanp to leave, but Hanp turns and attacks him 'with fist and claw', and we are shown how wrong Arghol was to think he could rid himself of his animal self by banishing Hanp when we see with how little resistance Arghol himself is changed from inactive intellect into 'the soft, blunt paw of Nature—taken back to her bosom, as a matter of course—slowly and idly winning her battle!' (p. 37) After knocking Hanp unconscious, Arghol collapses and sleeps and 'a dark dream begins valuing, with its tentative symbols, the foregoing events'.

The claustrophobia is intensified by the dreams because they reveal to Arghol how he has always been the prisoner of his 'parasite self'. He sees the books that influenced him as a student as 'parasites... Poodles of the mind', and tears them up. He sees that his student friends are 'all companions of the parasite self' and prepares to disown them too. The settings in this section of the play are, paradoxically, less surreal and we are particularly encouraged to see Arghol as Lewis at this point when we learn that he, like Lewis, spent his student days in Germany. The parasite self here is not, as it had been in the earlier exchanges with Hanp, primarily the physical body. It is rather the much-edited and inauthentic social self assumed so habitually for the purposes of social interaction with friends and acquaintances that it has taken on an identity of its own which has begun to seem more substantial than the real Arghol. Arghol in this dream-sequence actually gives this social self the name of Arghol and realizes that 'that creature of two-dimensions, clumsily cut out in cardboard by the coarse scissor-work of the short-sighted group-spirit—the social mind—that impudent parasite had forgathered too long with men, borne his name too variously, to be easily abashed much less ousted'. He continues, anticipating the ending of the play, 'Why, he was not sure, even had they been separated surgically, in which self life would have gone out, and in which kept alight' (p. 40). In his dream, Arghol, when he meets one of his student friends, tries to disown the platitudinous charade of socially sanctioned interaction and to establish some more authentic communication, but he quickly realizes that 'such a superficial fellow as this would never see anyone but the customary Arghol of his acquaintance' (p. 40).

At this point Lewis has made the only change which represents a real departure from the *Blast* version. In 1914 he had written, with what by 1932 had apparently come to seem either wishful thinking or a sign of weakness: 'This man would never see anyone but Arghol he knew—Yet he on his side saw a man, directly beneath his friend, imprisoned, with intolerable need of recognition' (p. 78). The main revelation of the dream is that there never has been any possibility of escape for Arghol. He thought that, by leaving the city and coming to live in solitude, he could rid himself of his false social self, but the 'Arghol he had supposed left behind in the city is suddenly here, who has followed him, almost a stowaway. And, lo, it is Hanp!'

Now Arghol lies asleep and as we see him through Hanp's eyes he appears increasingly repulsive and the claustrophobia intensifies. Hanp feels 'a great sullen indignation' against Arghol for having resorted to action after having always before advocated stoic passivity: 'the heavy body, so long quiet, flinging itself destructively about—face strained with the intimate expression of the act of love—what a repulsive picture was that, as it shot up in retrospect' (p. 41). In his long meditation over the sleeping Arghol, Hanp acquires authenticity and presence to precisely the degree that his former master, now powerless because asleep, loses his dignity. He is ready to become the victim, not, as before, by his own choice and on his own terms, but on Hanp's terms. Arghol's very apearance as he lies asleep becomes, to Hanp, an incentive to murder: 'Lying there by the door, he heaves. It is in a sickly pneumatic pumping of stale wind. Death the refrain of his being, Arghol lies now, like a corpse (fitted with a wheezing pump' (pp. 42–3). At the sight of the sleeping Arghol, Hanp, with lethal clarity, sees through the mask of Arghol's self-deception, understanding that 'the great humbug's preparation for extinction, in which all his days are passed, is a ritual to scare it off if anything, rather than a going-out to meet it!' Once Hanp sees the fear of death at the heart of Arghol's stoic posing, he has his former master entirely at his mercy. 'Why not tip him over into the cauldron into which he persistently gazes? It is an irresistible notion' (p. 43).

This, it seems to me, stands as a devastating and courageous piece of self-analysis on Lewis's part. The Enemy mocks others because they shut out from their minds the spectre of human mortality and prides himself upon his own ability to look unflinchingly at the depressing spectacle of the human lot. Yet he is here suggesting that his supposed ability to cast a cold eye on death is not so much an act of brave defiance as an evasive manoeuvre intended to mask his own fear.

Everything is stripped away from Arghol as the trap closes and in the final refinement of claustrophobia he reaches a state of ultimate vulnerability and becomes the victim of the involuntary operation of his own body. As he sleeps he snores and the snoring is first the means of stripping away all his dignity and humanness and then, in Hanp's ear, a fly searching for dead flesh on which to lay its eggs and finally 'a trumpet-call ... to murder':

> Bluebottle, at first unremarked, hurtling stealthily—a stout
> snore rises into the air. Clotted, soulless and self-centred, it
> compels hysteria ... as Hanp listens ... a peachy, clotted tide
> of sound, gurgling back into the viscous shallows. It is the
> snorting of a malodorous, bloody sink, emptying its water ...
> All the majestic sonority of this voice that in the past some-
> times has subdued him, suddenly turned into music of the
> disrespectful Abyss, anti-human rhapsodies of the waste-pipe
> and water-closet. (p. 43)

Lewis is careful not to allow Hanp to be elevated by the
degradation of Arghol—making sure that there will be nothing
to relieve the bleakness of the conclusion. Hanp as he commits
the murder and then drowns himself is once again the crude,
repulsive and clumsy lout that Arghol saw: 'Peeping in a dim
puppy-stare, through tumefied slits of blackened flesh, he sways
and groans a little. A booze-hound collecting his wits ... he
stretches and strains like a big toy in the act of being wound up.'
He has one brief moment of elation when he is 'the darling of the
sky', but 'a galloping blackness of mood overtakes the lonely
figure'. At this point he encounters a 'lounging idle shadow', a
'faceless super' with 'a mask of inexpressive clay'. In *Blast*
Lewis had written, 'It was his master', but later, 'It is Sfox'.
His name suggests that Sfox represents the 'Not-self', the principle of non-existence, the antithesis to the intellect of the living
Arghol and now all that remains of him.[4] Sfox watches as, 'with
a clumsy recklessness, like a bad actor ... Hanp springs off the
parapet of the bridge'. In this, 'the poorest suicide that was ever
staged, he might have been jumping into a swimming bath in a
fit of ill-temper' (p. 47).

Lewis's decision to externalize and objectify his own state of
mind by making the two conflicting drives within him into two
characters and by creating for them their own surreal world
which would be proof against his own authorial intrusion enabled him to be self-analytical with a steadiness of gaze that he
did not try to achieve again. Frequently after this he would
describe the repulsiveness of his characters as though the cause of
his revulsion lay entirely in their shortcomings rather than

largely in his own nihilistic and claustrophobic view of the human condition. Yet, with a great deal of courage, he refused to opt for a less painful, more optimistic philosophy. He continued to be the 'Enemy of the Stars'.

9

Tarr: A Nietzschean Novel

ALISTAIR DAVIES

Ezra Pound, who persuaded the *Egoist* to serialize Lewis's *Tarr* after publishing Joyce's *Portrait of the Artist as a Young Man,* expressed, with characteristic flamboyance, his sense of the importance and originality of the two writers. Their work was 'the insistent utterance of men who were once for all through with the particular inanities of Shavian-Bennett and with the particular oleosities of the Wellsian genre'.[1] Subsequent commentators on Lewis have repeated, although less extremely, Pound's view that Lewis had, with Joyce, staged a revolution in modern English fiction. They have acknowledged Lewis's radical departure from the prevailing conventions of the comic and realist forms of Shaw, Bennett and Wells by defining *Tarr* as a tragi-comedy or as a tragic satire in the manner of Chapman or Shakespeare.[2] The terms used convey the sense of the dramatic and theatrical presentation of scene and character in Lewis's fiction. For such commentators, the amusing but ultimately doomed progress of Otto Kreisler is the tragic or tragi-comic action at the centre of the novel.

However, the same commentators have been less willing to accept Pound's judgement that Lewis's hard, objective prose or his cool, conceptual approach in *Tarr* are preferable to the leisurely flow of Joyce's novel. They have argued that *Tarr* is ultimately too brutal, too objective, as it becomes, in the final stage after the death of Kreisler, the mouthpiece for Lewis, who projects himself into the figure of Tarr. Tarr, formerly a character caught up in the human relations represented by the novel, becomes, in the final stage, the Lewisian exponent of icy detachment in life and art. He is, accordingly, no longer able to express any sympathetic appreciation of the plight of the other characters with whom he had been involved, or, indeed, to reflect upon the special isolation of his own position. The final and most objective stage of the novel destroys the structural and emotional coherence of the work, as Lewis, in order to suggest the super-human quality of Tarr, detaches himself and his character from the emotions aroused by Kreisler's death. Lewis had not yet learned, as Joyce had, how to distance himself as a writer from his creation, or how to invent the dramatic situations in which his characters might fully reveal themselves.

But this negative assessment of *Tarr* by its commentators does not seem adequate. The striking and confident style, the un-apologetic but effective presentation of types, the underlying intellectual coherence, do not suggest a writer who was either ignorant of literary methods or unsure about his purposes. In this essay, I wish to argue that *Tarr* has been found wanting in structure and characterization because it has been judged by conventions of tragic or dramatic action which are inappropriate. Lewis, who had spent several months of study in Munich in 1905, makes use of and adapts to his own ends as a novelist the form employed by the two leading German avant-garde writers of the period, the Nietzschean novella.

Thomas Mann, in *Tonio Kröger* (1903) and *Death in Venice* (1912), and Rainer Maria Rilke, in *The Notebooks of Malte Laurids Brigge* (1910), were concerned with Nietzsche's analysis of the creative and destructive forces of culture and society that operate upon the individual. They questioned the nature and the possibility of autonomous life, particularly for the artist, in a bourgeois environment. To do so, they established the Nietzschean novella. What was unusual about the Nietzschean novella, as a form depicting the forces operating upon the individual and society, was that it was not concerned with the analysis of character, or of relationship, or of human action. It reduced characters to social, psychological and sexual types, and distinguished between the sick and the healthy, the weak and the strong. Those who were weak were unable to transcend the destructive social and psychological forces impinging upon them, while the strong did so through successive acts of rebellion and creative rebirth.

Tarr is not, as critics have suggested, an incoherent work in which the final apotheosis of Tarr destroys the emotional and moral focus of the novel in the tragic action of Kreisler. The un-conventional structure is that of the Nietzschean novella, which presents the development of the central hero, Tarr, marked out by his superior vigour and vitality, as he breaks through and transcends the sick and destructive forces which surround him. This process, rather than Kreisler's tragic fate, forms the central adventure of the novel. Indeed, the decline of Kreisler, who in Nietzschean terms is a sick and pathological creature, deliberately parallels the rise of Tarr. Kreisler's doom arouses neither pity nor awe: it is as inevitable as it is deserved.

However, before a detailed examination of *Tarr* as a Nietz-schean novel, it is necessary to define Nietzscheanism, and to show how it affected the work of the most important novelist of the German avant-garde, Thomas Mann. Nietzsche believed himself to be the philosopher whose ideas would enable the great prophets of tomorrow—artists, poets, leaders—to be born. But they had to suffer in order to free themselves from the values of the intellectual, religious, moral and artistic traditions of the Greco-Christian West, whose common origins he traced, in *The Genealogy of Morals*, to the repression of instinct and of the powers of life by mind and conscience. Consequently, the sexual drive, enfeebled by such repression, found its outlet in the sentimentality of Christian love and pity, in the idealized adora-tion of women, and in various forms of Romantic sensibility and art. 'Oversubtle modern man is the heir to the conscience-vivi-section and self-torture of millennia.'[3]

The schools and universities taught the principles and values of this moral ascetic tradition. History was believed to possess an intelligible, moral purpose, which modern man, at its culmina-tion, could comprehend. Bourgeois ideas of justice and pity represented the fullest practical expression of Christian teaching. The modern, democratic state, and its liberal institutions, were the instruments to redeem mankind. Consequently, the schools made the young aware of the moral development of history, and of its fulfilment in the present, by instructing them in an encyclopaedic body of historical knowledge, which, it was believed, was the sum of civilization.

For Nietzsche, such a view was fundamentally misguided. Instead of representing the culmination of history, modern

society and culture, based upon repression, revealed only de-
generation and sickness.[4] The morality of justice and pity arose
from herd morality, from pathological weakness and not from
strength. The cosmopolitan and encyclopaedic knowledge incul-
cated by the schools resulted only in a hybrid, exhausted and
uncreative culture. The perversion of the creative impulse by
mass education led only to charlatanism, theatricality and sexual
morbidity.[5]

Having diagnosed the sickness of modern man and of modern
culture, Nietzsche also offered his own solutions. In *The Gay
Science*, Nietzsche mocked systematic German philosophy which,
in Hegel, had delineated the forms of existence through which
modern man had progressed to achieve freedom. Such freedom,
Hegel argued, came through the recognition of social identity in
and obligation to the community. For Nietzsche, however, such
freedom was the sick and sentimental consciousness of the herd
animal, which had not escaped from the banal, and whose
instincts, sapped by the self-torture of Christian asceticism, found
their outlet in forms of dementia, cult worship and mass fantasy.[6]
Only the aristocrat of the spirit, who was free from the self-
torture of herd morality, and who, consequently, combined great
instinctual energies with great creative energies, had the potential
for true freedom.[7] For he could sublimate his sexual drives
through creativity rather than repress them. In this way, he
could become a Self, creating his own style, assuming his own
rather than a group identity, expressing himself in a unique
way.[8] Unlike the herd animal, he was not afraid of isolation.[9]
Equally, unlike the Christian, whose fear of death was allayed by
the belief in immortality, the aristocrat˜of the spirit was not
afraid of death, for he could oppose it by creating, through the
sublimation of the powers of life, enduring artefacts. The response
of this free spirit was a carefree and annihilating laughter, a kind
of metaphysical gaiety.[10]

German writers in the pre-war period found in Nietzsche
sanction for a variety of purely negative responses to bourgeois
culture, whose inner sickness they believed had been fully diagnosed by Nietzsche. One was the exaggerated mockery of
Christian morality by the George circle, which, at its height
during Lewis's period in Munich, produced perverse, sadistic

rituals in dramatic verse. Another was the irony of Thomas
Mann, who had begun to attract a wide following in Munich
from 1900. Perfecting the Nietzschean novella as the dominant,
avant-garde form of German culture, Mann showed in *Tonio
Kröger* and *Death in Venice*, the psychological and physical
stages of the estrangement and decline of the over-subtle individual, of the ironic artist, who pre-figured in his own over-
sensitivity and lethargy the fate of the class from which he came.
Its traditions and values, so robust on the surface, were no longer
capable of sustaining or of renewing life. This was left to the
crude, unreflective vitality of the parvenu.

For Mann, bourgeois values were the constricting and uncreative forces against which the artist rebelled. But he could not
go beyond them because his own will had been wasted by them.
As he showed in his portrait of von Aschenbach, the ironic artist
could only reflect upon the exhaustion of culture. The artistic
vocation might free the individual from the narrow imaginative
horizon of bourgeois life, but it placed him instead in the un-
bounded realm of historical culture, which, despite its abundant
reference of image and symbol, was no longer able to maintain
itself. Such symbolism had become decorative, disguising the
inner emptiness of the culture which adopted it.

A similar fatalism affected the discussion of the nature and
condition of art. As we see in von Aschenbach's pursuit of the
idealized Tadzio, adventure for the ironic artist is reduced to the
adventure of art. It is through dreams, illusion and idealization
that individuals seek release from the values of an ailing culture
and seek transcendence in the pure order of art. But Mann was
equally conscious of the ambiguous nature of this transcendence.
The artist's wish to transform the real into the ideal, to structure
life through a framework of perfecting symbol, was itself tied to
the exhaustion and morbidity of bourgeois life. Nietzsche had
stated that the repressed sexual drive, which formed the basis
for creativity in art as well as life, could only find its outlet in
sexual idealization, in sentimentality, in illusion. Mann repeats
Nietzsche's analysis in his portrait of von Aschenbach. The
creative drives of the writer can only find their expression in
sentimental adoration, in sterile and uncreative homo-erotic fantasy. Tadzio, at first idealized as a timeless and transcendent

platonic symbol of Beauty, appears at the end as the Angel of Death. For Mann, the imagination could only assume, in a period of decline, effete, obsessive and hyper-refined forms: it could only yield, with rapture, to the voluptuousness of disintegration and death.

Lewis, with *Tarr*, introduced into English literary culture the structure and themes of the Nietzschean novella, which he adapted to full-length novel form. He was concerned, like Mann, with the creative and destructive social, cultural and psychological forces which weigh upon the artist in the modern world. He presented, through the biography of his hero, a study of the nature and conditions of art in a society indifferent to its values. But, unlike Mann, he did not show the life of the artist to be one of estrangement, sickness and death. Tarr represents vitality, abundance and the powers of creative regeneration, although Tarr's actual greatness as an artist we need to take on trust. Indeed, Lewis was anxious in his novel to establish, as we shall see, a central contrast between the vital artist, Tarr, and the pseudo-artist, Kreisler, who resembles the ironic figures presented by Mann. Like Tonio Kröger, Kreisler is a bourgeois who had turned to art, but without the promise of authentic life or expression.

The reasons for the difference between the pessimism of Mann and the optimism of Lewis are to be found in the latter's positive reading of Nietzsche. He understood Nietzsche, 'whose influence', he wrote, 'was paramount at this time', not to be, as Mann thought, the fatalistic analyst of sick culture, but the prophet of a new world, of new forms of life and expression. Nietzsche's *The Gay Science* was 'among my favourite reading in those years'.[11]

Indeed, the very structure of *Tarr* reproduces the stages outlined by Nietzsche in *The Gay Science*, by which the individual realizes his Selfhood and becomes a true creator. First, he struggles with the banal, mediocre and sentimental modes of feeling of herd life. Second, he struggles with its empty, theatrical rituals and modes of behaviour. Finally, by struggling against and by transcending these modes, he comes to achieve freedom as a Self, as an artist able to assert his own feelings and to make his own rules of behaviour. He moves from the shared

level of sentiment to the exceptional level of metaphysical gaiety.
In the first stage, Tarr rests upon the level of play, upon the
level of sporting, good humour. Good humour, as he explains, is
the national characteristic of the English, who hesitate to suggest
either difference or uniqueness, and who endeavour, through
the conciliation of humour, to project a comforting mediocrity
which ties them to their fellow men. Humour in relationships
allows men to disguise the inequalities of Nature. It provides the
principal means of illusion by which the English disguise the
cruelty, indifference and ruthlessness of Nature in the social
and cosmic order. It is this playful quality which informs
Tarr's encounters with Hobson, Butcher and Lowndes, the three
acquaintances with whom he discusses his problematic affair
with Bertha Lunken.

Alan Hobson's originally manly body, we are told, has been
disfigured by its Cambridge cut; Guy Butcher, still an adolescent
romantic, enjoys life on the level of schoolboy adventure;
Lowndes is a fussy and self-important gossip. They are all the
anti-vital products of Cambridge and Oxford, of the cultural
circles of the English Liberal state, in which the weakened
sexual instincts are transformed, in life, into maudlin romance
and the cult of friendship, and, in art, into prettiness and decoration. In conversation with Hobson, Tarr excoriates such groups,
and the Liberal state which nurtured them, specifying, as he does
so, the sterile psychological, sexual and moral forms Nietzsche
had diagnosed as symptoms of cultural morbidity:

> The Cambridge set ... is, as observed in an average speci-
> men, a cross between a Quaker, a Pederast and a Chelsea
> Artist ... Your Oxford brothers; dating from the Wilde
> decade, are a stronger body ... You represent, my dear fellow,
> the dregs of Anglo-Saxon civilization. There is nothing softer
> on earth. Your flabby potion is a mixture of the lees of
> Liberalism, the poor froth blown off the decadent nineties, the
> wardrobe leavings of a vulgar Bohemianism with its head-
> quarters in Chelsea.[12]

The prevailing English good humour is the communal expression of a feminine and exhausted culture. Although Tarr is not,
by background or education, a member of the Oxbridge and

Chelsea set, he becomes conscious, through his encounters with those who are, that his attachment to Bertha is based upon good humour, upon maudlin romance. He loves Bertha because she is mediocre, and so allows the artist, as a human being, access to the comfort and reassuring banality of the ordinary world. Yet, to continue to play his part in this relationship, to maintain the illusions on which good humour is based, Tarr would have to blind himself to the radical differences which separate them. The risk, clearly expressed, is that Tarr's masculine vigour, associated with the brutal and steadfast temperament of the artist who could confront the cruelties and inequalities of Nature without the consolation of illusion, might itself be sapped by maintaining the illusion at the heart of their relationship. The threat posed by the relationship is consistently described in terms of sickness, disease and debilitation: 'We are all sicknesses for one another. Such contact as he had with Bertha was particularly risky' (p. 61).

The first section of the novel ends with Tarr giving up humour and indicating to Bertha that their relationship must end. He looks about her room at its contents: 'She seemed so humble in it —the appeal of the little again. If only he could escape from scale' (p. 62). This is the first stage in his Nietzschean recognition that he must, as a human being as well as an artist, accept a qualitative difference of consciousness, experience and human response in order to maintain his full creative vigour and masculinity: 'The price of preoccupation with the large was the perpetual danger from the little. Brutality was no doubt necessary for people like him' (p. 62). The phrase, 'no doubt', points to the complex but decisive psychological moment of awareness, regret and final assent. We see, in this moment of the recognition and transcendence of the banal, the fundamental Nietzschean structure of rebellion and transformation which lies below the level of narrative and plot in Tarr.

In the second stage, Tarr moves from the playful level of individual encounter to the more objective level of social relationships, in which he can maintain more easily the detached and brutal relationship to others he has chosen for himself. Lewis presents, in this stage, the bohemian social circles of Paris and the part played within them by an art-student acquaintance of Tarr,

Otto Kreisler. The consistent vocabulary used to describe the bohemians and Kreisler is that of performance. Of the most fashionable group, the Lipmann circle, Lewis writes:

In this assembly, almost all exuded a classic absurdity. There were two sisters named von Maag, from the Baltic provinces. They were very 'grande dame'. There was a German countess. One of the initiatory ceremonies in this society was to sit for the Countess. If anyone shied from this, it was a very bad mark. Two girls from Dresden, who professed a sort of adoration for Fraulein Lipmann were present. But the most noticeable thing in this group of women was their pretence to be, one and all, in love with each other. (p. 132)

The bourgeois-bohemians live in a sickly and feminine world, in which men and women act out various fantastic and exaggerated social and erotic roles for one another.

Otto Kreisler is a type who embodies in his own person the contradictions of modern culture. His clothing is a mixture of the conventional and the bohemian, showing both the will to rebel and the will to conform: 'a military morning suit, slashed with thick seams, carefully cut hair, his German high-crowned bowler-hat and plain-cane' (p. 89). His moods, as he plays out a self-conscious role in bohemian society, are volatile and inconsistent, ranging from eager self-advertisement to sullen depression. Although he has broken away from authoritarian society, rejecting through his bohemianism the patriarchal structure of German society, he is still submissive and obsequious to others: 'At the Berne he had lost his nerve in some way; he clowned obsequiously some evenings, and depressed and slack the next, perhaps resented his companions' encores' (p. 84). His solitary life is interrupted by such angry and disruptive forays into society. Although the rumour of his seventeen children in Germany suggests a pleasure-seeking man, he is also a fantasist, transforming women into idealized objects of adoration.

Indeed, the story of Kreisler in the middle section of the novel shows how he transforms into his ideal object the beautiful Anastasya, whom he meets by chance in a café. He will play the role of hopeless, chivalric lover to her, 'for the sake of the Invisible Audience haunting life' (p. 177). His yearning to meet her again is satisfied by an invitation to the Lipmann circle, which she frequents, but while visiting a café earlier in the evening he sees her in the company of another man, Soltyk. Overcome by jealousy and despair, he turns to drink, and arrives at the party in a dishevelled and drunken state. His scandalous behaviour evokes only a derisory laugh from Anastasya. When the party breaks up to go on to a nightclub, Kreisler too leaves. En route, he encounters Bertha, who has been drawn to him by his isolation. Bertha takes the opportunity to show public infidelity to Tarr by allowing the drunken Kreisler to kiss and embrace her. In this way, she justifies, in the eyes of his friends, Tarr's abandonment of her. This further scandal completes Kreisler's effect on his bohemian audience.

This narrative linking of Kreisler and Bertha completes a consistent element in the presentation of Kreisler. He is the ridiculous, pathological type against whom we can measure the strong, vital and creative type, Tarr, whom he replaces in Bertha's affections. Kreisler behaves throughout the scene at the Lipmann party like a mechanical doll. The image establishes for us not only the degree to which he is detached from the natural powers of life but also the degree to which he lacks shaping power over the energies he does possess.

What distinguishes the weak from the strong? In truly aristocratic society, as represented for the West in the Russian novel, the custom of the duel, in which the individual showed his self-mastery in the face of death, was the ritual which distinguished the true from the false. The climax of the second stage of the novel is reached when Kreisler's challenge to Anastasya's half-Russian companion, Soltyk, is accepted. The Russians organize a duel, although Soltyk hopes to resolve the dispute honourably. Kreisler, too, offers to withdraw his challenge, but his offer to kiss his opponent is so insulting that he is deemed an unworthy adversary. Kreisler, in a sudden change of mood, is unwilling to be humiliated by such a withdrawal, and tries to force the duel by training his pistol on the Russians. Struck contemptuously in the face by one them, his pistol discharges and kills Soltyk. Kreisler fails the test of the duel, because he is a man who has never achieved self-mastery, has never become a Self. He has lived, even in rebellion, in an uncreative, weak and submissive state. Having broken the law, he submits, in infantile terror and dependence, to the judgement of a society whose rules he has broken. His suicide, in the police cell in which he has taken refuge, is moving, not because it is tragic, but because it expresses his profound bewilderment and defeat.

Kreisler's death concludes the second stage and prepares for the third and final stage of the novel, which is set against the background of Death: 'Death, real living death, was somewhere upon the scene' (p. 309). Tarr, who had transcended the unmasculine world of good humour and the inauthentic world of bourgeois-bohemian rites, had achieved independence, had become a Self, but had yet to achieve full Selfhood. It is the aristocratic Anastasya, with whom Tarr has an affair, and who had spoken with businesslike calm about Kreisler's death, who teaches him how this is to be done. The artist confronts and surmounts Death and Nothingness through the masculine powers of formation and creativity. In their sexual relations, the masculine spirit of the artist must shape and subdue feminine matter: 'His Mohammedan eye did not refuse the conventional bait. His butcher's sensibility pressed his fancy into professional details' (p. 314). The lesson is quickly learned, as Tarr transforms Anastasya into a clean and solid object beneath his eyes. The definite form imposed by his new, aristocratic and masculine will is far from the shapeless mess associated with the peasant-like Bertha. Anastasya releases Tarr's full, masculine and formative instincts, for, in his subsequent sexual relations with other women, he fathers three children. He becomes a literal source of formation and of regeneration.

From Anastasya, Tarr learns a lesson which he can apply to his art. If the ultimate force over everything is death, the true artist, like the potent man, achieves freedom by negating death through creation. Death, Tarr states, is the thing that differentiates art from life, because life, in its manifestation in human beings, is transient and discontinuous (p. 316). The art object, however, endures in time. Unlike men and women, it does not live and die: 'art is identical with the idea of permanence' (p. 316). The artist who works in materials which endure, words, paint, stone and metal, imprints his masculine powers of form upon these amorphous, feminine materials, in order to convert

them into something which is permanent. To achieve permanence, the created object has to be fashioned from material which
itself is not liable to decay: 'Art is Paleozoic matter, Dolomite,
oil-paint and mathematics' (p. 318).

As he achieves creative Selfhood, Tarr fulfils his role, outlined
in Nietzsche's *The Gay Science*, of sign-making animal, fashion-
ing, as an artist, those signs necessary for communication and
deciphering the essential signs by which others express themselves. He thus achieves joyful wisdom. Christianity, Nietzsche
had argued in *The Gay Science*, rested upon a deep distrust of the
nature of existence and of man, and, accordingly, sought to
idealize both, to impute a reality beyond appearance. Romantic
art, with its emotional excess and its idealizing transport, tried to
reveal and communicate this world beyond. The Nietzschean
artist, who repudiated such idealization by accepting his animal
nature, who confronted the cruelty and brutality of life, also
produced signs to communicate the order which he imposed upon
the world. But he did so without believing that the created object
was a vehicle to a higher realm, beyond appearance. 'Deadness is
the first condition of art', Tarr states, because its deadness is based
upon 'the absence of soul, in the human sentimental sense'
(p. 317). The art-object is a sign-in-itself: 'the lines and masses of
the statue are its soul' (p. 317).

I think we must infer from Tarr's thorough exposition of the
nature of modern art and of the appropriate reaction to it, that
our response, as readers, to *Tarr*, and to the final stage in particular, must be one of metaphysical gaiety. This requires us, as the
difficult and unconventional form of the Nietzschean novel intended, to amend our usual conventions of reading. We must not
attribute to Tarr that inner spiritual depth, that moment of tragic
insight, that glimpse of resolution or immortality with which
classical or Christian fiction concludes. For these conclusions are
those of a sentimental, banal, herd culture. We, as readers aware
of our own physical being, recognize the distinction of Tarr.
We understand him, from his appearance, from his surface, as a
true Self, who has been able to release his sexual energies into
modes of human and creative response which, on the one hand,
fashion enduring works of art, and, on the other, surmount the
banality and inauthenticity of the culture which surrounds him.

In writing *Tarr*, Lewis employed and explicated the Nietzschean novella's exceptional conventions of structure and of response. From this comes the strength and coherence of Lewis's novel; and from this comes the history of its misreading in a literary culture to which Nietzschean forms are strange and alien.

10

A Reading of *The Childermass*

ALAN MUNTON

The Childermass (1928) is by far the most difficult of Wyndham Lewis's fictions to explain. Its obscurity prevents the reader from being sure what is happening, and makes him uncertain how to place those events that he can recognize; yet in another way it seems perfectly clear what is happening—Lewis is dramatizing the arguments of *The Art of Being Ruled* and *Time and Western Man*. This view is the usual one among critics, though I do not accept it; it accounts for very little of the text. Since my interpretation of the book is in places complex, I shall set out here a summary of my conclusions.

The setting of *The Childermass* is an imaginary afterworld controlled by a figure called the Bailiff. It is a satire upon an intellectual, Pullman, who is deceived by the Bailiff, who represents all those forces in Western European democracies which diminish freedom. Instead of opposing him, as Lewis believes he should, Pullman accepts the Bailiff's view of the world, and concedes his authority. *The Childermass* shows what it is like to experience the demands of a ruler who pretends to be a democrat, but is in fact a ruthless exploiter of all the means of persuasion available to him. Pullman abjectly renounces all those critical powers that the intellectual should possess; we see him betray the intellect and, in effect, the intellectual community. Pullman's companion Satters, despite his apparent stupidity, has a surer grasp of the realities of the afterworld than has Pullman; he sees through the Bailiff far more readily. Lewis exposes the working of an ideology in *The Childermass*, which is a radical and humane work, having none of the reactionary tendencies usually attributed to Lewis.

The Childermass presents an entirely male afterworld. In an unfamiliar landscape Pullman (who bears a remarkable physical resemblance to James Joyce) meets Satterthwaite, who on earth was his fag at school. Both are recently dead, Satters (as he is called) killed in the First World War. They walk together through a landscape which is subject to changes caused by time, and eventually reach the amphitheatre where the Bailiff, apparently the ruler of this unstable world, hears appellants who wish to enter Heaven, a city lying in the distance across the river Styx. The Bailiff is opposed at these hearings by a group of men, all homosexuals, known as the Hyperideans, after their leader Hyperides. A series of debates ensues, and the work ends just as the Bailiff comes under powerful argumentative attacks from two of Hyperides' spokesmen, Alectryon and Polemon.

The first question is that of genre. 'The "Apes" [*The Apes of God*] is not a novel, nor is "Childermass" ', Lewis wrote.[1] Both are more accurately described as satires, and we should not read *The Childermass* with the same expectations that we bring to a novel like *The Revenge for Love*. The satire is a mixed form, so capacious that it can deal with almost any subject, and it is appropriate that it should include public debate. Lucian uses the journey between the world of the living and the underworld as an opportunity for satire in his story 'Menippus', which attacks false philosophers and includes a guided visit to the underworld. It provides a precedent for both parts of *The Childermass*. 'Menippean satire', a term proposed by Northrop Frye, places such works as *Brave New World*, Samuel Butler's Erewhon books and the satires of Peacock and Voltaire in a tradition which goes back 'through Rabelais and Erasmus to Lucian'.[2] Frye describes the 'short form of the Menippean satire' as 'a dialogue or colloquy, in which the dramatic interest is in a conflict of ideas rather than of character' (p. 310), and this clearly describes the latter part of *The Childermass*, where the form is much expanded. The clothes that Pullman and Satters are given in the afterworld express the maturity and immaturity of their respective minds when they were on earth. This witty exploitation of the doctrine of *karma* relates *The Childermass* to the satiric tradition of 'clothes philosophy' that includes *A Tale of a Tub* and *Sartor Resartus*: 'what is man himself but a microcoat, or rather a complete suit of clothes with all its trimmings?', asks Swift's ironic narrator. There is little substance to Hugh Kenner's objection that *The Childermass* is 'simply *The Art of Being Ruled* dramatised',[3] for it has many of the attributes of fiction, while we should expect this form of satire to be associated with works of theory, rather than otherwise. As a satire, *The Childermass* has impeccable credentials.

The Childermass falls into two clear parts, the first describing the wanderings of Pullman and Satters in the ever-changing 'Time-flats', the second describing the debates and other events at the hearings held by the Bailiff. If we read the first of these parts as fiction, two things slowly become apparent: that Pullman is a devotee of the Bailiff, while Satters is not; and that Lewis is exploring the social uses of degraded and worn-out language. These two processes are related.

In the early pages, Pullman appears to be well-informed about the nature of their surroundings and acts as mentor to Satters, who is full of admiration for what Pullman seems to know: 'Everything is different since we have met it all seems to have a meaning', he says.[4] However, it gradually becomes clear that the 'meaning' Pullman finds is one that he has derived wholly from the Bailiff; what he tells Satters is the Bailiff's truth, and Satters eventually realizes this. Pullman's learned reference to 'the dantesque purgatory' (p. 93) should alert us to his actual role: he is an incompetent Virgil.

The first time that Satters mentions the Bailiff, Pullman reacts possessively: 'At the word *Bailiff* Pullman withdraws into a hypnotic fixity of expression, as if something precise for him alone had been mentioned under an unexpected enigma' (pp. 9–10). Pullman believes that he has in the Bailiff the source of authoritative knowledge. When Satters asks, three times altogether, what the 'peons' are, Pullman replies each time in almost the same words: ' "It is the multitude of personalities which God has created, ever since the beginning of time, and is unable now to destroy" ' (p. 41); he prefaces his first explanation with the words 'What they say about them is that' (p. 30), while on another occasion he says ' "That's how the Bailiff explains it he ought to know" ' (p. 83). These appeals to authority betray Pullman, for it is the Bailiff's explanations that he is repeating, and as his confidence grows when Satters insists on his own stupidity, he begins to repeat the Bailiff's jokes: ' "That was the Bailiff's way of putting it" ' (p. 80).

This admiration for the Bailiff emerges cautiously; but when Pullman enters into a justification of the Bailiff, the language of admiration can also be read as the language of self-deception:

'The Bailiff encourages jokes', mildly expansive, he proceeds, warming to this congenial instruction. 'If you want to get into his good books you will find that that's the way. He's really not so black as he's painted. Haven't you ever gone down there and listened to him? I mean for a whole morning, say? When I feel a bit under the weather I go there. He cheers me up remarkably. I was very surprised at first to find—you hardly expect to find a sense of humour in such a person. He really can be extremely entertaining at times'. (p. 64)

There is not a living phrase here, yet it fascinates. The confidential tone, the uneasy refutation of a point that has not been made ('not so black as he's painted'), the half-sentences that betray the effort to suppress an initially unfavourable reaction, all express the will to accept the Bailiff struggling against the awareness that a quite different conclusion about him is possible. In these sentences we see at work the process of values being internalized.

It is necessary for the Bailiff to find supporters, for he does not have full control over his world; it is unstable and subject to sudden changes. Pullman is fully aware of the difficulties of negotiating the 'Time-flats', where objects move, not in space but in and out of different times. As he guides them forward he is

on the *qui vive* for the new setting, fearing above all reflections, on the look-out for optical traps, lynx-eyed for threatening ambushes of anomalous times behind the orderly furniture of Space or hidden in objects to confute the solid at the last moment, every inch a pilot. (p. 48)

Because he has to do this, Pullman knows well that his admired Bailiff has limited control. To sustain his admiration he has to deceive himself, and try to deceive Satters too:

The distance to the city varies: Satters repeatedly looks over, lunging his head to catch it at its changes and at last says:
'Doesn't that look smaller sometimes?'
'What?' Pullman looks round indignantly.
'Sometimes it looks smaller to me than others'.
'Certainly not! Whatever makes you think!'
The whole city like a film-scene slides away perceptibly several inches to the rear, as their eyes are fixed upon it.
'There!' exclaims Satters pointing.
'Oh that! I know, it looks like it. But it isn't so. It's only the atmosphere'.
Satters leans heavily upon the sage Pullman's arm. (p.32)

The irony is clear enough, but it throws the reader upon the perceptions of Satters, and he is likely to resist this, because they emerge from a podgy sweating schoolboy who smells of 'the sticky vegetable odour of small babies in a close room' (p. 15). Nevertheless his reactions are the commonsense ones, and the closest to true perception that we have.

It is Satters who recognizes one of the Bailiff's primary tricks, that he has chosen the outfits in which all the appellants are dressed, and that the identity they suggest is the only identity each person is allowed. Satters wants to undress, but Pullman will not allow it. ' "It's best to have them on, that's all, they prefer it here" ', he urges. Satters becomes angry: ' "And why is it I have to do that? Because we're held down to this magic we are enslaved" ' (p. 146). Pullman tells him he shouldn't listen to what people say (he means the Hyperideans), and Satters eventually replies:

'Rot. You talk rot. . . . It's you who listen to what people tell you not me my poor old son you're potty. . . . Why shouldn't we leave off our coat if it's too hot to wear it?. . . .
'Yes, it's easy to leave off. But you leave yourself too'.
(p. 147)

Pullman is committed to the idea that what people appear to be, they are. The sartorial signals made by an individual constitute his whole identity. To believe this is to support the Bailiff's view of reality and to assist him in controlling the afterworld. Throughout *The Childermass* Lewis is concerned to expose the

way in which cultural materials are used as part of overall
political control.

There is another level of control, which has been identified
and described by Fredric Jameson in his essay 'Wyndham Lewis
as Futurist'. This concerns the disclosures effected by the degraded language used by both Pullman and Satters; the peculiar
absence of punctuation is part of this procedure. Lewis's 'stylistic
practice', Jameson writes, testifies to 'the inescapable contamina-
tion of the collective mind and the language itself'.[5] Lewis's
writing is

> a reflection of the increasing and inescapable influence of mass
> culture in modern times . . . that systematized network of cul-
> tural code and representation which preexists the individual
> and which speaks and invents him just as surely as language
> itself. In such a situation, indeed, there no longer exists any-
> thing like a personal or individualized speech. (p. 320)

Lewis himself had made the same point in an early work, *Enemy
of the Stars* (1914):

> The process and condition of life, without any exception, is
> a grotesque degradation, and 'souillure' of the original soli-
> tude of the soul. There is no help for it, since each gesture and
> word partakes of it, and the child has already covered himself
> with mire.[6]

The child is integrated into the social world as its own gestures
and speech receive a response from the people around it; there is
no opportunity to be isolated from the process of socialization
that invents the personality and gives it a language. It is this
process that is dramatized in *The Childermass*. Recently reborn,
Pullman and Satters, in the very act of trying to understand their
surroundings, internalize the Bailiff's power through an acceptance of his definitions of reality, using a language that they
believe to be their own, but which is riddled with the terminology of subjection.

In *The Art of Being Ruled* (1926) Lewis discusses the way in
which power is exercised through the control of ideas, and he
displays a debt to the French political theorist Georges Sorel
(1847–1922). Lewis makes it clear that he is not interested in

Sorel as a theoretician of violence or of the general strike, or in the usefulness of his ideas for reactionary political movements, but in his speculative writings,[7] and he discusses primarily *Les illusions du progrès* (1908), a product of Sorel's brief Marxist phase. The argument of this work is that 'democracy', by which Sorel meant bourgeois democracy, is the political means used by the bourgeoisie to exercise power in its own interests. This is achieved, in part, by the imposition of philosophic and scientific ideas which accord with the conditions of bourgeois life. For example, the thought of Descartes was accepted in the salons of the literary world because it justified existing circumstances; it was 'a very remarkable example of the adoption of an ideology by a class that has found in it certain formulas to express its class propensities'.[8] When Lewis writes, in *The Art of Being Ruled*, that 'the intellectual domination of certain schools of thought today' would seem 'amazing' to a future critic, he is interpreting Sorel. Lewis writes: 'In every epoch thinkers of different, opposite types occur: there is always a Leibniz and always a Locke. It has been the political tendencies of the time that make one or the other prevail' (p. 416). Similarly, Lewis's statement that 'The ideas of a people are always the ideas of the class in power' (p. 368) is based on Sorel.

The emphasis in *The Childermass* upon clothing as an indicator of identity becomes clearer when we examine the metaphor Lewis uses in *The Art of Being Ruled* to develop his Sorelian insights: 'The ideas of a time are like the clothes of a season: they are as arbitrary, as much imposed by some superior will which is seldom explicit. They are utilitarian and political, the instruments of smooth-running government. And to criticize them seriously, especially today, *for themselves*, would be as absurd as to criticize the fashion in loofahs ... or soft felt hats' (p. 419). The Bailiff succeeds in imposing both the clothes of a season (usually as a malicious joke), and a group of utilitarian political ideas. He is a satiric realization of that 'superior will' in the politics of Heaven. In *The Childermass* Lewis exposes the contingency of the real by setting events in an imaginary landscape where the forces at work in the real world can be discerned, but also isolated and stripped of the plausibility that their very existence confers upon them.

Lewis was explicit about the way in which all systems are invented structures analogous to games: 'According to my view, all intellectual endeavour is in the same contingent category as a game of cricket or billiards.'[9] He demonstrates this by undermining the bases of reality in *The Childermass*, so that the contingency of the fiction itself is persistently demonstrated. This occurs most notably in Lewis's treatment of the opening description of the city and the plain. It is one of the most remarkable openings in twentieth-century fiction:

> The city lies in a plain, ornamented with mountains. These appear as a fringe of crystals to the heavenly north. One minute bronze cone has a black plume of smoke. Beyond the oasis-plain is the desert. The sand-devils perform up to its northern and southern borders. (p. 5)

Once the reader is embroiled in the uncertainties that follow, he looks back to the solidity of this opening with assurance, for it is so slow-moving that it demands attention, so detailed that it receives assent. It therefore comes as a surprise when the Bailiff claims to have invented these mountains:

> 'We've got a mountain range in the distance and things generally have quite a normal appearance; they *look* all right, anyhow, even if on closer inspection they still leave much to be desired and that's half the battle, my tempting little titters!...
> 'The mountains were an idea of mine!... Yes, I thought of them one day as I was sitting here!... They are as a matter of fact from Iceland, volcanic as you see I daresay'. (pp. 209–210)

A concrete reality that seemed to be endorsed by the fiction-making activity itself turns out to be an invention in which the author allows us to believe only for as long as it suits his purpose. By not honouring the convention that the openings of novels are reliable, Lewis insists upon the contingency of all his fiction, and demonstrates its reliance upon a tacit agreement between author and reader. The reason for betraying this agreement is not simply to create a rule-breaking text, in the manner of the *nouveau roman*; Lewis wishes us further to understand that all forms of political structure are as dependent upon the creative will of the ruler as a fictional form is dependent upon the will of its author. *The Childermass* is unsettling to read once we realize that nothing in it can be trusted. It is equally unsettling to realize that all political structures depend for their persistence upon the forms of deception satirized in the Bailiff. By bringing his fictional reality into doubt, Lewis brings the political reality into doubt.

The background to Lewis's objections to what the Bailiff is made to stand for is again to be found in *The Art of Being Ruled*, where Lewis brings together his political and cultural analyses in a crucial theoretical statement. Political organization under capitalism is related to cultural life because 'the *capitalist state* is . . . an *educationalist state*' (p. 111), and all the various methods of education then existing—the press, cinema, radio and theatre, education in schools, and literature itself—promulgate the ideology of liberal-democratic capitalism: 'Education', Lewis wrote, 'plays, and will continue to play, a much more important part in government than physical and exterior force' (p. 98). It is these techniques of non-violent ideological control that Lewis satirizes in the second part of *The Childermass*, though the Bailiff can turn to violence when he needs to, as capitalist states do.

This part of the work is greatly clarified if we see it as a large-scale development of the final question put to the Bailiff by Polemon, to the applause of the Hyperideans: ' "Who is to be *real*—this hyperbolical puppet, or we? Answer, oh destiny!" ' (p. 400). Throughout his writing career Lewis gave a privileged place to the word 'real'. In fiction it meant a quality of presence, of particular force; and in Lewis's fiction no figure is more real, in this sense, than the Frenchman Bestre:

> His tongue stuck out, his lips eructated with the incredible indecorum that appears to be the monopoly of liquids, his brown arms were for the moment genitals, snakes in one massive twist beneath his mamillary slabs, gently riding on a pancreatic swell, each hair on his oil-bearing skin contributing its message of porcine affront.[10]

In art, the function of the artist is 'to show you the world, only a realler one than you would see, unaided'.[11] In life Lewis means by 'real' a complexity and inconsistent variousness which must (for him) also incorporate a necessary imperfection, which distinguishes the human being from the machine: 'the state of limitation of the human being is more desirable than the state of the automaton'.[12] Even the Bailiff speaks of empirical life as 'that crusted fruity complex-and-finite reality' (p. 184), but what he stands for is the empirical real alone: 'there is no mind but the body' (p. 185), and in Lewis's scheme this is not adequate. Possession of 'the real' is a question of cultural dominance: 'who is to be real?' By his satire Lewis hoped to release the western democracies from a form of control which he deplored; once released, a period of cultural regeneration would follow. Absurd as this ambition now appears, Lewis wished intellectuals to have a prominent and influential place in society, and regarded his own critical writings as an active intervention in culture and politics. It was, in the 1920s, an honourable delusion.

In *The Childermass* there is a rising scale of reality amongst the figures we meet. At the lowest level are the peons; the force of a glance can make them disappear:

> Here and there their surfaces collapse altogether as his eyes fall upon them, the whole appearance vanishes, the man is gone. But as the pressure withdraws of the full-blown human glance the shadow reassembles. (p. 23)

It is possible to become 'more real' during the time spent waiting in the afterworld to be passed into Heaven. This is the reason the appellants are heard: they have to establish their reality before the Bailiff:

> 'This is my third bloomin turn'.
> 'Notyor third Bert? . . .'
> 'Ah! I ain't the goods notyet'.
> 'Ere Bert was yew ere Bert was yew——'
> 'I aint Bert Moody not yet not by a long shot get me?'
> 'Isn't you straight?'
> 'Nar-boy not proply'. (p. 299)

The 'most real of these imperfectly formed men', as Lewis describes him,[13] is Tormod Macrob, and in the Bailiff's dealings with him Lewis shows a full human identity under threat.

Macrob is the Bailiff's most substantial opponent among the appellants, and this strongminded Scot is both the object of Lewis's admiration and a sufficiently realized fictional creation not to be simply a stand-in for Lewis's point of view. He insists on questioning the Bailiff about his own reality, with a moving intensity: 'A darker expression of confused despair comes into the face of the Macrob. Painfully and steadily he drags the words one by one out of his mind, building up a sort of morose soliloquy' (p. 276). He insists: 'Am I an entity? Can I be put into Space and Time or taken out again, as you would put a pea into a glass of water and take it out again? Do I belong to empirical existence?' (p. 279). The Bailiff's reply is Bergsonian: every object is interfused with every other object, human or otherwise, in an undifferentiated process of becoming: 'I am a part of you at this moment: those battlements are becoming you' (p. 280). Macrob remains unsatisfied. 'The Macrob doggedly proceeds, his mind visibly grinds down upon its bone, his head canted and thrust out in tense mastication' (p. 285), and as the Bailiff continues his replies, the reader begins to feel the human degradation and humiliation that must follow from being viewed, not as a full and complex identity, but as a part of everything else that exists. The contempt for human identity embodied in such theories is insolent and cruel:

'No one cared in the least what became of you. You happen to have turned out as you have. The process is quite mechanical and absolutely impartial, Space-Time got the habit of you Macrob and threw you up here. What after all is your history? You persisted for a certain number of years like a stammer . . . the great Mother of all things . . . began saying "Macrob" and she went on stammering "Macrob" in a continuous present for the period of your natural life. The present "you" is the echo of that strange event . . . it was not a very lively chapter in world-history I can promise you, the life of "Tormod Macrob Esquire"'. (pp. 283–4)

In the system created by the Bailiff's God (even the Bailiff is dependent) it is impossible to die. Macrob wishes to do so, but the Bailiff cruelly refuses. In an exhilarating moment of slowly realized revolt, the Scotsman grasps the Bailiff by the nose:

The slow mind of Macrob leaves its shell inch by inch, horned blind and dazzled: then it is out, the shell stands apart statuesquely from its soul at last, staring and stark for a queasy second, and the unmitigated Macrob-clansman clicks into action ... up sweeps the gaunt Scottish arm with beaked talon and then thumb and index snap-to upon the snish-tickled twitching snout, wallowing in its black bath of snuff. The powder from the snuff-box, batted upwards, explodes into the Bailiff's face, blackened like that of a man doctored by an apache on the sneeze-racket, and the body of the squealing nose is stuck fast like a fat rat in a trap. (p. 293)

Macrob is torn to pieces by the Bailiff's supporters, the fragments thrown into a basket to be reconstituted inside the walls of Heaven. Eternal life, on the terms of the God of Space-Time, is an act of eternal cruelty. In this remarkable episode Lewis gives full emotional expression to the experience of an innocent consciousness suffering the bleak reality of an inhuman theory. The abstractions discussed in *Time and Western Man* have been recovered, fully realized, as fiction.

Macrob has threatened the Bailiff's authority as the Hyperideans, for all their arguments, have failed to do. Hyperides and the Bailiff are 'the oldest opposites in the universe' (p. 188), and their debate will never be resolved. Despite possessing many of the correct Lewisian arguments the Hyperideans' reality is limited by their chosen 'Greek' identity as homosexuals; they can never become sufficiently complex to be 'real'. The only person capable of reordering the life of the Bailiff's court is the artist Potter, whose revolt is internal, as he fixes upon 'this new object', the Bailiff, and disembowels it, 'rearranging everything in a logical order' (p. 254). This is the full extent of the artist's power; by imagining the world otherwise, he changes it fundamentally, but his objections do not threaten the political power that sustains the world as it is. Potter is passed quickly into Heaven.

The limitations of *The Childermass* are sufficiently apparent. There is an occasional crudity of exposition, as when the Bailiff is made to say 'I prefer hot-blood to your beastly intellects' (p. 386). If the reader is already familiar with Lewis's arguments from *Time and Western Man* and elsewhere there can be a certain tedium in their redeployment as fiction. Nevertheless, although we know that Lewis regards all that goes on in the world of *The Childermass* as false, it is rendered with a remarkable concreteness; the falsity is never skimped. The game is played with conviction, and it is the knowledge that apart from this game there is nothing, for on all sides there is a void, that makes the fundamental difference between the theory, which is argued out amongst the alternative possibilities available in the real world, and the fiction, which makes an absolute claim to be seen as the only reality.

The difference between *The Childermass* and the two later volumes of *The Human Age* is that in the first volume Pullman is treated, not exactly with contempt, but as someone who culpably allows himself to be taken in; like Joyce as he is presented in *Time and Western Man*, he is a victim of the *Zeitgeist* who should know better. In the note written for the dust-jacket of the 1955 reissue of *The Childermass*, Lewis describes Pullman as 'Man at his imperfect best', but this is not so. Sympathy for Pullman, and the willingness to make God's forgiveness of him part of his subject had to wait until Lewis belatedly realized that the intellectual who is hypercritically alert to the ideological pressures submitted to by other writers may himself be taken in, all the while believing that his superior theoretical equipment makes him invulnerable. Within three years of *The Childermass* Lewis had written *Hitler*; this and the inept political books that followed exploded his claim to detachment and a sense of political realities. These failures are particularly distressing because *The Childermass* is a work in which there is a basis of theory that makes a radical and successful critique of the 'educationalist state', and is sympathetic towards those who have to suffer the degraded reality it offers. Lewis's imagination transforms this basis of theory, infusing it with an hallucinatory power so great that it is not the intellect but the imagination that finally persuades us of the truth of what he has to say.

The Apes of God: Form and Meaning

PAUL EDWARDS

> For art is, in reality, one of the things that Revolutions are about, and cannot therefore itself be Revolution. Life as interpreted by the poet or philosopher is the objective of Revolutions, they are the substance of its Promised Land.
>
> *Time and Western Man*

The Apes of God was first published in a limited edition of 750 signed and numbered copies in 1930. It took Lewis about seven years to write, but is now, with *The Childermass*, probably the least read and enjoyed of his major fiction. A large and mannered satire, it seems at first sight to be a product of the will and intellect; by blocking the springs of human sympathy within him, Lewis also blocked the springs of his creative imagination, producing a book that is awkward and monumentally trivial.

The book's awkwardness seems to have been calculated. Physically, even, on account of its size and weight (in the first edition) it is taxing to read. On a more literary level, the fact that the intensely idiosyncratic and polished style describes the activities of a collection of contemptible puppets has given the book a reputation for unreadability. But it is only unreadable if you expect things from it that it does not promise. It is, after all, a satirical book, and though its humour is neither warm nor genial, it is at times wild and infectious. Objections against *The Apes of God* on account of its lack of human interest are objections to satire as such rather than to this particular book. There is a linguistic zest and imaginative invention in almost every sentence that makes the book as entertaining in its way as many more popular novels. Nevertheless, the verbal inventiveness will repel many readers because it precludes any relaxed immersion in the created world of the book, and draws attention to its own artifice. This artifice is important to the meaning of *The Apes of*

God, as I hope to show; it is not a self-indulgent display of one of the platitudes of modernism.

The Apes of God is a satire on 'artistic life' in England during the period Lewis later described as 'the insanitary trough between the two great wars'. It is picaresque and episodic, the *picaro* being the beautiful but moronic Irish youth, Dan Boleyn. This simpleton is conducted round various salons and visits numerous pseudo-artists (the apes of God), under the wing of the sixty-year-old albino Horace Zagreus, whom he reveres, and who in turn is captivated by the youth and 'genius' of his protégé. Unlike the usual *picaro,* Dan is desperately shy and reluctant to undertake any adventures, learns virtually nothing from those he is forced into, and, as if Lewis were mocking the responses of his readers, is painfully and paralytically bored by the constant lecturing and explaining that he has to sit through, most of which he is unable to understand. These explanations and lectures ('broadcasts' as they are called—Lewis was a keen student of the effects of new communication media) are retailed mainly by Zagreus, but their ultimate source is the mysterious philosopher-artist, Pierpoint. Pierpoint never appears in person in the book, though his words and ideas are constantly quoted by others.

The story begins and ends at the great town house of the Follett family, there being competition between relatives for the Follett inheritance. Ninety-six-year-old Lady Fredigonde Follett, whose toilette is described in the book's prologue, favours Horace Zagreus, who needs money to finance his Ape-hunting, while Fredigonde's equally ancient husband, Sir James, favours a nephew, Dick, who is rich already and, being an amateur professional artist, is a specimen Ape. There is also rivalry between Zagreus and Melanie Blackwell over the person of Dan Boleyn. Dan's relationship with Horace Zagreus reaches its zenith in Part IX, 'Chez Lionel Kein, Esq.', and its nadir in Part XIII, 'The General Strike', when Dan learns that he has been replaced in Horace's affections by the Jewish cockney, Archie Margolin, and is abandoned to Melanie Blackwell. During most of the book, the plot is in abeyance, being mostly present in Parts I, II, and XIII.

More significant than the plot itself is its formal disposition. This is a pattern in which the resolution of the plot (actually not quite complete by the end of the book) is a mirror image of its statement at the opening. Lewis draws attention to this pattern by frequent verbal echoes of the opening and by situating some of the minor characters in the same parts of the Follett house in both sections of the book. The result is that progress seems to be non-existent; the book finishes more or less where it started. In Part I, Zagreus, warned by her ladyship, pre-empts Dick's and Sir James's lunchtime consultation with the family lawyer by button-holing him in the hall. Because the expectations created in the reader by an atmosphere of intrigue are left so long suspended, the middle five hundred pages or so are experienced as a hiatus filled with purposeless activity. In various ways this hiatus is suffused with the atmosphere and themes established at the opening, the most important of which is not intrigue, but death.

The first page of the Prologue (entitled 'Death-the-Drummer') establishes an uncertainty about the line separating life and death:

> The antlers of the hall suggested that full-busted stags were embedded in its substance. A mighty canvas contained in its shadows an equestrian ghost, who otherwise might have ruffled the empty majesty of the house with confusing post-humous activity. . . .
> In a room upstairs a dead domestic, sneezing behind his hand because of the chill he had received as he entered the vast apartment, placed heavy chiselled blocks of coal within the grate, armoured with a transverse grating two inches thick. (pp. 7/11)*

In the description of Lady Fredigonde's toilette that follows, the line becomes even more blurred. She is presented so that what Lewis calls 'her differences with matter' (pp. 10/14) are seen to be slight:

> —it seemed a toss-up if she would come-to. Her fixed eye was bloodless and without any animation, a stuffed eagle's sham optic in fact, or a glass eye in the head of a corpse—though

---

* Page references are to all editions of *The Apes of God*: thus '(p. 7/11)' refers to page 7 of the first and all subsequent editions of the book except that published by Penguin Books in 1965, where the reference is to page 11.

the bellows plainly worked still, the shoulders slowly grinding on, blown up and let down with the labour of the breath. Gradually however her personality made its appearance. Fragment by fragment she got it back, in rough hand-over-hand, a bitter salvage. (pp. 23–4/29)

It is a 'toss-up', a trivial matter, whether she is actually alive or dead. Death is announced by the itinerant jazz band busking outside the Follett mansion and transmitting a shiver to Lady Fredigonde. The Holbeinesque dance of death is an appropriate image for the activities of the Apes that will fill most of the book, and Lady Fredigonde is their paradigm. As the band strikes up again on the last but one page of the book, Lady Fredigonde begins to expire. The blurred line, then, between life and death, is where the intervening 'hiatus' is situated; it is not completely crossed by Fredigonde in the book, but death, approaching nearer and nearer, is certain to arrive, and can be assumed to claim her immediately after the last word of the text. The form of *The Apes of God* thus resembles one of Zeno's paradoxes. The arrow never actually reaches its target; time is spatialized.

There is a subdued undercurrent of politics in the Prologue of *The Apes of God*. We are aware that the pampered, cantankerous and childlike Lady Fredigonde depends upon an army of domestics in order to survive and to indulge her whims. There is a policeman outside in the street, not as yet an insistent presence, but to become one during the General Strike, when he guards the mansion from non-existent rioters. Lady Fredigonde fantasises about herself and her collection of caps as exhibits in a future museum visited by a troop of Bolshevik Boy Scouts. The hints are sufficient to inform us that this is a book about the condition of England. The Follett mansion and its inhabitants are emblematic, much as Bladesover House at the opening of *Tono-Bungay*, or Chesney Wold in *Bleak House*. It is worth noting that there are several echoes of *Our Mutual Friend* in the text; Lewis's method of endowing inanimate objects with more vitality than 'live' people is clearly influenced by Dickens' portrayal of the Veneering circle. Lady Fredigonde is of the right age and class to have been a member of that circle; she would have been in her late twenties when *Our Mutual Friend* was published. Other works that will help a reader understand and place *The Apes of God* are the *Cena Trimalchionis* of Petronius, *The Dunciad, A Tale of a Tub,* and *Ulysses.* The range of these literary relationships, coupled with Lewis's selection of the General Strike as a conclusion to the work, reinforces the notion that *The Apes of God* is far more ambitious than the description of it as a satire on artistic life suggests.

The phrase 'artistic life' is misleading in another way; there is only one true artist in the book: the elusive Pierpoint. It is his commentary that provides all the 'meaning' in the book, without which it would be a collection of discrete apearances. This is, Lewis is suggesting, the function of the artist. 'Life' in itself is nothing (Lady Fredigonde is the representative of life); only art gives it meaning and value. *The Apes of God* is a portrayal of a 'time without art', as Zagreus calls it (pp. 294/308). Consequently it is a portrayal of a world in which there is a disjunction between meaning and appearance. One of the major achievements of Lewis in this book is to create a style capable of depicting such a world. It is not a world from which meaning is completely absent, but one in which the categories imposed on naked experience are second-hand and ill-fitting. The superfluity of imaginative material with which the artist informs reality is, in the social life of the Apes, replaced by a series of hastily assumed conventional façades. It is as if they were constantly signalling to each other, but the signs never mean anything of value.

'Peters,' he lisped in complaining falsetto—'Peters—don't you think you could possibly manage to get a few of those logs off? The heat is beyond description. I know it's cold sometimes, but it's particularly warm tonight.'

Lord Osmund addressed Peters with a coaxing appeal but with the customary nasal peevishness, and the servant, with a mixture, as well, of impatient contempt and of slovenly obedience, began removing the uppermost of the logs. Lord Osmund twitched his nostrils, curled his lip, sniffed very slightly—looking whitely at the Sib, his hands upon the table at either side of his plate, the hard-goffered cuffs coming down over them, a flowered handkerchief overflowing his chest from beneath the brocaded flange of his doublet.

(Peters removes the logs from the fire and pours water over them, to extinguish them.)

'I wish you could think of some other way of disposing of the logs Peters!' hissed and puffed Lord Osmund in still louder expostulation, simulating a man choked with the fumes of charcoal. (pp. 368–9/385–6)

The puppet-like rigidity of Osmund (he 'simulates' a man choking) is also found in most of the dialogue in the book; the characters all seem to be acting as their own impresarios rather than to be engaged in what they are ostensibly doing. This displacement of meaning has infected what works of art do exist:

Upon the walls the pictures revealed the strange embrace of Past and Present—of so casual a nature as to produce nothing but an effect of bastardry. There was a picture of two buffoons by Giovanni Cassana, a late Venetian: two Magnascos of a mock trial in a cavern of witches and gipsies—a Chirico of a carthorse surprised by ruins, springing into the air—a Tiepolo sketch of the abdomen of a horse and a platter—a Max Ernst of two disintegrated figures in frenzied conjugation—a Modigliani of two peasant morons, both girls, one depressed upon her left flank with a ponderous teat. There was an equestrian sketch of Lord Osmund by Munnings (an apotheosis of the Georges One-to-Three of super-hanoverian squirearchishness). (pp. 491/512)

This is a sort of debased version of the modernist eclecticism embodied in the 'tradition' of Pound and Eliot; the paintings are in no vital relation, either to life, or to each other.

Two further examples of this disjunction between meaning and experience may be cited: the first an example of an attribution of too much meaning to inanimate objects, and the second an instance of a speaking human figure that seems to have no meaning at all. Matthew Plunkett (in Part II, 'The Virgin') is obsessed by shells, and regards the Shell petrol van that crosses his path occasionally in Bloomsbury as intensely significant. The second example occurs at the end of Part IX, 'Chez Lionel Kein, Esq.'. At the entrance to a mews, Zagreus, Dan and their companion pass a man who shouts into the mews three times

'I shant-get-a-bloody-break-down-not-a-goin-on-as-I-'ave-bin-lately' (pp. 313/328). None of the questions that this curious figure might provoke are asked in the text, and he remains puzzlingly emblematic of the area in which communication occurs, or fails to occur, in *The Apes of God*. Having passed him by, the three spend the next few moments attempting to fix conventional meanings to other figures they see in the street, such as 'youth', 'health', 'race', and so on.

The most important art in *The Apes of God* is literature; it is the lack of an adequate language that divorces the Apes from engagement in reality. The theme, like most others, is introduced in the Prologue by Lady Fredigonde, whose random thought-stream happens to throw up an idea she has heard from Zagreus (its ultimate source is Pierpoint):

> But we survive by *words* he says—*things* perish. He got that most likely from one of those Smart Alicks he goes about with.
> —In some respects he is a master of paradox.
> By words, this is it seems the idea, we are handed over to the tender mercies of the Past. That is that parasitic no-longer-with-us class of has-beens, he cleverly calls it. In other words the dead. (pp. 15/20)

The points made here are these: first, that all experience is 'fictional', the *Ding-an-sich* being inaccessible, and, second, the point already discussed, that the categories and fictions that human beings use are second-hand and out of date. A connection is also made with the prevailing theme of death. The idea is phrased more politically in Pierpoint's 'Encyclical': 'The *novelty* of any time enables people to pretend that they are existing in the state of society that in fact they have superseded' (pp. 118/126). Hence Lord Osmund Finnian Shaw's guests are invited to attend his Lenten party dressed up as famous characters in fiction, while the gardens of his country house are modelled on the long-vanished Vauxhall.

The most extensive treatment of this theme is in Part IV, 'Chez Lionel Kein, Esq.', where Zagreus describes his fellow dining-guests as

> '*Sixteen characters in search of an author!* . . .
> 'It would be better to say sixteen characters in search of a

real author' said Horace 'to replace the sixteen false-authors, or the *faux-auteurs* that this lot probably are. All to a man, I'll wager (like Pirandello's *six characters*) are characters of Fiction. That they can claim right enough: for they have all been written about in their own or their friend's books—upon that you may rely. But of what Fiction? It is a Fiction as dependent upon reality—*such a poor reality and so unreal*—that they are neither flesh nor fowl—they are *fictional mongrel facts* (that is Pierpoint's expression). . . .

'How portentously they suffer for the want of a great artist to effect that immortal translation—how they suffer!' (pp. 293–4/307–8)

The fictions created for these people accept the values of the gossip column; not only do they create no new values, but they succeed only in pandering to the vanity of their subjects and in insulating them within a dead and unreal world. Lewis's reference here is to such 'satire' as Aldous Huxley's and Michael Arlen's, but also to Gide, and above all to Proust. The 'objectivity' which such 'social news-sheets' parade is actually highly selective, and even those characters who are 'satirized' (as against those who are treated indulgently) never have the objective truth told about them: 'Obviously that would involve the heroes as well in the disgrace of the villains' (pp. 265/278). This is because

'none of us are able in fact, in the matter of quite naked truth, to support that magnifying glass, focussed upon us, any more than the best complexion could support such examination. Were we mercilessly transposed into Fiction, by the eye of a Swift, for instance, the picture would be intolerable, both for Fiction and for us. No more than there are "good" and "bad" people, are there such people on the one hand as can pass over into a truly inquisitorial Fiction with flying colours, and those, who, upon the other hand—so translated—are disgraced. *Every* individual without exception is in that sense objectively unbearable.' (pp. 257/270)

A passage like this clearly invites us to apply it to a consideration of Lewis's own satire. Lewis rightly perceives that if satire exposes people's pretensions to physical beauty (and he has a

Swiftian sense that all such pretensions are vain) it can hardly leave their inner mental life intact, even if it wished to do so. Our other pretensions are bound to be implicated to some extent in the disgrace of our bodies. But such pretensions, physical and mental, are necessary simply to carry on living; an acceptance of them to some degree certainly underlies all the great novels that have been acclaimed as life-enhancing. This is implied in Zagreus' admission that truly 'objective' satire is intolerable 'both for fiction and for us'. Such reflections remind us that the role of fiction in life is complex; the 'truth' that Zagreus is talking about may be a result of stripping off all the human accretions that make life tolerable, but it requires an act of creative, indeed visionary, imagination to arrive at that truth and expose the Fredigondes that we all ultimately are. Also, it is, to say the least, debatable whether this creative imagination might not be better employed in inventing new 'pretensions' or fictions that serve to extend life's possibilities. One's answer to this question will determine one's opinion of the value of much of Lewis's work, of *The Apes of God* in particular, and of the value of satire in general. There is no simple answer to the question; to pronounce that 'life-enhancement' is the only valuable task of the imagination is surely to argue in favour of self-deception (as Swift saw), and to ignore an important side of the human condition. It is not surprising that writers like Wyndham Lewis and Swift, who provoke such fundamental questioning of art and life, should be unpopular with moralist critics.

The Apes themselves, no less worldly than the moralist, could fairly ask why they should be obliged to accept the unflattering portraits Lewis paints as true likenesses, or could at least object that Lewis really has no justification for satirizing them rather than anyone else; their own affectations, on Lewis's admission, are, *sub specie aeternitatis*, no worse than anybody else's. If philosophically minded, they might frame their objections as a rejection of Lewis's epistemology; what makes Lewis's version of them any more reliable than their own idea of themselves? Especially, they might add, as Lewis is motivated by malice.

Lewis is aware of such arguments, and creates his art under the pressure of them, with the result that the art is pulled strongly in two opposing directions. First, so that no competing epistemology can offer a different version of the world he portrays, he emphasizes that world's fictionality; it is a new world essentially different from the one we inhabit and not, like the fiction written by the Apes, 'dependent on reality'. As Zagreus puts it:

> 'The world created by Art—Fiction, Drama, Poetry etc.—must be sufficiently removed from the real world so that no character from the one could under any circumstances enter the other (the situation imagined by Pirandello), without the anomaly being apparent at once. (pp. 265–6/279)

It is a matter of judgement whether the world of *The Apes of God* is sufficiently realized for Lewis to be able to claim such autonomy for it. This cannot be finally decided by means of a single quotation, but certainly the figure described in the following paragraph could not possibly have any existence outside the words with which Lewis created him:

> In colour Lord Osmund was a pale coral, with flaxen hair brushed tightly back, his blond pencilled pap rising straight from his sloping forehead: galb-like wings to his nostrils—the goat-like profile of Edward the Peacemaker. The lips were curved. They were thickly profiled as though belonging to a moslem portrait of a stark-lipped sultan. His eyes, vacillating and easily discomfited, slanted down to the heavy curved nose. Eyes, nose and lips contributed to one effect, so that they seemed one feature. It was the effect of the jouissant animal— the licking, eating, sniffing, fat-muzzled machine—dedicated to Wine, Womanry, and Free Verse-cum-soda-water. (pp. 355/ 371)

The second and opposing pull of Lewis's art is also present in this passage. This pull is towards verisimilitude, realism and almost documentary accuracy; Lord Osmund Finnian Shaw, unique creation though he is, is strongly reminiscent of Sir Osbert Sitwell. The effect (and it is the same effect in passages where such resemblances to real people are no longer evident) is one of hovering between two worlds, neither of which can be granted absolute primacy. The same effect is apparent, and more easily demonstrated, in the designs that are reproduced on the title-pages of each of the thirteen parts of *The Apes of God*. One of the best is that which announces Part III, 'The Encyclical'. What strikes the eye at once is the vitality and visual interest of this compact of blocks and curving lines. It is only on closer inspection that the mind constructs the figure of a tortoise out of these shapes; the design hovers between pure form and representation. It is not only the ambiguity that pleases, but also the fact that it is the slowly-plodding tortoise rather than some more vigorous creature that is thus energetically projected. In a similar way the effect has meaning and produces satire when it occurs in the writing. The figure that the prose creates is an unmistakably mechanical doll which, if our pretensions about ourselves are justified, should under no circumstances be mistaken for a living human being. The deep disturbance that it causes a reader to discover that quite a large portion of his life could be convincingly performed by a mechanical doll issues in laughter. It might also cause him to consider what parts of life could not be so performed; two examples might be love and the creation of imaginative art.

The two contradictory pulls seen in individual passages such as the one just discussed can be seen in *The Apes of God* as a whole. A new world is created, much as it is in Pope's *Dunciad*; clearly not the real world, but one which could pass as a fairly adequate substitution. Every care is taken by the author to show which world it is he is creating a substitute for; it is London, England, the West in 1926. The glosses on the activities of the Apes that Pierpoint provides bridge the two worlds and apply equally to both. Within the fictional world itself various characters put Pierpoint's ideas and observations to different uses (usually merely trivial, or socially advantageous), but no-one's behaviour is fundamentally affected by them. At the same time, the 'broadcasts' provide for the reader a complete anatomy of the purposeless world in which the Apes live (their similarity to the ideas and observations of Lewis in *The Art of Being Ruled* has often been noted). As explanations their epistemology is no doubt open to the same objections that we have imagined the Apes making to Lewis's portrayal of themselves. But just as the nature of the fictional world removes those objections to a level on which it would hardly be profitable to pursue them, so the different nature of the long explanations in the book anticipates similar objections. They happen to be the only explanations available in the book (and, the implication is, in the world), and, should any alternative ones be offered, they would similarly be open to objection themselves. As Pierpoint writes in his 'Encyclical', his theories pretend to no absolute validity or truth:

> I rather insist upon than seek to slur over the fact that I am a party. But it is from amongst the parties that the acting judge is ultimately chosen. Where else should you get him from? The supreme judge is constantly absent. What we call a judge is a successful partizan.... The finding of the supreme judge would automatically dissolve us all into limbo....
> —Things however that I have put forward as facts—not as fair comment—will be verified by you in due course. Fortunately there no one can balk the truth of my evidence. (pp. 118/125–6)

Lewis draws our attention to Pierpoint's participation in the world of the Apes in other ways. We learn that one of the main sources of his income is Zagreus, who buys ideas and 'broadcasts' from him. He is thus implicated fairly directly in the competition for the Follett money, since Zagreus's own money is now nearly all spent. It is also worth noting that Pierpoint's constant absence from the action finally leads him to misinterpret events; the version of Lord Osmund's Lenten Party that his lieutenants supply him with is a travesty of what the reader has witnessed himself. This does not discredit all he has said before, but confirms that he is not a god-like and infallible figure, and that his observations do indeed (as he says) need to be checked against the evidence. His absence also shows him to be a little the 'Ape' of God himself, as does his use of the word 'encyclical'. As an artist, too, he is God's ape, since his creativity is modelled on God's; God's Ape is of course the Devil, and there is nothing unusual in the idea that human genius is diabolic. It is certainly an idea that Lewis was familiar with, since it was later to become one of the main themes of *The Human Age*. Beyond Pierpoint can be discerned another Ape of God, Lewis himself, the creator of this alternative world and its puppets. These theological issues are peripheral, and worth noting here mainly because they show that

Lewis did not, as is sometimes asserted, consider himself to be excluded from the satire he wrote; his hell is certainly not just for other people.

The Apes of God who are the main objects of Lewis's attack are the prosperous amateurs who have monopolized the artistic world and frozen out those with real talent, making the creation and survival of true art virtually impossible. Lewis's ideas about this are clearly stated in 'The Encyclical', and the examples he gives in the rest of the book need little comment. It perhaps needs noting that Lady Fredigonde is the epitome of the Apes we are shown. The art which the Apes produce serves the same purpose, and serves it as ineffectively, as Fredigonde's toilette: it is an unconvincing mask on the death's-head; these are people with no future. At the same time they represent the future, since no-one is producing imaginative fictions upon which an alternative future might be modelled. The Apes are important not as relics of the bourgeois era soon to be superseded; on the contrary, they are actually a sample of the future:

> The dreams of the economist-utopist in a sense are already realized, upon a small scale, today. In that respect the society of the future is already with us. He could study, in its full working effect, one of his favourite and most attractive theories, and upon a considerable scale: namely that of Everyman possessed of leisure and means to enjoy the delectations of Art. (pp. 118/126)

This is a point that must be understood when the final part of the book, a portrayal of the General Strike, is read. We must also notice that we are shown the strike through the consciousness of Dan Boleyn, and that Dan has absolutely no idea what is going on. This contrasts with a passage in 'Lord Osmund's Lenten Party' where he is shown to have a visionary gift. His vision is of a park planted with spikes (a premonition of the role of Hyde Park during the strike), and, beyond that, of violence and war. It seems to be a part of Lewis himself speaking, or at least Dan is portrayed here comparatively sympathetically:

> Nothing could live thought Dan, or *love* thought he and sighed, where he had been looking, where alas he had looked and seen the battle-parks and the spikes planted for trees, he

thought.—He would never look again! Never of his own free will would he look again for years! (pp. 418/436)

The occasion of Dan's vision is a Pierpointian harangue from Zagreus, and it is from this invective that the vision acquires its violence. Dan's turning his back on his own gift and on Pierpoint's ideas (or the use to which they are put, since he does not understand the ideas themselves) is done in the name of 'love'. Whatever our sympathy with the character at this point (and I think it is, although undermined to some extent by the satirical context, quite strong), we must acknowledge that his rejection of ideas and vision is the cause of his failure to understand the General Strike.

It has already been suggested that the character of Dan is in some respects a kind of parody of the reader of this 'unreadable' book, and that his boredom and inattentiveness anticipate a reader's similar reaction. His bewilderment during the strike is a mockery of the plain reader's reception of the last part of the book. But the reader's bewilderment will take a different form from Dan's, and result from disappointed expectations raised by the ambitious-looking title-page to the last part, with its broad working-man's hand slung defiantly out of use. The revolution visualized by Lady Fredigonde in the Prologue and alluded to occasionally later in the text has come at last, it would seem, to bring down the curtain on the Apes and their trivial doings. Literary taste demands an Apocalypse here, but a reader who has properly understood the book thus far will not be surprised that the End is deferred. There is a reinforcement of the Zeno's paradox of Fredigonde's approaching death in this treatment of the strike. The 'revolution', we should realize, whatever its reported violence, could change nothing, since, in an art-less society, it cannot escape from the limits of what it appears to be about to sweep away; the paradise of the Apes of God is the only future imaginable for it. This can be seen in the only passage of direct reporting of the strike that appears in the text, where the collocation of death-like passivity and violent activity already made familiar in the earlier sections is repeated in the first sentence:

The whole townland of London was up in arms and as silent

as the grave and it was reported that in its eastern quarters, in the slum-wards such as Poplar, a Police-inspector and two Specials had been kicked to death and there were more and more violent riots in Hammersmith, where trams had been wrecked and street-rails torn up by the mob, and the Police stoned and injured: while it was confidently stated that in the North crowds had sacked the better quarters, in the big factory-towns, mines were flooded, mills were blazing, and the troops were firing with machine-guns upon the populace. (pp. 618/643)

Meanwhile, in the street where the Follett mansion stands, 'all was dead and pleasant'; the contrast suggests that elsewhere things are dead and unpleasant. A lot of the unpleasantness is anyway fictitious; the syntax of Lewis's report mimics wildly-spreading Rumour. The whole account is ironically underscored by the reader's knowledge that the General Strike failed in its purpose, and that it was not (nor did its leaders want it to be) a revolution. These and other ironies are nicely encapsulated in the song the buskers sing outside the Follett mansion at the close of the book:

> Whoddle ah *doo*
> Wen *yoo*
> Are *far*
> *Away*
> An I
> am *bloo*
> Whoddle ah *doo*
> Whoddlah DOOOO! (pp. 624/649–50)

Fredigonde and the Apes have not departed yet, and it seems that these unemployed men do not want them to go; they would be left at a loss not knowing what to do if the Apes were finally swept away.

The Apes of God is one of the major pessimistic achievements of literary modernism. Its pessimism is rooted in the political and philosophical study which Lewis undertook when he realized that his revolutionary optimism in The Caliph's Design would not be justified by history, and which led to books like The Art of Being Ruled and Time and Western Man. I have not discussed the links between these books and *The Apes of God* because I believe it is important to show that the work of fiction can stand as an independent work of art. Its formal peculiarities express and shape the book's meaning, which is recoverable from the text itself rather than from a knowledge of Lewis's 'ideas'. The phrase 'neglected masterpiece' is used too often, but it justly describes *The Apes of God*.

12

On Lewis's Politics: The Polemics Polemically Answered

WILLIAM M. CHASE

> Again let me do a lot of extraordinary talking.
> Again let me do a lot!
> *One-Way Song* (1933)

In a small book now some twenty-five years old, and to which proper attention has never sufficiently been paid, Hugh Kenner speaks in defence, oddly, of Wyndham Lewis's *Hitler* (1931). He recognizes that it is, for Lewis's career, a troublesome item. Noting one of its most prominent features, its discussion of German Jews and of German anti-Semitism, Professor Kenner submits that Lewis's 'naivete' in the 1930s as to things German, nationalistic, contemporaneous and political, 'must be weighed against Lewis's taste for system and his temperamental indifference to persons'.[1] Kenner is more than right, of course, to focus discussion on this particular aspect of *Hitler*, for it is *the* volume exhibiting to Lewis's readers, and to many of his critics who have heard only rumours of the book, his truest ideological allegiances. Read or un-read, it cannot be forgotten, nor should it be. Lewis in Germany, Kenner goes on to say, saw Jews and Gentiles as people who 'had cheerfully turned themselves into racial stereotypes'; their mutual animosities, Kenner gently argues, were 'no more sanguinary than Dr. Johnson's sparring with the Scots'.[2] Saying this, Kenner then underscores a fundamental principle of understanding in his little book, that 'in those days, and for thirty years thereafter, people susceptible to worry, pain, and frustration didn't exist in the universe to which [Lewis's] sensibility was attuned'.[3]

We may with reward linger over this illumination. It offers us a new vista on the resources of literature and on Wyndham

Lewis as a writer. We might otherwise have thought we were done with Lewis on Hitler, having found in his book only the erroneous ('Hitler is not a gratuitously warlike individual at all'),[4] the anti-Semitic (Jews are 'a glib metropolitan product' with 'an ancient and dissimilar culture'),[5] and the deluded (racial purity in Nazi Germany in the 1930s 'would secure greater social efficiency').[6] With it to guide us, Professor Kenner points our way to something about literature we might never have suspected: that in the right hands, it can tell of the lives of people touched not by worry, or by pain, or by frustration. In some of his books, Wyndham Lewis found such people in the world and attuned his sensibility to them. On peril of permitting our imaginative lives be less than they might be, we must attend to this triumph.

Indeed, we may extend Professor Kenner's remarkable critical observations a bit further. We may consider the enviable prospects of a novelist and a political thinker endowed with a 'temperamental indifference to persons'. Novelists and ideologists have for long been burdened with all the messy complexities of human beings (humans who ruinously resolve themselves into entities Lewis found deplorable, such as 'women', 'negroes', 'jews', 'pacifists', 'feminists', and lovers of 'jazz'). As a writer, Lewis easily lifts this burden from his own shoulders. He will have people who are a little less than human and a little more than imaginable; they will thus be appropriate to his 'taste for system'. They will have, moreover, only that 'external' aspect to which his mind so easily turned; they will not be bothered by the 'internal' realities he found so distressing. He frequently reminded his readers that the 'ossature', and not the 'intestines', of his characters was the more attractive side of things. And during those thirty years Professor Kenner mentions —years empty for Lewis of people susceptible to worry, pain and frustration—Lewis developed his most handsome and useful tool as a writer: his 'carapace'. Thus shielded from the obvious vulgarity of his surroundings, he could draw ever more elaborately on the fierce and energetic insensitivity that was his calling-card as a writer. The result would be the peculiar 'hard' unreality and willful unpleasantness of all his prose. The world Lewis thus went about constructing for three decades or so would be a monument to the belief he alone among 'the men of 1914' had—that it is possible to write of the world of events, entanglements, aspirations and disappointments from a point of view at once menacing and omniscient. 'We hunt machines, they are our favourite game. We invent them and hunt them down ... [he wrote in *Blast* of 1914] Our Vortex is proud of its polished sides.'

Professor Kenner can again be of help to us as we proceed across this odd terrain; he points out that 'Lewis has always specialized in unreality' and that his characters are, all of them, suspended 'over a void; and are radically unaware of the existence of any things or persons except themselves'.[7] That their happy deprivation in this respect is owing to the generosity of their creator is a thought that must occur to readers as they familiarize themselves with the world of Lewis. His authorial solicitude consisted in withholding from his characters any enlargement of understanding, compassion or refinement that he himself had been able to resist. In *Enemy of the Stars* (1914 and 1932), the 'character' Arghol puts it in this memorable way: 'Anything but yourself is dirt. Anybody that is.' Of Lewis's manifest and unambiguous candour on this point and many others we should not have the slightest doubt.

Prominent among the productions of unreality that Lewis gave to the world is his novel of 1937, *The Revenge for Love*. Many critics rightfully consider it to be his masterpiece. It is a 'political' novel, or rather a novel that aspires to engage contemporary political phenomena without betraying either a sentimental concession to the human or a developed interest in the ideological. Novels to which it might be compared (by readers uninstructed in the ways of Lewis and therefore stunted by their fascination with the merely human, the merely ideological, and their merely alarming connections) are two by André Malraux: *La Condition humaine* (*Man's Fate*), 1933; and *L'Espoir* (*Man's Hope*), 1937. The latter, published in the same year as *The Revenge for Love*, provides an illuminating comparison. But both of Malraux's books, handicapped by his lack of the severe obtuseness under which Lewis laboured, are concerned with the ways in which individual lives gain meaning and find identity amid political situations of maximum intensity. The first Malraux novel takes place during the 1927 Shanghai revolution; the second during 1936–7 amid the Civil War in Spain and before the final defeat of the Republican cause. *The Revenge for Love* is also concerned with the war in Spain and features characters affected by its violence. But the violence of Malraux, and the devastation it causes to the lives of people, is merely absurd. In Lewis it is ridiculous. Malraux brings to an almost unbearable point of tragic understanding the conflict between a person's immense capacity for violent action and the pitiable waste of violence. In *Man's Hope*, we are forced to see certain well-known abstractions, such as the Nietzschean will to power, the dark beauty of 'Destiny' and 'Fate', and the attractions of fraternal responsibility, lose their merely academic life and take on genuine life in a real historical situation. And in *Man's Fate*, we are made to witness what human self-transcendence might be all about when one character, Katow, gives his own cyanide pill to two doomed fellow-prisoners so that they will be able to experience death less horribly than he.

In *The Revenge for Love*, Lewis attempts to provide us with a gallery of people who are, by contrast, silly, cannot be taken seriously, and who are seen even by Lewis himself as negligible. They are, by turns, talky fellow-travellers, artists without particular talent, marginal operators who combine gun-running with painting-forgery, and one very nasty representative of bourgeois life. All behave badly. Everything is arranged by the author to make inappropriate, even impossible, any sympathy on our part for anybody's situation. One critic of the novel, Peter Dale, has spoken of it in a manner so subtle that he must be quoted lest his attitude be misunderstood as negative:

In *Revenge for Love* the obvious intention is to satirise old school-tie, drawing room socialists by confronting them with a working-class socialist who had suffered for his beliefs in putting them into action in Spain. In the course of this, however, Lewis's magpie vision is distracted by other bright ideas. Several things hinder his purpose. First, his habit of making all characters 'objective' by continuous satirical comment and authorial intrusion renders every character ludicrous. The confrontation occurs between parties neither of which command any respect or sympathy. Hypocrisy is everywhere and everyone is stupid—except the author.[8]

Mr Dale's words echo those of Frank Swinnerton, who long ago said that Lewis 'must all the time, so tiresomely, melodramatize everything, enlarge it to the proportions of sensational intrigue or monstrous perversion, proclaim a betrayal or a disaster, and denounce all who are not of his party. Since that party consists of Lewis alone, he is never done with mares' nests and dirty linen'.[9]

Only a churlishly eager sensibility would seize upon these observations as hostile to Lewis. Surely Dale and Swinnerton are of the party of Kenner ('*The Revenge for Love* is a great novel. It is not only, despite flaws any schoolmaster could indicate, a great piece of writing, it has a genuine plot. . . .')[10] and Marvin Mudrick ('the most humane and the most comprehensive political novel of our time').[11] For Dale and Swinnerton grasp what is essential to grasp about Lewis: he alone is important in his books. His inventions do not count, but he omnipresently does. In writing his great novel, therefore, he is wise enough to eliminate any characters he cannot dominate or scorn. And thus left with himself, he is left with wisdom.

This wisdom comes out most clearly in what he does to one of the characters in *The Revenge for Love*, Percy Hardcaster. Attempting to escape from a Spanish prison in the 1930s, Hardcaster is shot and one of his legs is amputated. Brought home to England, he becomes a hero to the left. Hardcaster is fatuous; his admirers, on the other hand, are feckless. One of them, a woman, becomes enamoured of Hardcaster and their liaison is described with that combination of detachment and revulsion that Lewis masterfully employed whenever he studied the human:

> Percy was perspiring. He lay back on the rotten couch in the Phipps's flat and mopped his massive pink forehead. He had been kissing Gillian and was hot and short of breath.
>
> He had implanted the tissue of his lips upon a real lady's drawling mouth for a quarter of an hour without stopping, and his desire to sip the nectar of social success, without being satiated, was in a mood to take some heed of time, especially in view of his overtaxed bodily condition. (London, 1952, pp. 181–2)

Their intimacy, such as it is, is interrupted by the appearance of Jack Cruze, businessman and lout. He has his own designs on

Gillian and so, in short order, far away from Spain, from war, from fascism and liberalism, the two Englishmen fight while the woman looks on. Jack wins, and in his own special way:

He sprang back as Percy rolled on the floor, and delivered a pile-driving kick at his fallen rival's weak spot, the mutilated stump. As the boot struck him, where the Spanish surgeon's knife had cut in, Percy Hardcaster turned over, with a bellowing groan, against the wall, and Jack sent in another one, after the first, to the same spot, with a surgical precision in the violent application of his shoe leather. And then he followed it with a third, for luck. (p. 182)

Obviously, from everything we have learned about Percy up until now, we cannot feel much sympathy for him. Nor can the woman in question. When she looks at Hardcaster, here is what she sees: 'his mouth fixed open as if he were singing some fruity patriotic song, which required the fetching up of deep notes from the pit of his abdomen' (p. 195). And hearing him, here is what she feels: 'She loathed the automatic voice out of the deeps, even more than the offensive discourses that had so recently issued from the same lips, that were now only a mechanical mouthpiece' (p. 195). It is an important moment, one typical of Lewis: unpleasant people, made to represent conflicting classes or ideologies, meet and behave with mechanical nastiness toward each other. The violence at the core of Lewis's intelligence as a writer is thus allowed to emerge.

One 'character' (in this case, Hardcaster) is so brutally abused that our sympathies vaguely, and momentarily, go to him. The novel ends, in fact, with Percy once again in jail, this time as the result of a low-minded Leftist scheme. He has plenty of time to think things over and comes to understand that he, a Leftist, has exploited people. Self-knowledge crowds in upon him: 'And the eyes in the mask of THE INJURED PARTY dilated in a spasm of astonished self-pity. And down the front of the mask rolled a sudden tear, which fell upon the dirty floor of the prison' (p. 195). This is actually a very big moment, for in a Lewis novel, even self-pity, much less pity for others who have been exploited, is hard to come by, so meagre of charity is the author. Lewis's wisdom, if we may return to that attribute for a moment, consists in rewarding his characters, no matter how desperate their circumstances, with nothing more than the chill of his attention. His wisdom partakes also of a fine impartiality: superiority goes neither to the Right (Jack Cruze, he of the three swift kicks), nor to the Left (Percy Hardcaster, he of much familiarity with Spanish prisons). It stays with Lewis. And this has the effect, which is perhaps his unique contribution to the political novel, of completely neutralizing ideology itself. Even the human aspiration to political life is rightfully seen as valueless.

As early as 1929 Lewis had in fact established a formula potent enough to devitalize any politics, even his own. In *Enemy 3*, he announced that his position was 'partly communist and partly fascist, with a distinct streak of monarchism in my marxism, but at bottom anarchist with a healthy passion for order'. This is essential Lewis, for while it introduces political possibilities, it cleverly does so only to have them summarily dismissed. It would be a fool's errand to try to resolve Lewis's communism with his fascism, melding it with his monarcho-marxism, and aligning it with his anarchic orderliness. Lewis mentions these isms only so that they may be seen through; behind them is revealed the intelligent authority of 'The Enemy' himself, Lewis alone.

And, of course, Lewis had superb reasons for wishing to belittle political life. In his long and prolific career as a writer, it is astonishing how often he was simply and unambiguously wrong as a political observer. This is not to chastise him, for surely his greatness as a writer rests on other grounds. We have, moreover, come a long way from believing our great writers are, in Shelley's words, 'the unacknowledged legislators of the world' and that we can look to them for wise advice. It is nonetheless remarkable how often Lewis lagged behind even the minimal level of political sensitivity possessed by his fellow-citizens of the same time, or of any time.

In discussing the *cause-célèbre* of Lewis's first book on Hitler, D. G. Bridson reviews all the damning evidence—the great haste in which the book was written, Lewis's belief in the pacific intentions of Hitler and his S.A., in the desire of Nazism to preserve the values of Western culture, and in Hitler as a 'typical' and peace-loving German—and then comments that 'Lewis may have made his monumental misjudgement, but it was shared by the majority of the British people, if not by the majority of his readers'.[12] Elsewhere Bridson accurately reports that Lewis regarded Churchill in 1936 as a 'firebrand' and an 'alarmist' for having warned against German rearmament.[13] Bridson then again ventures the opinion that most British people of the time shared Lewis's notions. Bridson is obviously a kind and generous critic, but his sympathy is not to the point: it belittles English citizenry while inflating the qualities of Lewis's judgement. After all, a sufficient number of English people knew Lewis was wrong at the time. Even the editor of *Time and Tide*, in which magazine the Hitler book was serialized, was careful enough to say that 'we do not find ourselves in agreement with Mr Wyndham Lewis's attitude towards the German National Socialist Party and the political situation generally'. And the Berlin correspondent of the *Manchester Guardian* wrote to *Time and Tide*, as Bridson points out, to say that Lewis was only the ignorant conveyor of Nazi propaganda.[14]

No, Lewis is not to be understood or 'excused' by the easy conventions of liberal tolerance. (Under the circumstances, that would hardly be appropriate.) One of the other 'men of 1914' —Ezra Pound—knew better and called him: 'the man who was wrong about everything except the superiority of live mind to dead mind, for which basic verity God bless his holy name.'[15] It is no small success to be wrong about *everything*, and perhaps Pound's praise of Lewis in this respect should be taken as no more than hyperbole stimulated by friendship. Nonetheless, it is worth remarking that the steadiness of Lewis's misreadings of political reality was, over the years, accompanied by just this preference for live mind over dead mind. In fact, so strenuously did Lewis prefer live mind over dead mind that he passionately detested the 'inferno of moronic idiocy and decay' surrounding him in England and elsewhere. The vulgar mass of people, those who had sunk into 'the sleep of the machine', were always to be scorned. Hence, while Lewis himself did not encourage violence, his thinking and his style expressed affinities with violence, and part of his genius consisted in recognizing how violent action could quickly reveal the difference between a 'live' mind and a 'dead' mind.

Thus *Blast* No. 1 (1914):

BLAST

years 1837–1900

Curse abysmal inexcusable middle-class

WRING THE NECK OF all sick inventions born

in that progressive white wake [and so on

for many pages of vilification].

Thus the collision of Arghol and Hanp in *Enemy of the Stars,* in which Arghol ('Central stone. Poised magnet of subtle, vast, selfish things') resists the vertiginous impulses that would reduce him to no more than an aspect of mankind. He wills that he remain a 'Self' in the pure and aloof Lewisian sense, but to do so entails the rigours, and the rituals of blood, that gave him such selfhood in the beginning: 'Self, sacred act of violence, is like murder on my face and hands.' Directly opposed to Self is Hanp, the merely social self: unheroic, sensual, derivative, unclean, embarrassing. Hanp is what happens when the true self ('live mind') condescends to mixing with other humans ('dead mind'): 'Men have a loathsome deformity called Self; affliction got through indiscriminate rubbing against their fellows.' Given this bleak and rebarbative situation, Arghol and Hanp first fight ('Arghol used his fists') and then die, the former stabbed, the latter a suicide. The world they depart is one in which 'the sickly houses oozed sad human electricity' and so their leave-taking cannot be seen, by Lewis or by his reader, as a matter of any real regret. The world, as Lewis saw it, is not a well-lighted tavern in a storm, but the grimiest of bus stations.

Lewis's excellence of sensibility is found also in 'Cantleman's Spring-Mate' (1917), in which war-time story violence and revulsion are again conjoined, but now in a setting affording the lonely hero of the piece, Cantleman, much more to despise than was given Arghol. Cantleman is one of the best of Lewis's haters; he hates women, war, Nature and his fellow-soldiers. He hates them by comparing them to hateful things: 'A. he hated because he found him a sturdy, shortish young man with a bull-like stoop and energetic rush in his walk, with flat feet spread out to left and right, and slightly bowed legs. . . . He had a swarthy and vivacious face, with a sort of semitic cunning and insolence painted on it.' (Cantleman seems to be of the opinion that 'the quarrels of jews'—as he charmingly puts it—are something the truly strong man must stand above.) The female character is hateful because she is female: 'all women were contaminated with Nature's hostile power and might be treated as spies or enemies. The only time they could be trusted, or were likely to stand up to Nature and show their teeth, was as mothers.' In this regard, Cantleman savagely and disdainfully obliges by impregnating the woman. Then, although caddishly refusing to answer mail from her that comes to him in the trenches, he turns his attention to other projects, but keeps her somewhere in mind: 'And when he beat a German's brains out, it was with the same impartial malignity that he had displayed in the English night with his Spring mate.'

Kenner, who quite rightly sees 'Cantleman's Spring-Mate' as 'the best of Lewis's early stories',[16] instructs us to understand that its irony involves the new-born infant back at home. Even the brutal and nature-loathing Cantleman, in helping to have created a child, has inadvertently participated in nature's processes. We may thereby infer from Kenner that in the world of Lewis a new-born child is just as despicable a datum as is a woman, a fellow man, or springtime itself. This is the truth of Lewis's admirable preference for 'live' over 'dead' minds, a preference that sought its appropriate definition in violence.

Indeed, Lewis's rhetoric in The Art of Being Ruled (1926) would prompt any reader to ask: for what good reason should coercive state violence be prohibited, given Lewis's description of people within mass democracy? If deep misgivings about the inherent qualities of human beings form one basic assumption of authoritarian rule, then the threat of violence is the necessary instrument of that rule. Absorbing both the Machiavellian distrust of political humankind and the Nietzschean separation of that humankind into 'master' and 'herd', Lewis argues that most people, all too willing to surrender their liberties, want only the security of being dominated:

... is it not what most people desire, to be dolls ... to be looked after, disciplined into insensitiveness, spared from suffering by insensibility and blind dependence on a will superior to their own?[17]

In pondering the many aspects of *The Art of Being Ruled*, Geoffrey Wagner, a patient scholar, comes to the conclusion that 'the general reader, unacquainted with Lewis's basic beliefs, is likely to find contradiction after apparent contradiction in his work. Even when one knows his beliefs, some of these remain insoluble'.[18] But Lewis, a genius, justified these defects by asserting the need to: 'Contradict yourself, in order to live. You must remain broken up.'[19] This, we remember, was advice acted upon once before when Lewis, pouring corrosive acid on ideology, defined himself as a communist-fascist-monarchist-marxist-orderly anarchist. In *The Art of Being Ruled*, it encourages him to elide Marxism (or his understanding of it) with fascism (his understanding of it): 'all marxian doctrine, all *étatisme* or collectivism, conforms very nearly in practice to the fascist ideal. *Fascismo* is merely a spectacular marinettian flourish put on to the tail, or, if you like, the head, of marxism'.[20]

But what does remain consistent amid all this vegetable confusion is Lewis's passion for having everybody else be coerced. Ten years later, in *Left Wings Over Europe* (1936), a tract composed with the coming of world war clearly in mind, Lewis asked his favourite question and again gave his favourite answer:

Do most people really ever desire 'freedom'? Do they indeed desire the *responsibility* that is entailed by all freedom? The answer to which is an emphatic No! *Freedom* and *irresponsibility* are commutative terms, where the average man is concerned. . . .
    Ninety per cent of men long at all times for a *leader*. They are on the look-out, whether they know it or not, for someone who will take all responsibility off their shoulders and tell them what to do.[21]

Over the years, this ideological consistency gave Lewis's somnambulistic automata a certain credibility. It also allowed him to transcend the moral qualms about political terror that were growing apace in the 1930s, qualms that other writers of the time faced with anxiety and profound misgiving. Two remarks of his from this decade can serve to illuminate for us the peculiar mixture of *hauteur* and sub-freezing rancour that was his. The first measures the extent of his compassion for almost everyone else: 'these masses of half-dead people, for whom personal extinction is such a tiny step, out of half-living into no-living, so what does it matter?'[22] The second presents for our admiration the kind of force—Hitler's Berlin followers—most useful in modern society:

> Their hefty young street-fighting warriors have not the blood-shot eyes and furtive manners of the political gutter-gunman, but the personal neatness, the clear blue eyes, of the police! The Anglo-saxon would feel reassured at once in the presence of these straightforward young pillars of the law. Everything is strictly legal—*nur legal!*—fair, square and above-board to the letter.[23]

This is all a far cry indeed from the tortured ambivalence of, say, George Orwell in the 1930s as he explored the political terrain of the Spanish Civil War. Where Lewis exercises his well-deserved moral superiority, Orwell can see little but difficulty, irony and the dense fabric of confusion:

> So much political capital has been made out of the Barcelona fighting that it is important to try and get a balanced view of it. An immense amount, enough to fill many books, has already been written on the subject, and I do not suppose I should exaggerate if I said that nine-tenths of it is untruthful. Nearly all the newspaper accounts published at the time were manufactured by journalists at a distance, and were not only inaccurate in their facts but intentionally misleading. As usual, only one side of the question has been allowed to get to the wider public. Like everyone who was in Barcelona at the time, I saw only what was happening in my immediate neigh-bourhood, but I saw and heard quite enough to be able to con-tradict many of the lies that have been circulated.[24]

Orwell's simple virtuousness, as many readers have observed, consists in no more than this: to be involved, to observe, and to try to tell the truth. The truth was hard for him to tell, even though he was in Spain, fought against Franco's forces, and was wounded. Lionel Trilling has given us a clue as to why, for Orwell, the truth was not easy to pluck out of the air: it is because Orwell insisted on respecting the old bourgeois virtues —integrity, honesty, humility. And he did so because 'they were stupid—that is, because they resisted the power of abstract ideas'.[25] Political reality was never ultimately ideas; it was ideas engulfed by events. The comparison with Lewis in this respect could not be more devastating to poor Orwell. Lewis wrote in England a book partly devoted to the war in Spain (*Count Your Dead: They are Alive!*, 1937), in which he favoured Franco ('no more a Fascist than you are, but a Catholic soldier who didn't like seeing priests and nuns killed'), [26] saw the entire struggle as Communist aggression, inspired by the Soviet Union, which must be stopped by anti-Communists (the Axis powers included), and attributed most of the Spanish trouble to the Soviet Ambassador to Spain, 'Don Moses Rosenberg'. Where Orwell patiently details the differences between the Communists, the Trotskyists, the Anarchists (the F.A.I. and the C.N.T.) and P.O.U.M. in Spain, Lewis's strength of mind prevents him from straining after such gnats. His diagnosis of the situation has an elegant simplicity:

> The solution to which we are being driven by our acquiescence in present events, is Communism. Consciously or unconsciously (it is the latter in Great Britain, where nothing is conscious) the puppets who pretend to govern us accept this solution.[27]

Orwell was 'stupid' in an old-fashioned way: he believed the truth, of war or of politics, was hard enough to tell by means of the old standards without searching for new ones. But stupidity is not all the same. Where Orwell laboured under one kind, Lewis obeyed the maxim of Nietzsche in pursuing another: 'Genius is a will to stupidity.' The obvious differences between Orwell and Lewis, a virtuous man and a genius, can be traced to the ease with which the will of Lewis flourished. It penetrated the most tangled of questions—war abroad, the rise of totalitarianism, anti-Semitism, the ideological validity of communism versus fascism, the strength of democracy—and immediately returned, book after book, with the answers. That they were never the same answers—that they were often at odds with each other—reflects only that Lewis was never as interested in the determination of the truth as he was in the exercise of his self-hood.

Lewis, of course, was not the only writer in the 1930s to be wrong. Where he was wrong about Hitler, the Jews, Nazism, Churchill, Mussolini (whom he saw only as a 'noisy ice-cream agitator'),[28] the correctness of the Italian invasion of Abyssinia,[29] and the appropriateness of fascism to England and America ('for anglo-saxon countries as they are constituted to-day some modified form of fascism would probably be the best'),[30] other writers were wrong in other ways. W. H. Auden, for instance, was also wrong about Spain and about violence. Briefly infatuated by the Communist appeal, he wrote poetry and prose expressing his rhetorical desire to take chances with his own and other people's lives so that revolution could succeed:

> Today the deliberate increase in the chances of death,
> The conscious acceptance of guilt in the necessary murder . . .
> We are left alone with our day, and the time is short, and
>   History to the defeated
> May say alas but cannot help or pardon.
>
> ('Spain', 1937)

Auden opposed fascism in Spain and in Britain and thought a fascist party in Britain intolerable. In 1939 he thought he knew exactly what he and others should do:

> . . . I think that the Socialists are right and the Fascists are wrong in their view of society. (It is always wrong in an absolute sense to kill, but all killing is not equally bad; it does matter who is killed.)

> Democracy, liberty, justice, and reason are being seriously threatened and, in many parts of the world, destroyed. It is the duty of every one of us, not only to ourselves but to future generations of men, to have a clear understanding of what we mean when we use these words, and to defend what we believe to be right, if necessary, at the cost of our lives.[31]

But Auden's convictions on matters such as these quickly

collapsed and, in time, he grew acutely embarrassed by what he had said. He repudiated 'Spain' and four other poems of the time. When, years later, he allowed them to be reprinted, he insisted on adding a note: 'Mr. W. H. Auden considers these five poems to be trash which he is ashamed to have written.'[32] And he called the entire period 'a low dishonest decade'. Politics at last sickened him.

Lewis, whose career was made up of a succession of apodictic pronouncements on all topics, politics included, came also to make apodictic political recantations. In *The Hitler Cult* and *The Jews, Are They Human?* (both 1939) and in *Rude Assignment* (1950), he acknowledged that he had been wrong about many matters. About Hitler he had been wrong, indeed had not known what he had been talking about, for he had fallen victim to current propaganda about Nazi 'cleanliness' ('I confess that in one respect I was badly taken in, in 1930. What more than anything else caused my judgment to trip was that unusual trinity of celibacy, teetotalism, and anti-nicotine ... To-day I have a higher, and not a lower, opinion of Herr Hitler than formerly, though I regret that in my rather contemptuous toler- ance of him I overlooked the danger latent in so much harmless- ness'),[33] and about Jews he had been wrong, although his revised opinions about them have the characteristically graceful Lewisian touch ('I shall make out a case for their humanity in these pages').[34] In reviewing his career, he proved as harsh as any later observer could be about his political writings of 1936 and 1937 (*Left Wings Over Europe* and *Count Your Dead: They Are Alive!*): 'ill-judged, redundant, harmful of course to me person- ally, and of no value to anybody else.'[35] Such candour is of course appealing, but actually of no importance in our understanding of Lewis. Good judgement is a most appropriate test of writers who lack his genius, for of such lesser writers we may ask: 'What are we to think of those events and forces beyond our powers and yet influential upon our daily lives? Tell us, for we respect a voice, such as yours, proven in such situations.' We would not think of subjecting Lewis to such a vulgar test. That is because we recog- nize that he had always been immured by the massiveness of his will and his self-concern from genuine human or ideological connection. His genius, that is, prevented him from ever having

a politics. He had an interest in its language only so that with it
he might raise his voice. The voice and the absolute conviction
were always what counted.

Professor Kenner, to whom we may now in conclusion return,
feels that Lewis's reputation as a writer has, largely owing to the
Hitler book, undergone 'an occultation from which it has never
recovered'.[36] One wonders, *pace* Kenner, if this could really be so.
Indeed, one wonders if Lewis's genius has not been given, over
the years, exactly the recognition it deserves. In fact, were
Kenner's general principle of black-balling correct, Lewis would
not have been its only victim. Ezra Pound, still read, annotated,
discussed, and admired by many for various reasons, would long
ago have dropped from sight, for his pro-fascist activities had an
inculpatory authenticity never matched by those of Lewis.
T. S. Eliot, whose own 1933 book, *After Strange Gods*, is a dis-
maying compendium of reactionary and anti-Semitic notions, is
still rightfully seen as a great poet.

But Lewis, after all, never had a *Pisan Cantos*, where humility
and recantation meet with lyrical splendour, and where utter
defeat joins with an aspiration given to Pound by the small and
the delicate things of a natural world external to the poet himself
('When the mind swings by a grass-blade / an ant's forefoot shall
save you / the clover leaf smells and tastes as its flowers'). And he
never had a *Little Gidding*, where the will is surrendered ('You
are not here to verify, / Instruct yourself, or inform curiosity / Or
carry report'), where exhaustion is acknowledged ('the cold
fiction of expiring sense'), but where the beauty of yet living in
a world about which one will perpetually be wrong is recognized
('From wrong to wrong the exasperated spirit / Proceeds, unless
restored by that refining fire/Where you must move in measure,
like a dancer').

No, Lewis has by now been awarded the reputation that is
quite properly his. A writer's political statements are, after
all, not his whole being, and he stays alive in the minds of his
readers by virtue of other things: his vision and his wisdom.
He stays alive because, in the deepest sense, he remains good
company. For some readers—Kenner, Mudrick and, latterly,
Martin Seymour-Smith: 'Lewis is without question the greatest
English-language writer of the century and one of the greatest in

world literature'[37]—he provides exactly that company. For other readers, however, genius of the kind that Lewis had is not company enough. And that is because genius can at times be constructed of insufficiencies, profound ones. An insufficient genius, Lewis did a lot of extraordinary talking.

13

Lewis as Travel Writer: The Forgotten
Filibusters in Barbary

C. J. FOX

'To be rooted like a tree to one spot, or at best to be tethered like a goat to one small area, is not a destiny in itself at all desirable', Wyndham Lewis wrote in 1945. 'I am just as much at home, if not more so, in Casablanca as in Kensington; feel in no way strange in Barcelona—like equally (when the circumstances are auspicious) Paris, London, or New York.'[1] Desirable qualities indeed for a travel writer. And although only one of the 40-odd volumes produced by Lewis, *Filibusters in Barbary*, was a full-blown travel book, his potential in the *genre* is obvious from the heightened intensity of the writing and keen sense of locale in evidence whenever any of his works—fiction, autobiography, criticism or socio-politics—takes him exotically far from his London lair. His great dream, Mrs Lewis once told this writer, was to visit China, whose art he considered supreme and where the spectacle of a huge human swarm emerging into modernity would surely have engaged all his powers as a consummate sociological 'eye-man'. But the fact is that, for all his itch to travel, Lewis ranged relatively little beyond the world of Europe-America, and even within that Western orbit his movements were largely dictated by economics rather than by his much-vaunted wanderlust. Finally the illnesses of his last years effectively 'tethered' him to Notting Hill Gate and, ironically, left this advocate of 'the Case against Roots' firmly identified in the public mind as a solidly entrenched denizen of that London village.

Through a combination of accident and intention, Lewis's lengthier segments of writing with settings overseas concern themselves with what might be termed colonial or frontier societies—Morocco, Brittany, Northern Spain, Canada. Such 'barbaric environments' lay far away from the ostensible centres of civilization but provided this fascinated 'specialist in savagery' with the engrossing spectacle of crude and violent forces openly in conflict. Back in metropolitan Anglo-Saxony ('the sleekest and smoothest of all worlds', as Lewis called it in a 1938 broadcast), that selfsame savagery concealed itself beneath urbane surfaces, though ready to burst out and swiftly reduce the brittle sophistications to ashes. It was in 1931 that Lewis visited Morocco, just as the West was sliding into the depths of the Great Depression. In the unruly life of North Africa, he found in full barbaric flower something of the fate that seemed to him to be overtaking Western society as, under the impact of the slump, it reverted to being 'a semi-savage sub-world of the down-and-out'. The shacktowns of Casablanca, for instance, struck him as a forerunner of the huge camp populated by nomadic unemployed then taking shape outside Chicago. 'Capitalism and Barbary breed the same forms—but how odd!'[2]

Perhaps Lewis was prompted to make his Moroccan trip by a premonition that it would provide just such a foretaste of the shambles awaiting the West. Filibusters in Barbary, the record of his visit, offers some of his most vivid and significant writing. Yet its stock with commentators on Lewis has never been high, to judge by the paucity of references. Now the time has come for Filibusters to be given its due prominence among Lewis's works since it contains so much vintage Lewisian prose, important statements of his political views and main general themes ('violence, the machine, the megapolis', as John Holloway would have them),[3] and the fascinating perspectives of a highly unconventional mind on that crucial phenomenon of our time, the last stages of colonial subservience to Western control. (Lewis's approach to Late Colonialism is of course the opposite of Fabianly solemn, he being on 'the laughing side of the world'.) The time has come in fact for a new edition of Filibusters, collecting all his writings on Morocco and complete with reproductions of the highly interesting drawings executed by the artist-author on his eventful journey from London to the fringes of the perilous western Sahara.

Quite apart from its contents, Filibusters in Barbary has a

history dramatic even by the standards of Lewis's career as embattled bookman. Precisely why he chose to go to Morocco is not wholly clear. Mrs Lewis, in conversation some forty-five years later, said her husband made the decision on the spur of the moment, as they were travelling through France in search of a home there. But Lewis's extensive preparatory reading on Morocco would suggest greater deliberation, as do his trying circumstances at the time (well worth escaping) and indeed his own words. The year before, in 1930, he had visited Berlin. The result was his first book on Hitler. This provoked a controversy which proved a major factor in the decline of Lewis's reputation. At the same time, he was contractually committed to produce the second and third sections of the *Childermass* trilogy for Chatto and Windus, a commitment he found difficult to fulfil. In the foreword to *Filibusters*, he speaks of being weary after six years of intensive literary work, and goes on:

> Then the atmosphere of our dying european society is to me profoundly depressing. Some relief is necessary from the depressing spectacle of those expiring Lions and Eagles, who obviously will never recover from the death-blows they dealt each other (foolish beasts and birds) from 1914–1918, and all the money they owe our dreary old chums the Bankers for that expensive encounter. I thought I would not take the beaten track to Russia (where all those go as a rule who require a 'breather' after too prolonged immersion in the fumes and fogs of 'capitalism') but to a less controversial spot. Perhaps nothing short of the greatest desert in the world, or its proximity, would answer the case.[4]

Lewis had long been interested in such addicts of the desert as Doughty and T. E. Lawrence, actually intending at one point to illustrate the latter's *Seven Pillars of Wisdom* and citing with what must have been approbation the former's remark that he had undergone his Arabian ordeal to rescue English prose from the slough into which it had fallen.[5] As a painter, Lewis had already ranged into the realms of an imagined Baghdad, a sphere touched on too in *The Caliph's Design*, and the region of Islam known as Barbary would have fascinated him as the setting for the exploits of some of the most daring buccaneers of the 'spacious' Tudor age he so much admired. (Notable among these was his semi-namesake Captain Thomas Windam sailing, as Hakluyt records in a phrase charged with Lewisian symbolism, 'a tall ship called the Lion of London'.[6] Master Windham—or Wyndham, as Lewis naturally makes him—scuds along the historical horizons of *Filibusters in Barbary* in his role as commander of the first English trading expedition to Morocco. Compared with him, Lewis suggests, the modern White freebooters to be found in Morocco, the 'filibusters' of his title, were a squalid lot.) Finally there was the possible lure of a stark landscape appropriate, one would have thought, as a backdrop to the still unwritten chapters of *The Childermass*. After weeks of wandering through Morocco, Lewis reassured his Chatto editor C. H. Prentice in a letter from Agadir that he had started work on the eagerly awaited Book II 'in consequence of the propitious scenery and circumstances'. A fortnight later, on 11 July 1931, he expressed surprise to Naomi Mitchison in another letter that D. H. Lawrence hadn't been drawn to Barbary. 'I have been to places, and broken bread with people, calculated to lay him out in a foaming ecstasy.'[7] Lewis himself may have felt a pang of nostalgia in this country, historically linked as it was with his old Iberian haunts.

The use of 'I' in his remark to Naomi Mitchison served to conceal the presence with him in Morocco of Mrs Lewis, a fact not divulged either in any part of *Filibusters* ('unaccompanied, I set out', he exclaims proudly at the climax of its first paragraph). Mrs Lewis could give no reason for her omission from the book when asked about it recently. One can only assume that it was merely another instance of her husband's initial secrecy about his marriage, or an indulgence, this time with poetic licence, of an inherent egoism.

Filibusters in Barbary: Record of a Visit to the Sous was published in June 1932, by Grayson and Grayson, London, and (without the subtitle) by the National Travel Club, New York, at roughly the same time. An American trade edition followed from McBride and Company, New York, in September. But that was by no means the end of the publishing story. A full eighteen months after *Filibusters* appeared, one Major T. C. MacFie of Agadir complained through his London solicitors that the book contained 'false and malicious matter of the most serious character concerning himself.[8] Indeed, in a chapter called 'The Filibuster of Tooting Beck', Lewis had waxed satiric about an 'odd, smug, highly respectable-looking filibuster [who] lives outside Agadir in a smug white "arab" house he has built for himself'.[9] This mysterious entrepreneur ran the principal estate office in Agadir, along with a dairy and bus service. Lewis, trying to see as much of the district as possible, fared badly with the pale-face potentate now revealed to us as MacFie. In fact Lewis believed (was this his famous paranoia at work again?) that the 'strange plump Cockney-Scot' regarded him as a bothersome 'nosy parker' and was out to frustrate his every attempt at sight-seeing around Agadir.

Although MacFie was not mentioned by name in *Filibusters*, his solicitors claimed that the description of 'The Filibuster of Tooting Beck' could be understood as referring to him and held him up to ridicule. The upshot was that Grayson and Grayson expressed regrets, withdrew *Filibusters in Barbary* from circulation and paid MacFie 'pecuniary compensation'.[10] All in all, Lewis (addressed as D. B. Wyndham Lewis in the first letters sent to him by MacFie's solicitors) fared badly with the English libel laws. *Doom of Youth*, also published in 1932, suffered a fate similar to that of *Filibusters* following complaints by Alec Waugh and Godfrey Winn. The American editions of both books, however, were not affected.

So *Filibusters*, in the Grayson edition at any rate, ranks among the rarest of books by Wyndham Lewis. (The New York firm of Haskill House issued in 1973 a photographic reprint of the American edition, complete with its textual variants from the English version, notably in capitalization, two typographical errors in the table of contents—which is in any case differently organized from the Grayson—and the original photo illustrations. These, not taken by the author, were a travesty of what might have been achieved with the use of Lewis's own drawings, some of which embellished the *Everyman* magazine serialization of the book.) *Filibusters in Barbary* takes us from Lewis's home base in Ossington Street, Kensington, to Paris ('That Mecca of the high-brow globe-trotter is down on its luck'); then by train through southern France (its skies 'blue and well, after the sick, moist countries'), to Marseilles (full of midget Japanese Jack-tars), and, aboard a veritable floating-Bedlam, to Oran, via an Alicante politically seething like a setting for *The Revenge for Love*. Once in North Africa, the Lewises headed first for Tlemcen in north-eastern Morocco, and on, via the old capital of Fez, to Casablanca on the Atlantic coast, then south through Marrakesh (Lewis used the French spelling, 'Marrakech') and Agadir into the uneasy 'dissident' country known as the Sous. This bordered on the Rio de Oro, at that time still under nominal Spanish control but (then as now) a violent wilderness. 'Upon the edge of this vast and perilous western desert I halted.'

Lewis spent four months of the spring and summer of 1931 in Morocco, an opportune time in its history for his visit. Most of the country was still under the French Protectorate, which had begun in 1912 and was to end, along with Spanish rule in the northern Rif, with independence for the whole of Morocco in 1956. The first and most renowned of the French Residents-General, Marshal Lyautey, had been brought home somewhat ignominiously in 1925 ('an insulting recall', Lewis claimed), and his replacement, Marshal Pétain, succeeded, where Lyautey failed, in putting down the rebel forces of Abd El-Krim. But there was still much 'dissidence' among the Berber tribes of Southern Morocco, while the neighbouring Rio de Oro served as an inexhaustible source of lurid café stories about the killings and kidnappings supposedly perpetuated by the fearsome 'Blue Men' of the desert.[11] Law and order extended into the southern regions of French Morocco only through the local feudal lords, notably T'hami El Glaoui, Pasha of Marrakesh, whom the French had left to conquer the local tribes. The pacification of the South, however, was not to be officially complete until three years after Lewis's trip. He thus was able to sample the atmosphere of menace that went with living in a country not quite at peace, where gun-running continued to be a thriving trade and foreign filibusters an established feature of the scene.

Among the *indigènes*, Lewis duly noted the occasional signs of gathering discontent with the French. Indeed the period of his stay saw the organized beginnings of the movement that ultimately led to independence through the skilful machinations of the sultan Mohammed V, who came to the throne in 1927. Of the Berbers, who made up a third of the mainly Arab population and predominated in the rural areas described in *Filibusters*, Lewis wrote sympathetically: 'Our Machine Age civilization has pushed its obscene way into the heart of their country: but for the Berbers nothing is changed, except that, by God's will, we are there, and they wish we would leave.'[12] If the Moroccan scene confirmed anything for Lewis it was his unflattering portrayal of contemporary Western civilization in the stream of books he published prior to *Filibusters*. And *Filibusters in Barbary* does carry on the polemical tradition of *The Art of Being Ruled* and *Time and Western Man* in its scornful approach to the shoddier manifestations of Western ways encountered in Morocco. (Significantly the travel book is included under 'Criticism' in some of the lists of Lewis's works attached to his subsequent publications.)

For a man generally associated with the political Right, Lewis's views on colonialism, as set out in *Filibusters*, are unusually critical. Indeed he concluded that the masses of Europe stood to gain as little from empire as those of the subject countries. And he derided the very notion that the White overlords could or should expect loyalty from people kept subservient by force.[13] For contemporary representatives of British colonialism he showed a particular aversion. Yet for traditional French imperialists— Lyautey and his soldiers as against the new civilian *colons* then threatening to sweep into Morocco from France—Lewis expressed the greatest admiration.

Lyautey's imperial principles were, naturally, high-sounding and have since been attacked as a mere paternalistic screen for French avarice. He believed in 'close association and cooperation between the autochthonous race and the protecting race, joined in mutual respect, and the scrupulous safeguarding of traditional institutions'. Yet he didn't conceal the element of French self-interest in all this, and assured his countrymen that no system of administration provided so effectively for 'the utilization to our benefit of the local institutions and the development of their resources'.[14] Lyautey's strategy of pacifying the rebellious South through the power of 'the Great Lords of the Atlas' showed the use he intended for local institutions in the unification of Morocco under the French Protectorate. Lewis, writing twenty-five years before the Protectorate finally collapsed, saw the disintegration of the Lyautey system as inevitable. While admiring the Marshal's regime, all the more so for its resistance to mass immigration by grasping whites from France, he argued that the powerful economic interests thereby alienated would not rest until they had destroyed it, just as they had already brought Lyautey's personal downfall.[15] The typical agent of this destruction, colonizing-pride of the 'radical' Third Republic, was as 'unfixed, restless and incalculable in everything as is the nomad, semi-nomad, "transhumant" or only technically "sedentary" population he is invited to boss. All that is essentially stable is the military.... And the civilization behind the military power, and upon which it depends [the author of *Time and Western Man* is speaking], has made a virtue of disequilibrium.'[16]

Against all this the 'Roman' Lyautey had stood, a beleaguered anachronism. 'This great 'Man-of-action' . . . is (how can one tell? but one has that sensation) perfectly scrupulous—a passionate *ambitieux* no doubt, but one whose hands have not been dirtied with money at least . . . this chivalrous monument is destined in history to stick up paradoxically in this african and levantine landscape, the gloved and booted statue of a typical Gentleman, in the military uniform of a radicalist Republic.'[17] Almost nowhere else in Lewis's work are so many admiring words expended on a public figure. His evaluation of Lyautey is far less ambiguous than Lewis on Hitler a few months previously and matched for warmth of approbation only by the chapter on Franklin Roosevelt in *America and Cosmic Man*.

Lyautey, born in 1854, was fundamentally a royalist, giving the Third Republic only a *de facto* acceptance.[18] The Lewis of *Filibusters* makes no such concession to the Republic. We have, for instance, his comically scathing treatment of one of its matriarchal representatives ('this bogus butter-and-egg marchioness—this enthroned charlady') observed on the boat trip to Oran.[19] Elsewhere in the book, the very thought of the Democratic Idea provokes a Lewisian expectoration while, in approaching the subject of Lyautey, Lewis pauses to declare: 'First I will divulge my bias. In so far as I can be said to have an opinion regarding french Politics, it would approximate to the *Action Française* outlook, rather than to that of say Mr Briand.'[20]

But fortunately *Filibusters in Barbary* is never heavy with politics. Its author is too fascinated by the novelty of Morocco for that, and too happily preoccupied with the myriad characters he encountered from Marseilles to Marrakesh and beyond. We are back in the world of *The Wild Body*—of decrepit country hotels and noisy cafés, the writer again contemplating a 'sun-baked ferment', watching with delight the great comic effigies which erupted beneath my rather saturnine but astonished gaze'.[21] We have the hysterical Signor Borzo and his Hotel Splendide-Astoria to prepare us for the mad 'whoopee' of the Hotel Blundell in *Self Condemned*. And although its author had, as philosopher, repudiated Time and all its trappings, *Filibusters* reeks delightfully of Period, with Aertex vests, bulbous Peugeots and tempestuous Tin Lizzies, pith helmets, Beau Gestes, the Aeropostale, Valentino, and shifty-eyed, poison-bearing Sheikhs. Then there is what G. W. Stonier, in his predictably lukewarm review of *Filibusters* for the *New Statesman and Nation*, called 'the lurking presence of its author'.[22]

Lewis must have looked strange in his large, sombre hat and dark London business suit, under the broiling Moroccan sun. He touches on his incongruous attire at one point: 'My headress was black—"Enemy" wide-awake, reminiscent of *Richmond Gem* packets.'[23] In Agadir, this was his explanation for his un-popularity with the filibuster community: 'All I can suggest is that I am not an ordinary man and it may be I dislocate the pattern of the personalities in my neighbourhood.'[24] But high spirits pervade *Filibusters*, even its account of the Berber tech-nique of computing time:

> The reader may recall the story in the Arabian Nights in which a wanderer returns to his native city and, as he enters it, feels so elated to be home once more that he addresses a poor woman and her child who were resting just inside the gate. 'What a delightful child!' he exclaims. 'How old is he, madam?' The woman replies, 'He was born, sir, in the year of the great Fart.' (This was the year in which the traveller had himself left the city. And, it may be recalled, the reply de-pressed him considerably, owing to the fact that it was he, as it happened, who had been responsible for this particular historical milestone.)[25]

The high spirits, however, do not merely make for entertainment for we are in the company of a satirist who was, one could say, a natural sociologist. Thus, Lewis seated in a Fez café among the visiting international film troupe who have come to make an epic called *The Three Unlucky Travellers*, instinctively begins computing the rhythms of the cosmopolitan social organism taking shape beneath his eyes. 'They arrived as a mere chaos of personalities upon the scene of the *Grand Hotel*. But at the end of three or four days they had separated out into well-defined classes. . . . It was an evolutionary pattern, supervised by Cupid, the *motif* divorce, of course.'[26] In presenting the champion cinematic sheikh-faker he encountered at Marrakesh, Lewis not only dissects that frantically self-inflating figure in his best *Wild Body* manner but simultaneously places him in the international context of the 'vast imitative Underworld of the Screen'. The chapters on the various film folk provide some of the most incisive 'socio-psychological' analyses one is likely to find of the narcissistic Show-Biz Personality, and of the Film business viewed as mass idiocy, all done in a serio-comic style that, as so often with Lewis, merges into the visionary.

Lewis was fortunate in chancing on his Marrakesh sheikh-faker, for he proved to be a highly representative and prominent figure in the film world of the time. Mrs Lewis identified him as Rex Ingram, the Irish-born American director, whose greatest claim to fame was the launching of Valentino as a major star, through *The Four Horsemen of the Apocalypse* (1922). But Ingram (1893–1950) as pictured by the film historians cuts a far less ridiculous figure than the ponderous creator of 'blood and thunder lollypops' portrayed in *Filibusters*. 'A fertile imagination for the pictorial . . . made his films striking, although they were often without dramatic form and devoid of solid film structure', one cinema historian wrote of him.[27] By the time Lewis encountered Ingram, the director's career was in decline due to the onset of sound. As Lewis noted, he was now starring in as well as directing his films, the last of which—perhaps the one in the making at Marrakesh—was released in 1933 as *Love in Morocco*.

But if Ingram was in decline, another prominent figure gracing the pages of *Filibusters* was still in steep ascent. Airman Antoine de Saint-Exupéry had published his first novel, *Courrier Sud*, in 1929 and was about to publish *Vol de Nuit* when Lewis met him in Morocco. Like Lyautey, 'Saint-Ex' was praised in *Filibusters* to a degree unusual for Lewis and in spectacular contrast to his treatment two decades later of another French adventurer-intellectual, André Malraux. Perhaps Lewis's admiration for Saint-Exupéry reflects, apart from his enthusiasm for *Vol de Nuit* as literature, his long-felt fascination with authentic explorers or pioneers of a new geographical dimension, going back to the Tudor heroes of Hakluyt's *Voyages*. He had already concerned himself with a theme of Magellan in paint, and declared through one of his early dramatic characters, well before his books condemning the triumph of Time over Space in Western thought:

> ... we suffer from [the] shrivelling up of our horizons. We need those horizons, and action and adventure as much as our books need exercise. We have been rendered sedentary by perfected transport. Our minds have become home-keeping. We do not *think* as boldly: our thoughts do not leap out in the same way ... We must contrive; find a new Exit.[28]

Saint-Exupéry had indeed found 'a new Exit'. An aristocrat and dabbler in literature, he had learned to fly as a conscript after the 1914–18 War and eventually joined the legendary Aeropostale company flying the air mail route between France and South America, via Northwest Africa and the Canaries. Those were the days when flying was still very much a 'Space' experience, with cockpits open to the elements. (Charles Olson could write of the plane, long after the pioneer years: 'It is a *time* experience, not of space. *Speed* is its value.... Flight does not turn out to be the conquest Daedalus and Da Vinci imagined it to be.')[29] Saint-Exupéry and his contemporaries never flew sufficiently high or fast to escape the perilous interventions of terrestrial conditions—the sand storms of the Rio de Oro, for instance. Lewis writes admiringly of 'the Air Men of the Rio de Oro, in their roaring air-skiffs, dashing along a burning reddish surface—the roof of the storm, in a fresh mildly sunlit world'.[30]

Lewis considered *Vol de Nuit*, which appeared while *Filibusters* was being written, an extraordinary work. 'I have read no book that imposed the same conviction of the high values involved in the psychology of human flight—in its first and epical period of course.' Lewis would naturally be drawn to a novel whose characters, as he put it, 'on account of the intensity of their experience ... are marked off from other men ... If all Air Men felt like this (perhaps it is lucky they do not) we should speedily have an Aristocracy of the Air'.[31] Some of Lewis's high regard for this new élite can be found in his powerful portrait drawing of Wing Commander Orlebar, done in the year *Filibusters* was published. The recent memoirs of one London socialite would indicate aeronautical fantasies of a sort on Lewis's part far back in the twenties, when, we are told, he appeared at a Hampstead fancy-dress party in the leather flight togs of a futurist airman.[32] For his part, Saint-Exupéry continued, in ways Lewis again would have admired, to prove his aristocratic worth, taking a forthrightly independent line on the issues of the thirties, and freely voicing his hostility to the dictatorial side of the wartime de Gaulle. Finally he volunteered, in middle age, for service with a high-altitude reconnaissance unit photographing German positions in southern France. From one such foray, made in an elderly Lightning on 31 July 1944, Saint-Exupéry—'one of the most unusual of this new tribe of the sky', as Lewis called him—never returned.[33]

Saint-Exupéry's old Aeropostale route across the Atlantic took him over waters where the search still goes on for the Lost Island of Atlantis, or a long-submerged ancient causeway between Africa and Mexico. Could there be a Mexican connection in the distant past of the 'mysterious Berbers'? 'I do not add to my other high-spirited heresies a belief in Plato's continent', Lewis wrote in an article published a year after *Filibusters*. But, he went on, it would be as unscientific to dismiss it as to embrace it.[34] Yet Lewis had no hesitation about marshalling the evidence gathered by his own sharp painterly eyes in support of the theory that the Berbers do not share the same racial origins as the Arab majority in Morocco. He even suggested the plausibility of a Celtic link. But such theories have been denigrated by post-colonial historians who regard them as a reflection of the efforts made under the Protectorate, by French experts in the tactics of 'divide and conquer', to drive a wedge between the Arabs and Berbers of Morocco.[35]

In any case, Lewis showed far more interest in the Berbers than in the Arabs. With characteristic independence, he paid scant attention to the cherished architectural landmarks of Fez and Marrakesh, preferring 'the monumental beauty of the Berber Kasbah, to the tiresome surface elaborations of the arab-born hispano-mauresque'.[36] His fascination with Berber building was so great that he planned a book, separate from *Filibusters*, on the kasbahs—or great castles—of the Atlas and the souks, or market-places. All that came of this was a single article, but one full of vivid description and speculations about the kasbahs. 'They are barbarous, if you like; but outside of China they are the greatest expression extant of the human being at this stage of the cycle of Earth-life.'[37]

Though Lewis was not enthusiastic about the aesthetic charms of Marrakesh, he at least found that 'huge, red, windy metropolis of mud and sand' organically real, in contrast to the 'kaleido-scopic unreality' of the freshly constructed port city of Casa-blanca. By the thirties, he had lost the fervour he once shared with the Futurists for great new cities assiduously created in a spirit of abstract logic. Hence he disapprovingly pronounced Casa 'not an organism, but a preposterous assemblage of discrete and self-sufficing cells, which would collapse at a touch, admin-istered with force enough, almost anywhere'.[38]

There is no suggestion of impending collapse in Lewis's account of Marrakesh, a city possessed—unlike the pseudo-Western Casa—of a solid historical personality. Its central square, Djemaa El Fna ('The Place of Destruction'), teemed with vigor-ous African crowds and provided glimpses of ancient rites still solemnly honoured—like that of the palmist 'before whom squats some silent mountaineer, drinking in the words of fate, while the prophetic quack holds fast the tell-tale hand, mesmerizing his victim as he whispers to him the secrets of the future'.[39]

A gratified Lewis could thus report that Marrakesh had not capitulated to European ways. We are left with the same impres-sion by a book about the city published more than three decades later by another European visitor, Elias Canetti. It is interesting to compare the two writers in this connection since so often they deal with similar themes. Like Lewis, Canetti has displayed a Swiftian taste for the grotesque, and has written of power, the crowd and great symbolic occurrences such as Fire (the hotel inferno in *Self Condemned* bears comparison with Canetti's treatment of the conflagration theme in *Crowds and Power* and *Auto-da-Fé*). *The Voices of Marrakesh*, though unlike *Filibusters* in tone, shares its achievement of focusing, through the Moroccan scene, on the world (or, in Canetti's case, the human condition) at large. Canetti's slim book is a classic of condensation, a series of pithy meditations inspired by the bizarre, often appalling sights of Morocco. Its author shows the same penchant as Lewis for total, almost mesmerized absorption in the least grandiose of local characters and events. But where Lewis isolates the weirder aspects of Moroccan life to coldly comic effect, Canetti concentrates on the painful, the unappetizing and the mysterious in a thoroughly sombre spirit. There is drollery, however, in his account of the starving, apparently half-dead donkey seen lolling dismally in the Djemaa El Fna but suddenly unsheathing, in rampant defiance of his wretchedness, a prodigious member: 'I wish all the tormented his concupiscence in misery.'[40]

'Misery' was not a subject particularly congenial to Lewis. His eye was always vulnerable to the dazzling visual seductions of the sheer surface of life, even when confronted with the sordid 'Petrol-tin Town' of Casablanca. A Lewis drawing of this shack-town concentrates almost exclusively on the fantastic circular patterns produced by the oil drums supporting the roof of one of its crude dwellings. A nomad encampment outside Casablanca becomes a procession of giant-sized beehives flanked by suppliant figures. A Foreign Legionnaire is transformed by Lewis's pencil into a uniformed totem topped by a raw-boned expressionless face. Lewis's drawings of Berber women linger over the rich detail of dress and adornment, just as in painting the kasbahs he so revered he is preoccupied with their summits 'spiked like a cactus' and other architectural forms that liberate his abstract fancy. Two Japanese naval officers in Marseilles become a pair of sword-bearing marionettes cavorting at the end of invisible strings.[41]

The painting and writing occasioned by Lewis's Morocco trip bear out the explanation he gave four years later of how his pictorial and literary functions proceeded in relation to one another. Referring to 'The Ankou', a tale about a blind beggar whom he also painted, Lewis says:

> The 'short story' was the crystallization of what I had to keep out of my consciousness while painting. Otherwise the painting would have been a bad painting. . . . There has been no mixing of the *genres*. The waste product of every painting, when it is a painter's painting, makes the most highly selective and ideal material for the pure writer.[42]

These remarks are equally apt when applied, on the one hand, to the chapter in *Filibusters* called 'Islamic Sensations', with its account of Turco-Berber musicians in feverish performance at a *café-chantant*, and, on the other, to the drawing of the same ensemble, entitled *Design for 'Islamic Sensations'*. The chapter is all hectic uproar, in Lewis's best comic vein. But the drawing is wholly different in spirit—in Walter Michel's phrase, 'a faceted profusion, as in an oriental rug'. Michel writes that it represents an interesting example of the almost total exclusion from a painting by Lewis of what went into a literary description by him of the same scene.[43]

So, while the realities of Morocco are, in Lewis's book, congealed with maximum fancy into comic or picturesque shapes, occasionally even painterly set-pieces (as with the palmist in Marrakesh or the elaborate rites of commerce in the Tlemcen souk), the process of abstracting is still more radical in the drawings. These are no mere 'illustrations' to the text. 'When a painter is also a writer, whether good or ill should ensue, artistically, upon this double birth—this twinship in the fashion of Siam of the literary and the plastic executant—depends upon how these partners are mutually balanced', Lewis said of his dual gift. 'With me, I am inclined to claim, the equilibrium was practically perfect.'[44] If this balance can be found anywhere in Lewis's work, it is in the memorable writing and painting that accrued from his expedition to the far ends of wildest Barbary.

14

Snooty Baronet: Satire and Censorship

ROWLAND SMITH

The 1930s were both productive and disappointing years for Wyndham Lewis. His output was large but real success eluded him. He repeatedly found himself at odds with publishers, the book industry and the public. His health was poor and he was short of money. His political views became increasingly unpopular. *The Revenge for Love*, his major novel of the period, caused a bitter dispute between publisher and author and sold only 2389 copies.[1] Two of his books were withdrawn from publication under threat of legal action in 1932: *Filibusters in Barbary* and *The Doom of Youth*. *The Roaring Queen* was withdrawn before publication in 1936 for fear of libel. *Snooty Baronet* was handled with less than enthusiasm by its publisher, Cassell, in 1932 when Boots' and W. H. Smith's libraries found it indelicate and ordered only twenty-five copies each.

Snooty Baronet itself offers a revealing insight into the way Lewis worked in these years and the habits which so often led him into trouble. Not only was the novel attended by extra-literary scandal and pique, but also its strengths as satire are typical of his work at the time.

Lewis's ability to portray the mannerisms of people he knew was part of his satiric art. Much of his satire has the effect of a literary cartoon, exaggerating the most pronounced characteristics of his subjects and vividly identifying them with the trait that has been disproportionately emphasized. This is a feature of his exterior technique. By presenting his characters from the outside, visually, rather than from the inside, through their thoughts, Lewis accentuates their external characteristics and fixes them in the reader's mind as internally empty, thoughtless, mechanical marionettes who are all teeth (like his Tyros) or all chin (like Humph in *Snooty Baronet*) or all flushed face and flashing eyes (like Val in the same book). Because the portraits were recognizable the joke was all the funnier for those in the know and the humiliation all the more bitter for those pilloried.

The Apes of God had caused anger among its victims. Its pot-boiler successor, The Roaring Queen, was never published by Cape even though it had gone through proofs. The withdrawal of the weaker novel in 1936, six years after the appearance of its classic prototype, is in itself an indication of Lewis's declining fortunes and a growing wariness of the furore which was likely to attend his satirical ventures. In The Roaring Queen, the portraits of figures in the book-trade-racket are often laboured. The plot is slight, the invention weak. Its satire depends on broad exaggerations of role and attitude rather than any finely observed depiction of manner or gesture. There is simply less artistry in the creation of objects of ridicule, although the farce itself offers a rollicking sketch of a valueless world of writers and reviewers. Lewis's comic invention was of a much higher order in 1932 when he produced Snooty Baronet, but he was already on the road to 'censorship'.

It is surprising how many of Lewis's interests and experiences are reflected in Snooty Baronet. The novel is an extended jibe at mechanized responses. Its absurd protagonist, Sir Michael Kell-Imrie, is a behaviourist author; the reader is led by him through a series of increasing frenetic adventures into an anarchic universe of thoughtless, intuitive behaviour. Its most effective scenes are comic episodes in which the puppets interact with one another. Several details are drawn closely from life. Lewis incorporated a great deal of his recent past into Snooty Baronet as well as many of his pet themes. The themes in the novel, and their relation to Lewis's other writings, have been discussed by other critics.[2] Few, however, have discussed its living models or the circumstances of its publication.[3]

In April 1931 Wyndham Lewis signed a contract with the publishing house of Cassell for three novels. The first was originally to be 90,000 words but at Lewis's suggestion this was cut to 80,000 words. The contract provided for an advance payment of £300 on the first book and £400 advance on the next two novels. When returning the signed contract to Lewis on 13 April 1931

Desmond Flower of Cassell asked that the three manuscripts be delivered at intervals of six months, beginning in October 1931, so that the novels could be published in three successive seasons.[4] This relationship with Cassell, begun so optimistically in 1931, was to produce three books, only two of which were novels, and to end six years later in acrimony. By any standards the expectation of a novel every six months had been unrealistic. A. J. A. Symons had introduced Lewis to Desmond Flower, son of the Cassell Director, Newman Flower. Cassell was 'a large educational firm' that also produced 'best-seller type of commercial fiction'. Lewis understood that the Flowers regarded him 'as something in the nature of the writer to succeed D. H. Lawrence' and that the firm wanted to add a 'high-brow' dimension to its list.[5]

His contract with Cassell concluded in April 1931, Lewis left shortly after for an extended journey to North Africa. He travelled from Oran in Algeria to Agadir on the Atlantic coast and moved among Berber tribesmen in the Atlas mountains and on the fringes of the Sahara. The work growing out of these travels was *Filibusters in Barbary*, but the landscape and customs which so fascinated Lewis in North Africa also reappear as the realistic backdrop to Snooty's Persian adventure. On 25 June 1931 Lewis wrote from Agadir to C. H. Prentice of Chatto and Windus: 'The country is most remarkable and the desert-cities, humped antelopes, Berber brothels etc. abound in suggestions of a sort favourable to the production of the major book' [*The Childermass*, on which Lewis was ostensibly working].[6]

Brothels, armed fortresses, semi-nomadic warriors and the social organization of Berber tribes are all topics in *Filibusters in Barbary*. And the experiences Lewis describes there obviously underlie the Persian passages in *Snooty Baronet*. Lewis was himself a guest in castles very similar to that in which Kell-Imrie is held for ransom in the final Persian scenes of the novel. In a letter from Agadir (11 July 1931) to Naomi Mitchison, Lewis links his own contacts with the Berbers to Lawrence's cult of the primitive: 'Berberig is probably just Barbary, and I am amazed that Lawrence (D. H.—not the Colonel) did not find it out. I have been to places, and broken bread with people, calculated to lay him out in a foaming ecstasy. At all events, these folks are *the*

Barbarians right enough, and they build the most magnificent castles, upon the tops of cyclopean rocks, in the heart of vast mountains.'[7]

Not only does the last sentence bring to mind Mirza Aga's castle in *Snooty Baronet*, but also Lewis's sneer at Lawrence presages the superb Lawrentian parody in *Snooty Baronet*. In the novel, published a year after this letter was written, Lawrence is the author of a Mithraic tract, *Sol Invictus—Bull Unsexed,* which the snooty narrator reads before undertaking his journey to Persia. On that journey he is ostensibly searching for Mithraic Persian tribesmen, and really waiting to be kidnapped as a literary publicity stunt.

Filibusters in Barbary was published in London by Grayson and Grayson in June 1932. Rupert Grayson, an editorial scout in the family firm, had also gained the rights to publish a cheap edition of *The Apes of God. Filibusters* was soon beset by difficulties, however, when a Briton in Agadir identified himself as the 'Filibuster' most scornfully treated in Lewis's account of local corruption. He issued a writ and the book was withdrawn. There is an undated letter at Cornell from Grayson to Lewis which is headed 'IMPORTANT' and asks for the 'low down' on 'the man MacFie out of Filibusters in Barbary', who has already issued his writ. Grayson assures his author that the firm does not want financial assistance from him, but merely information.[8]

By 10 February 1934 the situation had deteriorated. On that date Lewis wrote indignantly to Rupert Grayson, having just heard that the firm had agreed to discontinue publication of *Filibusters in Barbary* permanently, to offer a public apology and to pay a large sum in damages. Lewis reacted angrily to the news that Grayson was annoyed with him for not having agreed to apologize himself and thereby diminish the amount of damages. The anguish in his outburst is typical of Lewis's plight in the thirties: 'you read *Filibusters in Barbary,* as you know (you and Curwen) and, as you will remember, you told me how you had fair died with laughter over many episodes in it (among others my account of the figure with whom Macfie [sic] identifies himself). It was because of *your* wanting the book especially that your firm took it—you had acquainted yourself fully with it's [sic] contents'.[9] A similar complaint was made to Wren Howard over *The Roaring Queen* and to the Flowers over *Snooty Baronet*. Relations between Lewis and Grayson and Grayson did not improve when on 2 July 1934, E. G. Taylor, Secretary, wrote to explain that they were holding royalties from *The Apes of God* in the hope that Lewis would allow them to be set off against the damages paid in connection with *Filibusters in Barbary*.[10] The nadir was reached on 24 January 1938 when Gordon Dadds and Co. wrote to Cassell on behalf of their client, Mr Rupert Grayson, demanding an apology, compensation, and the withdrawal from circulation of *Snooty Baronet*. Their client, say Messrs Gordon Dadds, has for some time been told by his friends that he is referred to in the novel, and recently he has become aware of serious imputations. It is the description of 'physical peculiarities' of the character 'Humph' which have caused their client harm. The author must have used his personal knowledge of their client as basis for his description.[11]

Such a response, five and a half years after publication of the offending novel, is grotesque enough to qualify for a scene in a Lewisian sketch of the period. Humph's physical peculiarities are the most pointed part of the satire and one which it is difficult to contest with dignity. His background in *Snooty* (Brigade of Guards, ex-King's Messenger) is of a piece with his preposterous, Old Boy, pipe-smoking manner and his absurd appearance: large head, short legs ('a big carnival doll—all costard and trunk, no legs to speak of'),[12] and enormous chin: 'When I look at Humph's chin I am reminded of a strong-box. The chap is all chin' (p. 57). Rupert Grayson's autobiography and its photographs reveal a manner obviously similar to that parodied by Lewis.[13] Grayson's own account of his role in the novel has an element of pathos. He is writing in 1973:

It was a curious preoccupation that compelled this brilliant but bad-tempered writer . . . (ready to shoot down, like Napoleon, any publisher who disagreed with him), to libel his friends . . .
. . . I too was awarded the ink-black badge of his friendship. He employed his usual weapon, a pen sharpened to dagger point with which he etched my likeness in *Snooty Baronet*, cutting lines jagged and deeper than scars and poisoned with

acidic brilliance; it was no joke unless you enjoy being ridiculed. As a friend of mine remarked when asked what he
thought of Lewis: 'Very funny if it isn't you.'[14]

Lewis's reply to the solicitors' letters in 1938 was to insist that
he had only known Grayson slightly as a publisher and that
'there are no "living models" for the characters invented by me
in "Snooty Baronet"'.[15] What is remarkable about the whole
incident is not only that Grayson should have bothered to take it
up so long after the event, but also that Lewis should have been
creating the satirical portrait in *Snooty* while *Filibusters* was
being published by its model. *Filibusters* was published in June
1932, *Snooty Baronet* in September.

It is the obtuse literary agent Humph who plans Snooty's
adventurous publicity trip. En route to Persia, Snooty is to visit
the poet Rob McPhail in France in order to persuade him to join
the expedition in search of Mithraic tribesmen. Mithraism was a
central interest of Lewis's friend Roy Campbell in the early
thirties. And Roy Campbell is the model from which Rob McPhail
is drawn in *Snooty Baronet*. He had taken refuge in Martigues at
the Bouches du Rhône (the model for Faujas de Saint Riom) in
1928. Like Lewis, he had clashed with the literary world, and like
Lewis he was becoming an isolated voice.

Lewis had met Campbell as a young man in London 'Bohemian' circles. The older man's ideas were appealing to Campbell.
On his return visit to his native South Africa from 1924 to 1927
he clashed with its cultural provincialism in as flamboyant a
manner as his master himself could manage. He edited a magazine
called *Voorslag* ('Whiplash') and adopted the persona of the
aloof, lonely poet scorned by the herd because of his individuality
and insight. So close was his outlook to that of Lewis that
Campbell's poem 'The Albatross' which first appeared in *Voorslag*, no. 1, in 1926, reappeared quite appropriately in *The Enemy*,
no. 3, in 1929.

Campbell left South Africa in disgust in 1927, but after experi-
encing English literary life for only a short period left England in
1928 equally dissatisfied with what he saw of the literary world.
He settled in Martigues, but carried on a battle with 'Bloomsbury' from there; first over the rejection by the *New Statesman*

of his favourable review of *The Apes of God*, and second when he delivered his own satirical attack on Bloomsbury, sex inversions, and the literary coterie-mind through the publication of his long poem, *The Georgiad*, in 1931.

On 2 February 1931 Lewis suggested to C. H. Prentice that Roy Campbell was the 'only person' to do 'the little book about me you had contemplated'.[16] Campbell reacted enthusiastically to the suggestion and worked on a critical study ('my W.L.' he calls it in correspondence) once *The Georgiad* was finished. He had little success with it, however. It was suppressed before publication by Chatto and Windus for fear of libel, and turned down by Boriswood (who published *The Georgiad*) and Cape. In a letter assuring Lewis that he is not half as ill or drunk as during Lewis's previous visit, Campbell talks of adding a preface to his W.L. on the intimidation of publishers.[17]

Arrangements were made for Lewis to visit Campbell at Martigues in the early summer of 1931. Martigues is only a few miles from Marseilles where Lewis boarded the packet boat for Oran on his North African trip. Campbell's Mediterranean home was a haven from the English literary world and also enabled him to enjoy a relaxed, outdoor life. Rob McPhail closely resembles Campbell in this respect. He spits at the mention of Bloomsbury and is clearly a popular local sporting figure. In a card to Lewis from Martigues postmarked '1929' Campbell frankly discusses his penchant for bullfighting. He confesses that he has given up any thought of fighting as an expert since his last attempt was a fiasco. He doubts that he can learn anything more than cocarde snatching.[18]

McPhail has an Asian (not African) background. Lewis's description of McPhail's total familiarity (since birth) with the vastness of Asia is gentle in its ironic recapturing of Campbell's frequent assertions about his own unfettered African past. The dialogue is a perfect example of the mannered comedy in *Snooty Baronet*:

'Good Lord' he said, 'you know Snoots mountains are all the same to me.' He beamed filmily sideways, out of his moist slant eyes of swimming green. 'I like Downs' he whispered huskily.

'A down? Not Sussex. *The Downs!*'
He nodded filmy-eyed. His favourite mildly uplifted sheep-
walks—I knew of course they were just his nonsense.
'Sussex. Or—Lincolnshire. It's green I like. A meadow—
a field! I never saw a field till I was—'
'When? Hadn't you really?'
'Not properly. When I first came to England that was the
same thing to me as what you are speaking about, the moun-
tains.'
'I see that. But height—girth—solitude!'
He nodded at solitude.
'Since I was a boy I'd seen nothing but!' he said. 'Whereas
a blade of grass! Mountains! I'd always seen them. The East is
full—there are millions of mountains.' (pp. 188–9)

Campbell's attachment to Provençal life was deep-rooted. In
1932 he published *Taurine Provence,* a short book celebrating the
bullfighting, equestrian culture of the area. Although he described
it as a pot-boiler in a letter to Lewis, joking that he had to be
drunk to write it in the style of a Baedeker,[19] his tone in the book
is fervent as he traces the classical roots of the athletic code he
loves ('for here the ancient life of Europe is all conserved')[20] and
describes the Mithraic element in bullfighting. He translates
Mistral's account of the wording on a Mithraic shrine with its
accompanying inscription 'Ad deo solo invicto Mitrae', repeating
the words on the last page of the book under a drawing of a
triumphant matador raising his arm beside a slain bull. There is
also a description in *Taurine Provence* of a 'charlotade or comic
bullfight' which resembles the Charlotade in *Snooty Baronet,*
and there are frequent sallies against pseudo-humanitarians and
animal lovers 'in their eternal belittling of the human being in
contrast to "Nature"' (p. 31). All these elements inform *Snooty
Baronet.*

On 1 February 1932 Lewis wrote to A. J. A. Symons thanking
him for reading the first part of the *Snooty* manuscript.[21] On
25 February Desmond Flower wrote to Lewis saying that he had
read part of *Snooty Baronet* with great delight but that there
were a few modifications needed to make the book 'tasteful' to
the public at which they were aiming. Another letter from

Desmond Flower on 4 April invites Lewis to come and talk about
Snooty. His father has read the book and liked it.[22]

The problem of causing offence was clearly part of Newman
and Desmond Flower's response. The sexual jesting in *Snooty*
was as likely to create trouble (on grounds of taste) as its recognizable portraits. Lewis reflects a new concern about hurting his
friends in a letter of 6 April to Campbell. In it he says that
although he enjoyed a recent visit to Martigues: 'it was too much
overshadowed by SNOOTY. Your appreciation of the book (outside
of the personal problem it gave rise to) pleased and encouraged
me', but there were still grounds for uneasiness. He reassures
Campbell that the passage in the *Snooty* manuscript which would
'generally be identified, more or less, with you, *as it first stood,*
was not a picture that anyone could interpret as unflattering'.[23]

The problem was many-sided. Not only does McPhail's death
in a local bull-ring appear futile to Snooty—and partially caused
by a desire to 'capture further applause' (p. 214)—but also
Snooty suspects that McPhail 'really was a priest of Nature and
only shamming antagonism to her horned representative' (p. 214)
as well as being 'definitely *pro-bull*' (p. 196). This characterization of the fictional Campbell character was most likely to upset
its *aficionado* model. Lewis explains to Campbell that one should
not kill off one's friends even in play, 'nor allow an ill-mannered
and lunatic puppet to sniff at his corpse—and put upon his
actions interpretations that are certainly not (need I say!) in my
view true ones—such as proclaiming that you fight bulls because
of your *hatred of Man*!'[24] Campbell's 'picture' in the novel has
been distorted by the 'necessity of altering and dislocating it if
[it] was to be used as "fiction", and the forcible fusion of it with
the drama of the preposterous "Snooty" resulted in the drama-
tisation of the things I borrowed from you.'[25] 'The things I
borrowed from you' would seem to include Mithraic interests[26]
as well as the setting of Faujas de Saint Riom with its bull-baiting
poet.

Snooty's distorted view of Rob's tastes is central to the theme
of *Snooty Baronet*. Although Snooty at first tries to present himself as a lone realist understanding the mechanical basis of human
actions, he becomes increasingly puppet-like himself. His instinctive, reflex responses to situations cause much of the humour in

the book. There are several ironic passages in which Snooty's observer-method is applied to himself. Lewis's wit is at its finest in these moments when his hero reveals himself to be as much an automaton as the subjects of his behaviourist researches. The critics compare his books on *people-behaving* to pictures by Rousseau the Douanier; his sketches are to be regarded as 'primitive masterpieces' and he himself as the 'perfect naif'. His response to this praise typifies the ease with which Lewis makes his Tyro damn himself:

> Between them they had succeeded in making a legend for me which did not at all suit my book. I knew, better than they could tell me, all my shortcomings. I was only too aware that I was in some respects preternaturally obtuse. If you like, a kind of inspired moron. I could have told him *that*. (I have to bore holes in my head before I can get an idea into it. I am a dullard with some cunning, that is all.) But it was most inopportune that they should have hit upon this inspired french painting moron to club me with. By transforming into mere *art* all my mock-science, they had made me a present of something I had no use for at all. An *artist* was the last thing I have ever desired to be. (pp. 67–8)

Snooty has been driven to the 'study of Man upon exactly the same footing as ape or insect' (p. 65) because of his disgust that 'Man, the little rogue, was compacting with the insects' (p. 64). He has come to hold this point of view—that mankind is 'engaged in an exultant carnival of overthrow, to commemorate the destruction of the last of the generation of the giants' (p. 64) —after reading *Moby Dick*. Once the book had 'passed into' him —'I scarcely can be said to *read*, like other people' (p. 61)—he had decided he felt like the whale and was not upon the side of man. Since he can do nothing single-handed about the odiousness of mankind he has turned to his behaviourist researches.

Naturally, then, Snooty is on the side of Nature, with the bull, when he is first introduced to Mithraism. And equally naturally Lewis's *bête noire* of *Paleface*, D. H. Lawrence, is ironically presented as another naif-primitive nature-worshipper whose tract on Mithraism reveals to Snooty 'that Lawrence was on my side and all steamed-up over the Bull. He made Mithras in love with the Bull because he always put himself in the shoes of any god he got interested in' (p. 93).

McPhail is one of the few characters whom Snooty likes and looks forward to meeting. Not only is he a 'Lord of Language' and 'one of the few authentic poets now writing in English' (p. 171), but also he is *solid*. 'He and I both love the four-square sensations, of things that are properly solid' (p. 166). As Snooty sees more of McPhail in his natural habitat he begins to have fleeting doubts about him. McPhail is the truly detached Lewisian artist. He lives in the backwater of Faujas de Saint Riom because to 'register the roar of storms you must yourself be just beyond their deafening circles' (pp. 169–70). But Snooty 'surprised as it were a technical secret of his upon this visit; for—how shall I describe it?—I caught the creature shadow-boxing, in the world about him, with the shadowy solids' (p. 170).

McPhail remains a sympathetic character even as Snooty becomes bored with him. And it is inevitable that the behaviourist will misinterpret Rob's misty-eyed sense of local honour—and yawn at it. So too his 'sixth sense' is what he has to rely on to assure himself that McPhail has no real interest in bullfighting. Snooty has already told us: 'I do not reason—I *intuit*. . . . What I feel to-day, I think tomorrow' (p. 108).

The violet-eyed Mrs McPhail, stoically caring for the dying Rob, is the final independent, human, anti-behaviourist facet of the Bouches du Rhône, and Lewis uses Snooty's attitude towards her to capture the obtuseness of his clockwork narrator:

Mrs. McPhail it seemed to me had the unpleasant fatalism of the highbrow-lady. . . . I was incensed, I recognize, against the very thing that made her a worthy wife for Rob. Is it because I like a bit of straightforward *Behavior*! I suppose so, it was that. Certainly from the standpoint of *Behavior* Laura was not behaving at all well, but deliberately obstructing her reflexes. (p. 220)

It is not surprising that Campbell should have been pleased by his fictional role in *Snooty Baronet*, and tell his friend that 'Snooty was grand'.[27] The McPhails remain gently and whimsically solid in a world peopled by some of Lewis's most superbly drawn automata. A fictional behaviourist's view of Rob would hardly agitate Campbell since he would remember its creator's attitude in *Time and Western Man*: 'behaviourism is rather a *biological façade* than anything else. The behaviourist is the *bravo* sent by positivist science over to psychology to make an end of consciousness once and for all . . . an impassioned mechanistic theorist, and a believer in the possibility and desirability of mechanizing men much further and more thoroughly than has been done even at present.'[28]

After McPhail's death the machine-people take over the novel even more frenetically than before. Snooty is increasingly devoid of reason and emotion as he jerks himself through his series of callous reflexes. Humph's fate, to be casually shot by Snooty, reveals the final 'logic' of the puppet-stage. Before travelling to France, Snooty has seen an image of himself in the mechanical gestures of a dummy figure advertising hats in a hatter's window. And his actions from that point are governed by the laws of a senseless mechanical universe. It is a tribute to Lewis's satirical skill that despite both the increasing waywardness of the plot and Snooty's bored unconcern, Rob McPhail emerges as painfully fragile, quaintly proud, and married to a beautiful non-puppet.

A similar humanity emerges, strangely enough, in the character of Val, the Chelsea enchantress 1930 model, who pays for Snooty's trip and is abandoned by him. Although her mannerisms and pretensions (particularly her insatiable urge to write) are the object of ridicule, Val's concern for Snooty in Persia and the appalling treatment she suffers from him create a curious sympathy. Absurd as she is, she is vulnerably human in the company of the behaviourist puppets. Unlike them she can be bruised; at least the reader flinches at the bruising she is receiving. In a way, the possibility of such a reaction presages the seriousness and humane concern that were to flood *The Revenge for Love*.

Val is also modelled from life. Marjorie Firminger, an ex-actress and author of one 'frank novel', *Jam Today*, published in Paris in 1930, met Lewis in 1929. On her death she left a typed memoir of her relations with Lewis, *No Quarter*, to the Lewis collection at Cornell. Its tone is extraordinarily reminiscent of Val's in the fiction. In *No Quarter* a second frank book, *Over Thirty*, is mentioned; it was abandoned because publishers considered it 'unsafe'. A third projected book was to be called *Love At Last*. In *Snooty Baronet*, Val's talk is a 'sex-dirge'; 'many of Val's expressions were quite unprintable, except in de luxe editions privately printed in Paris or Milan' (p. 10).

Val's 'mayfairish and mannish' (p. 18) manner is captured in marvellous passages of comic dialogue in the novel. *No Quarter* provides a footnote. Marjorie Firminger had played the part of a society girl, Penelope Foxglove, in a play entitled *The Letter of the Law*. 'I felt I had been playing an older version of Penelope, now chaperone to the beautiful Bright Young Person', she writes in her account of meetings with Lewis in 1929 and 1930: 'I had already begun to play her—at first almost unconsciously—at parties given by Bright Young People. And I was to play her with gusto during some of my meetings with Lewis.'[29]

In the novel Val is to be found in a maisonette for which the rent is paid by her lover. In the memoir Marjorie Firminger explains that she was helped with the rent of her maisonette by her lover: 'I lay sleepless that night asking myself what I was doing being the mistress of a man I could only see once a week' (p. 5). Such is the revelatory tone of *No Quarter*. But there are also moments of vulnerability. An early meeting with Lewis is described in this way: 'in the personal-appearance chat about mutual acquaintances that followed—as in his novels Lewis had an uncanny, almost nightmare, way of bringing them to life, you absolutely saw them, heard them and even smelt them—I was able to make a few contributions' (pp. 13–14). Val's chat about acquaintances becomes high comedy in *Snooty*.

Marjorie Firminger's excitement at Lewis's interest in her is frankly admitted in *No Quarter*:

As I entered my room I felt the crimson blush flooding up. Since a child I had flushed deeply and painfully whenever I got excited about anything, the result of being 'so highly strung' I was told. And when I realised that he [Lewis] had looked in to ask if I would by any chance care to come to see him at Ossington Street alone one evening, the flush deepened. (pp. 18–19)

Poor old Val's face is notable for its 'swarthy massaged flush' (p. 17).

The list of sources in *No Quarter* is unending. Marjorie Firminger describes telling Lewis of a lesbian friend of hers whose favourite phrase, like Val's, was 'got him in the bed' (p. 27). She recounts that she introduced Lewis to the original Kell-Imrie, a baronet whom Lewis called Sir Mike, a man of 'physical oddities and violent anti-social behaviour' (p. 30), who had been wounded in the war. For all her excitement at her relationship with Lewis, however, the pain of being depicted by him is rather primly recorded: 'I was so to be upset by the novel that it was to be taken away from me by the man I was to marry and I have never read it since' (pp. 31–2).

It is surprising that *Snooty Baronet* should have such stylized vigour when so much of it comes from life. In *Self Condemned* Lewis incorporated personal experiences into a profoundly moving novel, but that novel is more realistic than the mannered farce he published in 1932. Ultimately it was not fear of libel that threatened *Snooty Baronet*, but its lewdness. Sexual appetite plays an important part in Snooty's intuitive responses. Not only does he interact behaviouristically with Val, but also with his English Lily and a Persian version. Sex as reflex is an organic part of the comic world created in the novel. And Lewis manages to make reflex sex appear lascivious.

In February 1932 Desmond Flower asked for modifications in the *Snooty* script on grounds of taste. On 13 April 1932 Lewis returned alterations in the text to Newman Flower.[30] They were insufficient, however, to appease the readers for Boots' and Smith's circulating libraries, who, according to Lewis, rebuked Newman Flower for publishing so coarse a book and 'banned it in the most unpleasant and effective of all ways—namely by taking only 25 copies each, and refusing to put it in their libraries'. The result was that Cassell dropped *Snooty Baronet* from its advertising lists shortly after publication and, again in Lewis's words, insisted that if they 'were to pay me my advances on the next two books as stipulated in our contract, those books must be of such a character as to pass the Library censors of Messrs Boot and Smith'.[31]

Lewis was desperate. Chatto and Windus had suppressed *The Doom of Youth* in the same year because of an action by Alec Waugh, one of Cassell's authors and a friend of Desmond

Flower's. The whole three-tier contract with Cassell was in jeopardy over the threat of Boots' censorship. And the issue—coarseness—was one that Newman Flower must have noted earlier. Lewis's indignation was controlled:

> You read *Snooty Baronet* personally, and I do not think I am exaggerating in saying that it impressed you very favourably indeed. A. J. A. Symons told me he had learned through your son, [sic] that you were exceptionally impressed by *Snooty Baronet*: you wrote me to that effect: you repeated upon numerous occasions your great interest in the book and high hopes for it's [sic] popular success.[32]

Popular success was never to be experienced by Lewis. But it is ironic that 'censorship' for prudish reasons should have been applied to a novel as actionable on other grounds as *Snooty Baronet*. Cassell submitted Lewis's next novel, *The Revenge for Love*, to a Boots' reader before publication. The result was a lengthy delay because the reader objected to its sexually outspoken quality as well as to the innuendo running through its imagery of false bottoms; in particular, the character of the philandering Jack Cruze was found objectionable. After many months and bitter dispute, the book, originally scheduled for publication in spring 1935 was quietly published in May 1937.[33] The Spanish Civil War had broken out in the interim and popular feeling was unlikely to be sympathetic to so cynical a treatment of political activity in pre-war Republican Spain. Cassell saw the novel as a liability.[34]

Lewis made many enemies in the 1930s. He could be malicious. And his luck was conspicuously bad.

15

Literary Criticism as Satire

WILLIAM PRITCHARD

Anybody who has travelled by train from New York to Boston, or from New York to Washington, will realize what I mean when I say that this part of the United States is a sort of desert. The tundra, or the dune, dotted with the eternal fir tree, comes right up to the back door of the last house in almost any Pennsylvanian or New England townlet, or small city either, for that matter. Half the houses, even today, again, are frame-houses, often with a brick flue and chimney running up outside the timber: . . . Professor Babbitt, for instance, to take a very concrete illustration, lived in a wooden house— *not* a log cabin—a very fine house of wood. However good looking these wooden buildings must be highly inflammable one would think, and convey a feeling of permanence much inferior to brick or stone . . .

Then, as most of the wooden residential houses are not enclosed with walls or fences (if anyone attempts to fence his house he is reported to the landlord, that is the rule, I believe, and compelled to pull it down), these houses stand, where they begin to thin out upon the edges of a town, or a city, in the middle of what is more often than not a steppe.

This description of life along the East Coast of America is not from the journal of a nineteenth-century traveller, nor from a work of science fiction, but occurs in Wyndham Lewis's chapter on Henry James in *Men Without Art*. Pretending to be an informative report, chock-full of first-hand evidence about the housing conditions obtaining from Boston to Washington, it is nothing of the sort. Admittedly the time was half a century ago, yet even in the early 1930s it may be admitted that if permissible for a Londoner to refer to New England and Pennsylvania as 'a sort of desert', there was no general agreement that 'tundra', 'dune', 'the eternal fir tree' and 'steppe' were the inevitable terms with which to persist in talking about such a waste land. As an American Easterner who has lived in frame houses for many years, I feel these edifices have enough permanence for my needs (as with Irving Babbitt, I do not live in a log cabin) even though they burn better than brick or stone. As for the matter of being compelled to pull down any fence one might have erected about the house—what does one say? Now recall that *Men Without Art* is Lewis's most devoted venture into literary criticism, and my reasons for beginning my discussion of his typical procedure with the above fantasy will, I hope, become clear.

In a previous book about Lewis (*Wyndham Lewis*, Twayne, 1968) I made a case for the significance of this literary criticism. On the basis of his treatments of the 'Men of 1914' (Pound, Joyce and Eliot) and his more incidental ones of other modern writers (D. H. Lawrence, Virginia Woolf, Hemingway, Sartre, Orwell) I claimed a place for him in a list of five major critics of modern literature—Eliot, Pound, D. H. Lawrence and F. R. Leavis. My way of dealing with Lewis was to bracket him with Pound and Lawrence as wild men inclined to mix in foolish or rash pronouncements with their brilliantly unsystematic perceptions about literature. The analogy with Lawrence still seems a good one to suggest Lewis's virtues and limitations as a critic of modern writing, since both were adept at reading through the lines of other men's books in order to expose the assumptions underlying them. Seldom encomiastic in their criticism, they are great at demolition work, at 'seeing through' their subject; this is undeniably exhilarating for the young, relatively inexperienced reader, but perhaps less so for an experienced one full of prejudices and developed tastes.

At any rate the practising novelist or poet has no time or business being an encomiast of someone else who is likely his competitor for prize stakes. Lawrence and Lewis were prolific writers who had neither the leisure nor comparative quiet that occasionally possess the academic literary critic. A continuous want of ready cash in Lewis's case makes even more unlikely the notion of him sitting down to turn out a disinterested appreciation of some other English, American, or Continental novelist. And a man who at the time *Men Without Art* was being written received his mail at the Pall Mall Safe Deposit ('What I ask you is SAFER', he wrote to A. J. A. Symons in 1934, 'than the PALL MALL "SAFE" DEPOSIT, answer me that!') wasn't likely to squander his substance in praise of somebody else down the block. So the vigorous strength with which Lewis criticized his contemporaries indicates how hard he was fighting for his own artistic values. Insofar as one of his fictions failed to sweep English readers off their feet, just so far were there 'tendencies' or fashions in the air that must be exposed and decried, even ridiculed. To note this very personal, interested base to his criticism is also to note where its distinctive flavour lies.

As a literary critic Lewis can be glimpsed in many places, but is most consistently visible in three of his books: *Time and Western Man* (in its first section, 'The Revolutionary Simpleton'); *Men Without Art*; and *The Writer and the Absolute*. The first of them contains criticisms of Pound, Gertrude Stein, and a long chapter titled 'An Analysis of the Mind of James Joyce'. The idea these writers are seen as expressing is one of capitulation to the flux, to the 'time-philosophy' Lewis spent many pages in unmasking and combating. More interesting than his general attack on this bogey, however, are the particular judgements and perceptions he makes about the poetry of the *Cantos*, or the character of Stephen Dedalus in *Ulysses*—perceptions which are the result of his excellence as a practical critic with superbly equipped ears and eyes. But there is more to it than that, as we see from a look at the four-and-one-half pages devoted to 'The Prose-Song of Gertrude Stein'. This prose-song is

a cold suet-roll of fabulously-reptilian length. Cut it at any point, it is the same thing; the same heavy, sticky, opaque mass all through and all along. It is weighted, projected, with a sibylline urge. It is mournful and monstrous, composed of dead and inanimate material. It is all fat, without nerve. Or the evident vitality that informs it is vegetable rather than animal. Its life is a low-grade, if tenacious, one; of the sausage, by-the-yard variety.[1]

Where would a friendly reader of Miss Stein's begin to argue with this characterization? How, in other words, does one take issue with cold, black suet puddings, with the alliterated 'mournful and monstrous' matter that, if it has any life, is 'of the sausage, by-the-yard variety'? On the next page Lewis changes metaphors, and after a sort of Wildean reversal of the 'brilliant' sort—'she may be described as the reverse of Patience sitting on a monument—she appears, that is, as a Monument sitting upon patience'—he substitutes for the suet-pudding an authoress who has relapsed into the habits of childhood:

> This child (often an idiot-child as it happens, but none the less sweet to itself for that) throws big, heavy words up and catches them; or letting them slip through its fingers, they break in pieces; and down it squats with a grunt, and begins sticking them together again. Else this far-too-intellectual infant chases the chosen word, like a moth, through many pages, worrying the delicate life out of it. The larynx and tongue of the reader meantime suffer acutely.[2]

Fascinated by this vivid creation we watch Gertrude Stein, as if before our eyes, squat with a grunt and begin once again her laborious disintegrative activity. The image is so memorable that it becomes truth; no one else has evoked her in so compelling a way.

Written in old age when he was going blind and when he was particularly depressed about the intrusion of politics into literature, *The Writer and the Absolute* offers a less striking brand of satiric fantasy than found in earlier Lewis. Nonetheless, and particularly with regard to the book's closing section on George Orwell, Lewis succeeds not so much in responsibly criticizing the books Orwell wrote, as in imposing a figure on us who, if less of a broad caricature than the portrait of Gertrude Stein, is nonetheless drawn with a strong and simple outline. Orwell is a 'romantic Scot' with a 'dour pig-headed New Statesmanlike social conscience'; he also has a streak of snobbery and is obsessed by bad smells, particularly as produced by the lower classes. Lewis quotes a long passage about smells from *The Road to Wigan Pier*, then follows it with a personal confession: 'Myself, I started life in a house with a bathroom, with a nurse, two servants, and a cook; therefore I had four stinkers under the roof with me in place of Mr. Orwell's one.' With such comic good sense we are invited to see Orwell's perception as excessive and

obsessive ('This *stink* business was obviously a first-class complex', says Lewis briskly) and to understand it as part of a parcel
of romantic attitudes toward poverty and class structure. The
later part of the section goes on to argue that in Orwell's best
books, *Animal Farm* and *1984*, he broke through to political and
social realism, saw things steadily and disinterestedly for the first
time. Yet the 'positives' celebrated in Orwell's career are perhaps
less interesting than the excesses Lewis criticizes in his earlier
work. Or than the virtues he fails to do justice to; we—or at least
I—are less convinced that *Animal Farm* is a good book than that
Homage to Catalonia is a superb one. Yet Lewis never even
bothers to mention the Spanish war book, in his unfavourable
treatment of pre-World War II Orwell.

My point is that Lewis, like his fictional hero Frederick Tarr, is
possessed by what that character called 'the curse of humour',
to the extent that as a literary critic he can no more get along
without it than Tarr was able to in his personal relationships.
And if we take this cursed humour not simply as a delightful
coating on the pill but as the absolute base of the pill's ingre-
dients, then Lewis's distinctive quality as a critic may become
clearer. With this caveat in mind, we may now turn to *Men
Without Art*, the book which displays his most vigorous and
entertaining performance as a literary critic.

It was published at a less than high point in Lewis's career.
The letters from 1934 show him early on in a nursing home as a
result of a 'bad bleeding'. In June he refers, in a letter dated
'Pall Mall Safe Deposit Box', to 'recovering from a couple of bad
operations' and to being 'ill for a year and half off and on before
that, with long spells in bed and much mental anguish'. *Men
Without Art* came out in the autumn and the reviews of it
provoked him into some two-fisted responses, as in a letter to the
TLS of 29 November complaining that Rayner Heppenstall,
'a Communist, or perhaps someone so highly sympathetic with
Communism as to be more Marxist than Marx himself' should
have been assigned his book for review:

That a member of the Society of Jesus would not be an appropriate person to choose to do a review of a reprint of Darwin's

Works is obvious—or that any good Catholic, even, would be incompetent to review the novels of a notorious agnostic, that also is plain enough. But surely a Communist or Marxist is disqualified in much the same way, for the purposes of 'literary' review. Communism is ... a religion and a particularly bloodthirsty and persecutory one at that.

Concurrently he found himself in a complicated and hilarious (at least for his part) exchange of letters regarding Edith Sitwell's *Aspects of Modern Poetry* ('this rococo palace of blunders, this wax-works divided into "giants" before whom you abase yourself, and sots or desperadoes at whose effigies you spit and jeer').

We should remember that the section from *Men Without Art* dealing directly with the nature of satire had been published previously as a pamphlet (*Satire and Fiction*) written in vigorous defence of the kind of literary creation Lewis thought he had achieved in *The Apes of God*. That mammoth work, easier to attack or ignore than to read through, along with the book on Hitler published in the next year (1931), were to preside over the decline of Lewis's reputation in the 1930s. *Men Without Art* then could be looked at as a desperate effort to get closer to the literary centre of things he felt himself drifting away from. He would do this by seeing through the facades presented by various writers of current reputation; then by defending satire on the grounds that it alone was adequate to deal with 'the disasters of the peace' as they revealed themselves in the 1930s. The assertion —it is more an assertion than an argument—is that satire is good because it is true, true because it shuns the 'idealism' or 'romance' of other kinds of fiction, and therefore necessary in order to deal with the modern world in a sufficiently inclusive manner. In Lewis's boldest exaggeration, satire *is* fiction, and obviously (is it not obvious?) there was no more vital and productive a satirist than Wyndham Lewis.

Men Without Art begins with full-dress essays on Hemingway, Faulkner and T. S. Eliot (as critic, not poet), next discusses satire as it was being practised by Lewis himself, then examines some notions of fiction by considering the examples of Henry James and Virginia Woolf. After this the book—never confined to any particular subject—launches out into rambling chapters on the terms 'classical' and 'romantic', on materialism and the artist, on the phenomenon of 'bad-timism' in literature, on the figure of Flaubert. As with the earlier *Art of Being Ruled* and *Time and Western Man*, a reader finds himself flailing about, never certain of what direction Lewis will next take; but just frequently enough encountering a saving comic touch or a perceptive remark about the social and artistic world. If Gertrude Stein was a Monument sitting on Patience, *Men Without Art* severely tries our patience, particularly when it ceases to focus on particular writers and deals with more general topics. But eventually, in a welcome appendix, we move very much back into the concrete, as the famous or infamous 'Taxi-Cab Driver's Test for "Fiction"' is conducted.

That appendix is usually taken merely as such, to be savoured as brilliant or condemned as superficial depending upon one's attitudes toward Lewis. I propose on the contrary to treat the cab-driver's test as an essential element of his critical style and procedure. At least since the publication of *The Childermass* (1928), Lewis had been making the point that if that book (and afterwards *The Apes of God*) weren't 'fiction'—and they certainly weren't 'fun' to read, nor would they do well at the Lending Library—then what were they? By what standards would they be reviewed and criticized? In hopes of making the world safe for writers like himself who wrote difficult books that were not to be trusted to the unsubtle hands of ordinary Fiction Reviewers, Lewis invented the cab-driver's test—an instant way of distinguishing between 'fiction' and that something else which is art, literature, or whatever. The assumption is that writing, to be considered art, must be good writing, as good as could be found, Lewis says, in the works of a Donne or a Dryden —even though the writer is a twentieth-century prose-man or woman. In his rather curious but appealing phrase for it, the book should be an 'intellectual object', and any book which could possibly fit into the scheme of things implied by the word 'fiction' will be of no value, except as 'an awfully good aphrodisiac or first-rate "thriller"'.

His demonstration of how to conduct the test is worth pausing over:

The *taxi-cab-driver test* can be applied, in the absence of a taxi-cab driver—though not so effectively—by merely opening any book of 'fiction', at the first page, and seeing what you find. I will now give a hasty demonstration of that method, selecting, for my purpose, two of the only 'fiction' books I have within easy reach. Here displayed intact upon the next page, is *first-page* No. 1.[3]

The intention seems to be to sound as much like a carnival barker or snake-oil salesman as possible, and a literal-minded reader—should we suppose one to have made it through somehow to the end of *Men Without Art*—might find himself muttering annoyedly, 'What is all this business about a taxi-cab-driver, and why can't the test be applied as effectively without him? Where was Lewis sitting that these particular two volumes were the only ones within easy reach, and can this be a responsible way to conduct such an important test?' The answer to our reader would be, I think, that here as elsewhere Lewis is writing satire, that satire is *good* in itself, and that a book in defence of it should properly conclude by practising what it preaches.

This is not at all to say that Lewis is not very serious indeed about the necessity of distinguishing fiction from art; just because it is a matter of such crucial importance to him, because he believes in art as play, he becomes playful himself, creating a fantasy which will charm and amuse only those who, as it were, already *know* the difference between art and fiction—flexible, clever, playfully-minded readers. A few pages previously he provided this summary definition of satire:

'Satire', as I have suggested that word should be used in this essay (applying to *all* the art of the present time of any force at all) refers to an 'expressionist' universe which is reeling a little, a little drunken with an overdose of the 'ridiculous'—where everything is not only tipped but *steeped* in a philosophical solution of the material, not of mirth, but of the intense and even painful sense of the absurd.[4]

So in its small way, the performance of the cab-driver's test reels a little, is 'a little drunken' with the ridiculous.

Further conduct of the test confirms this sense. One of those

books Lewis easily reached out for and came back with was
Aldous Huxley's *Point Counter Point*, and much play is made
with how he will not reveal the title of 'the most important work
of "fiction" of a very famous author, published in 1928, and
regarded as one of the landmarks in English literature of the last
decade'. (The alert reader will note that indeed Huxley is a good
deal more famous than Wyndham Lewis, and that *Point Counter
Point* surely sold incomparably better than did *The Childermass*,
published in the same year.) After the first page of this landmark
is produced as Specimen A, Lewis breezily assures us that it's all
we need look at to see how no book 'operating upon this tone of
vulgar complicity with the dreariest of suburban library-readers'
could—whatever happens in its next 600 or so pages—be anything but a 'dull and vulgar book'. He then proceeds to object to
the 'cozy sound' of the name of Huxley's character, Marjorie
Carling, and the 'sentimental repetitive' in his 'she knew that
her importunity would only annoy him, only make him love her
the less'. That is the extent of Lewis's demonstration of how dull
and vulgar Huxley's novel must be. In no sense has he provided
an objectively convincing, damagingly adverse criticism of the
sort which might convince an open-minded, rationally inclined
reader. And yet in my view he is quite right about *Point Counter
Point*, a dull and sometimes vulgar book, read now by almost
nobody.

The other book at the critic's elbow, Specimen B, begins this
way—

> It was but a question of leaving their own contracted
> 'grounds,' of crossing the Avenue and proceeding then to Mr.
> Betterman's gate, which even with the deliberate step of a
> truly massive young person she could reach in three or four
> minutes. So, making no other preparation than to open a vast
> pale-green parasol, a portable pavilion from which there
> fluttered fringes, frills and ribbons that made it resemble the
> roof of some Burmese palanquin or perhaps even pagoda, she
> took her way while these accessories fluttered in the August
> air, morning freshness and the soft sea-light.[5]

—and is the opening of Henry James's uncompleted late novel,
The Ivory Tower. Lewis is no more concerned to delineate its

status and qualities as art by indulging in comparison and analysis, the function of the critic, than he was with the Huxley 'fiction'. After all cab-drivers don't spend much time at comparison and analysis, and Lewis is simply filling in for the absent driver. His sole comment about the paragraph from James is: 'That is a rather different kettle of fish, the most unobservant must detect.' But surely the most unobservant will *not* detect it as that, nor will they be persuasively led by the phrase 'different kettle of fish' to see clearly what before they had missed. It is you and I, observant readers who don't depend on the circulation libraries, don't look forward to the equivalent of Hugh Walpole's *Miss Gracie Smith* (a 'fiction' title Lewis uses as exemplary) who will upon reading the opening of *The Ivory Tower* know how different a kettle of fish it is. Though I am personally no great admirer of that gaseous late Jamesian piece of self-parody (for so it seems to me) it is surely Art, to be wondered at if not delighted by. Lewis may have been delighted by it because of the similarity, in mannered over-elaboration, to the kind of writing he had cultivated in his recent *Apes of God*; at any rate it makes a striking contrast with the Huxleyan novelese of Specimen A.

The point is that as a literary critic Lewis most typically plays this role by making scenes, creating fantasies, identifying himself in playful seriousness with the equivalent of cab-drivers—no nonsense, ungenteel fellows who don't have all the time in the world but are filled with honesty, common sense, and the rough capacity not to be taken in by the fashionable article. It is of some interest that a man with his delicacies of perception should clothe himself in self-protective homespun myth, the better to see through junk masquerading as literature. It should also be admitted that mockery, at the very least some strong teasing, is endemic to his procedure. The most memorable things from the long essay on Joyce in 'The Revolutionary Simpleton' are the broad and extended ridicule directed at the character of Stephen Dedalus, the weary poet, and the characterization of *Ulysses* as a cathartic outpouring, 'a monument like a record diarrhoea'. In a previous chapter Pound had been celebrated for supposedly giving up literature in favour of music; Lewis salutes this as a wise decision since Pound has nothing to say anyway and his effective work as a poet is finished. While in *Men Without Art,*

Hemingway and Faulkner become respectively 'The Dumb Ox', and 'The Moralist with a Corn-Cob'; mythical identities derived from Lewis's notion of how a Hemingway hero speaks and thinks, and from turning Popeye's violation of Temple Drake (in *Sanctuary*) into a metaphor for Faulkner's brand of literary instruction.

The two essays on these important American writers were written when they were far from fully-established values, less safe to admire than they are today. Certainly it was unusual for an English writer in 1933 to have read Faulkner's novels, let alone to see them as significant. To be sure Lewis mocks the 'poetry' in Faulkner, saying that it tends to occur when the atmosphere is getting thin and some new material needs to be pumped in:

> His characters demand, in order to endure for more than ten pages, apparently, an opaque atmosphere of whip-poor-wills, cicadas, lilac, 'seeping' moonlight, water-oaks and jasmine— and of course the 'dimensionless' sky, from which the moonlight 'seeps'. The wherewithal to supply them with this indispensable medium is as it were stored in a *whip-poor-will tank*, as it might be called: and he pumps the stuff into his book in generous flushes at the slightest sight of fatigue or deflationary listlessness, as he thinks, upon the part of one of his characters.[6]

It 'might be called' a *whip-poor-will* tank, yet no one but Lewis would have thought to call it that and so make memorable Faulkner's rhetorical habits. These expressive excesses don't obviate his interest as a novelist (as they pretty much did for F. R. Leavis, who reviewed *Light in August* dismissively in *Scrutiny*) since Lewis insists that we care about novels for something more than their well-written qualities. After all, was *The Apes of God* 'well-written'? By contrast Lewis quotes from Hemingway to demonstrate an art of writing that doesn't seem like 'writing' at all, rather seems lifted from nature. This is an artful trick, and should be exposed; but Lewis admires the subtle way in which Hemingway carries it off.

Making your subject the centre of a creative fantasy rather than evenly and responsibly discussing one book after another usually turns out, in Lewis's hands, to be something more interesting than mere denigration. Apropos Eliot's portrait of the young man carbuncular from *The Waste Land*, Hugh Kenner has remarked that if such a young man existed and read those words 'how must he have marvelled at the alchemical power of language over his inflamed skin!' This is handsome toward Eliot, but could work only if the young man were such a good reader as to consider the miseries of acne quite transformed by words cleverly employed. Hemingway should have appreciated his lead role in *Men Without Art* but in fact he was infuriated by it. Lewis had insisted that it was Hemingway's typical fictional character, and not the subtle author himself, who merited the 'dumb ox' label—'this constipated, baffled, "frustrated"— yes, deeply and Freudianly "frustrated"—this wooden-headed, leaden-witted, heavy-footed, loutish and oafish marionette— peering dully out into the surrounding universe like a great big bloated five-year-old—pointing at this and pointing at that— uttering simply "CAT!"—"HAT!"—"FOOD!"—"SWEETIE!" '. But, Lewis suggests, Hemingway has not been immune to this fellow's charms; and the implication might have been that to be taken in by such an ox is less than admirable. At any rate, whatever it was that most annoyed Hemingway (he later described Lewis as the nastiest man he had ever seen) Sylvia Beach reports that he punched the heads off three dozen tulips in her shop, spilling water all over the books.

By contrast Virginia Woolf, also accorded a chapter in *Men Without Art* and discussed in less than flattering terms, made a noble effort to delight in the alchemical power of Lewis's language over her inflamed psyche. She confides to her diary that his attack made her ill for two days; but she also rose to an appreciation:

This morning I've taken the arrow of W.L. to my heart: he makes tremendous and delightful fun of B. and B. (Mr. Bennett and Mrs. Brown): calls me a peeper, not a looker; a fundamental prude; but one of the four or five living (so it seems who is an artist). . . . If there is truth in W.L. well, face it: I've no doubt I'm prudish and peeping. Well then live more boldly, but for God's sake don't try to bend my writing one way or the other. Not that one can. And there is the odd pleasure too of being abused and the feelings of being dismissed into obscurity is also pleasant and salutary.[7]

Others were not as high-spirited as Virginia Woolf managed to be about herself (though in saying that Lewis places her as 'one of the four or five living' who is an artist, she finds more praise than the essay actually makes). Reviewing *Men Without Art* in the *Spectator*, Stephen Spender commended the attacks on Hemingway and Faulkner, but found the treatment of Woolf 'malicious'. Lewis replied in a letter defending himself against the charge; yet one can't deny I think that his way of presenting her is highly disingenuous.

He tells us first that he is 'compelled' to 'traverse the thorny region of feminism' and that he has 'chosen the back of Mrs. Woolf—if I can put it in this inelegant way—to transport me across it'. It is surely an inelegant way of putting it but all the better since the subject puts things, in her novels, in such elegant ways. Yet

I am sure that certain critics will instantly object that Mrs. Woolf is extremely insignificant—that she is a purely feminist phenomenon—that she is taken seriously by no one any longer today, except perhaps by Mr. and Mrs. Leavis—and that, anyway, feminism is a dead issue. But that will not deter me, any more than the other thorny obstacles for my purpose: for while I am ready to agree that the intrinsic literary importance of Mrs. Woolf may be exaggerated by her friends, I cannot agree that as a symbolic landmark—a sort of party-lighthouse—she has not a very real significance.[8]

This significance lies partly in her clash with nineteenth-century scientific realism as carried over in the Edwardian novelists— Wells, Galsworthy and Bennett. But Lewis's performance here is such as to divert attention away from serious critical issues on to the outrageously entertaining writing he is providing. First he presents us with the unlikely image of himself, transported on the back of Mrs Woolf; then are summoned up non-existent critics who (it is claimed) will instantly object that she is insignificant, taken seriously only by old-fashioned writers like the

Leavises. (Here Lewis gets in a swipe at the tendency of this literary couple to be insufficiently appreciative of his novels and critical studies.) Undeterred by these critics, he is bravely ready to forge ahead with his inquiry, even though he agrees that Woolf's 'intrinsic literary importance is exaggerated'. What more than such intrinsic matters could Virginia Woolf have cared about? Instead she is reduced to a sort of 'party-lighthouse'; by looking at her apology in 'Mr. Bennett and Mrs. Brown' we can find out the going Bloomsbury line on modern literature.

Using the materials that Woolf's essay provides, Lewis proceeds to exaggerate and caricature her as a 'little woman', a 'peeper', an 'orthodox idealist' suffocated by the three Edwardian 'bullies' (particularly 'the big beefy brute, Bennett') whose art is inadequate to convey the feelings of 'Mrs. Brown'—'longing to "bag" the old girl, and yet completely impotent to do so, because no one was there on the spot to show them how, and they could not, poor dears, be expected to do it themselves!' Then referring to the list of post-Edwardian writers Woolf had brought together to illustrate the necessarily fragmentary character of modern fiction, Lewis puts the following apology in her mouth, speaking for them all: 'You will never get anything out of us except a little good stuff by fits and starts, a sketch or a fragment.' By rendering Woolf's apology in this casual way, he shows how inapplicable it is to full-bloodied artists, writers like Joyce and Lawrence who, along with herself, Forster, and Lytton Strachey, make up her list of serious modern writers. And of course since she would be the last person in the world to employ the phrase 'a little good stuff', it is essential to the sharp fun of Lewis's attack that he put such inappropriate words in her mouth. Satire, as he kept reminding us, was deliberately unfair, did not try even-handedly to see both sides of the argument. And we can't but feel that Lewis found unacceptable Woolf's omission of his name from her list of significant contemporaries; it is this which may have been her real 'significance' as a party-lighthouse.

Virginia Woolf's novels are mentioned only casually, almost as an afterthought, and then only to designate as a 'pathetic crib' a section from Mrs Dalloway which bears affinities to Ulysses. Like his criticism of other literary figures, the chapter on Woolf is in no sense a responsible analysis of and judgement about that writer's creations. Yet, as with his criticism of those other writers, Lewis's portrait of her has permanent value in that it can be re-read with delight, with keen appreciation of the partial truths which satiric performance can bring. It should be read also with a recognition that there is a continuity between the portraits and scenes from Lewis's novels and paintings, and his portraits from life—as in the description of the housing situation on the East Coast of America, or the safety of the Pall Mall *Safe* Deposit. In no writer are the divisions between literature and life, words and reality, criticism and creations, more subtly—that is, artfully —confused.

16

Enemies of the Absolute: Lewis, Art and Women

VALERIE PARKER

> 'Are there no women who really understand—
> who can take part in a sacrifice?'
> 'How can they take part? They themselves
> are the sacrifice. They're the idol and
> the altar and the flame.'
>
> Henry James, 'The Lesson of the Master'

(i)

From the beginning Lewis was obsessed by art and the conditions necessary for creation. All his writings spring from a sense of his unique creative self, threatened by hostile opponents. In the political books the enemy is mass society, in his satires the bourgeois cultural king-makers. In *Tarr* the protagonist's enemy is woman, or rather the Nietzschean Woman, who represents the claims of ordinary sensual life which drag the artist down into the mass. As he wrote in his manifesto, 'The Code of a Herdsman' (1917): 'As to women: wherever you can, substitute the society of men ... treat them kindly, for they suffer from the herd, although of it, and have many of the same contempts as yourself.... But women, and the processes for which they exist, are the arch conjuring trick.' Lewis argues that people who are merely 'in' life, who cannot transcend ordinary existence, are mechanical because natural processes reduce them to mechanisms. Tarr echoes the doctrine of *Blast* 1 when he says that artists discharge themselves in Life by satisfying their bodily appetites, in order to keep themselves pure for Art, that pursuit of the Absolute. Women, he says, are the enemy of the absolute: if you cannot do without them, use them; you have to cheat nature if you intend to act creatively and individually. Surrender to a woman, proclaims Tarr, is 'a kind of suicide for an Artist'. Yet in his three best novels, *Tarr*, *The Revenge for Love* and *Self Condemned*, Lewis gives women central roles to play.

Lewis was not hostile to women but found it necessary to adopt this stance because he was trying to reject the ideology and structure of the English nineteenth-century novel. He shares with the writers of the 1890s, especially Wilde and James, the idea of two planes of being, the higher for art and the lower for life. Wilde said: 'I treated art as the supreme reality and life as a mere mode of fiction'; and he urged the artist to 'Create yourself; be yourself your poem'. Tarr echoes these ideas. In 'The Code of a Herdsman' Lewis advised the would-be artist to create various *personae*, to diversify the personality deliberately, even to adopt different dress and manners on various occasions. Lewis argues against social and individual harmony, against the family and the integration of the personality for the sake of society, values implicit in nineteenth-century novels. Even Wilde's *Dorian Gray*, a precursor of Lewis's divided and conflict-ridden hero, depends on the ideal of wholeness in man for its tragic force. Because Lewis places the emphasis on man the artist, the creator of new patterns for living, he rejects the suffering, developing, self-sacrificing intuitive heroine (the pattern which persists from Fanny Price in *Mansfield Park*, Maggie Tulliver in *Mill on the Floss* and Little Dorrit down to the heroines of Meredith and James). For Lewis, women adhere to dead values; their kind of 'creation' conflicts with the artist's creativity: they want consistent mates, not diverse individualists who are constantly in the act of self-creation.

Tarr is Lewis's first attempt to explore the psychological difficulties inherent in his hostile elitist position. Tarr and Kreisler represent two opposite resolutions to the conflicts of the Lewisian protagonist: between his desire to belong to the world and his hatred of it, his need for sex and wish to repudiate women. Tarr is intellectually poised, strong in his isolation; the only child of an adoring mother, he is accustomed to the service of women. Kreisler shares Tarr's self-love, resentment against women and hostility to the world in general. But he is poor, jilted by his girl-friend who has married his powerful father, upon whom he

is precariously dependent for love, money, security and even for
sex. Kreisler cannot be indifferent to women. He discharges his
creative energies in unhappy love-affairs, purging himself 'periodically of the too violent accumulations of desperate life'. He
goes out into the expatriate society he despises in a mad rage,
assaulting several women at the dance. In his anger and self-
consciousness he feels he is 'standing in filth'. Bertha calls him
'the Enemy' as she sees him from a window. Kreisler is a recurring *persona* in Lewis's fiction: bitter, isolated, ridiculous,
comical if he were not so dangerous. He rapes Bertha and commits murder and suicide. Tarr interprets his actions as part of a
sex-tumult, 'an attempt to get out of Art back into Life again. . . .
Back into sex I think would describe where he wanted to get to;
he was doing his best to get back into sex again out of a little
puddle of art where he felt he was gradually expiring'. He con-
fuses the two planes of being, art and life, and consequently fails
at both. Kreisler, without talent but full of 'cheap, stagnating
passion', embodies a theme which recurs in Lewis's writings: the
strain of trying to create while living in poverty and threatened
by failure. The would-be artist tries to turn his back on the comforting illusions of life, but finds neither artistic success nor
financial security. Kreisler is cursed with art because he is second-
rate. He is driven by passion as Tarr is dominated by ideas, but
while Kreisler struggles to integrate the parts of his life, Tarr
divides them and conquers.

Unlike Kreisler, who craves acceptance by society, Tarr regards
himself as an elite of one. He struggles with desire for Bertha; but
succeeds in tearing himself away; when he feels like sex he thinks
of the pox and represses his desire; he has life under control.
For Tarr, sex has to be got out of the way before he can begin his
art; he divides his personality into the intellectual and the
physical. Tarr says: 'I do not mean that sex is my tragedy, but
only art.' Like Wilde and Proust's Swann, Tarr believes that the
more ascetic an artist, the cruder his sexual tastes will be; his
taste in women is therefore slovenly. He isolates the aspect of
women he needs and degrades them into machines to relieve him
of his tensions; sex with Bertha, he considers, was 'some such
soothing milking process that nature wished him to have in place
of passion', merely a pleasurable release. Life is art's rival, says

Tarr, and woman is 'the arch-enemy of any picture'. Art is permanent and continuous; life is an individual spasm. 'What is life?' asks Anastasya. Tarr replies: 'Everything that is not yet purified so it is art.' Women are the prime example of the impure. Tarr believes that 'soft quivering and quick flesh is as far from art as it is possible for an object to be'. Tarr reifies the body (including his own) to release his mind from the body's chaos of instinct, emotion and decay. Art is a product of mind.

Tarr's affair with Bertha structures the novel, and we see her through his contemptuous eyes. Ordinary, romantic, ample of bosom and prone to tears, stolidly capable of putting up with Tarr's gibes, Tarr sees her trapped in Time, and he with her, as he looks at the photograph of them together: 'What abysms of all that was most automatic and degrading in human life: rubbishy hours and months formed the atmosphere around these two futile dolls!' She is also limited by her biological weakness: she is a sexual trap for Tarr, the victim of Kreisler's passion and recipient of his seed. She is a creature of illusion, who comforts herself with mementoes. Time-bound, she is deathly and surrounded by dead objects. Her romanticism is contrasted with Tarr's determination to treat her as an object. Even her fleshiness seems dead to him:

> He drew her ungraciously and roughly into his arms, and started kissing her mouth with a machine action. Docilely she covered him with her inertia. He was supposed to be performing a miracle of bringing the dead to life.

The portrait of Bertha is external but not wholly negative. Her attractions are real, and Tarr's conflict is conveyed by a vivid image of dismemberment. Bertha's love has penetrated him, and he feels his blood flowing out as they part. Though utterly conventional, she is not calculating, and her kindness to Kreisler is rewarded by rape. After the attack the narrative contrasts the workings of her mind, as she tries to reconcile her romantic assumptions with the reality of Kreisler's indifference. This ironic effect is clinched by his hypocritical apology. He convinces her that some spiritual good has resulted for him, and converts her depression into exaltation by cynically trading on her penchant for self-immolation.

In *The Art of Being Ruled* (1926), Lewis developed the opposition of male and female, art and life. The adjectives 'feminine' and 'womanly' represent the 'ordinary' level of human development which the person who wishes to be truly individual (and thus an artist or ruler) must surpass: 'the masculine is not the natural human state, but a carefully nurtured secondary development above the normal and womanly.' Lewis's ideal ruler is identical to the artist in his labouring, aspiring, lonely existence: 'The ruler must be completely disillusioned—a suspicion of belief and he would be lost.' Only females (of both sexes) believe in the values of their culture. Lewis does not say that women may not be artists, but insists that artists must be 'male' in character and mode of life. Early in the novel Tarr says to Butcher that he does not see the point of 'an exceptional woman, a particularly refined and witty animal'. Anastasya is such a person, and she seems a perfect mate for Tarr. Intellectual and independent, she summarizes Tarr's sexual problems in her witty complaints about the prison of the body. But in his internal debate he rejects her as too male. 'God was man; the woman was a lower form of life.' Anastasya has crossed the line. Thus Lewis dismisses the possibility that Tarr's conflict can be resolved by a Lawrentian truce or transcendence of the sexes. At this point in his career Lewis was content to argue that sex belongs on a lower plane of being than the intellect, and that is the only place where it can be enjoyed. The intellectual goes slumming for sex.

No true resolution can emerge, because Tarr and Kreisler have opposite destinies which both preclude women. Kreisler is destroyed by passion; Tarr's absurd marriage keeps him aloof from both women. He remains detached, finding a temporary solution in a supply of accommodating women. Lewis seems intent on positing persistently and completely, the view of women expressed in his portrait of Bertha. He never really gave up this view: that women are time-bound, earthy, infinitely desirable yet destructive of creativity. Lewis asserts that male and female interests are completely opposed: woman is an erotic object who can only distract and degrade the artist. A woman who is clever and creative is simply male, not woman at all. In *Tarr* a woman is raped, illegitimate children are dismissed with a shrug, and the novel ends with a marriage that mocks the conventional happy ending. Bertha escapes, but other women in Lewis's novels never live happily. In later novels Lewis allowed himself to see the psychological cost of being a companion to the Enemy.

(ii)

Despite the gap of nearly twenty years between *Tarr* and *The Revenge for Love* there is considerable continuity in the characters and theme. In the later novel there are again two male characters who represent two radically different modes of life. Lewis returns to the theme of art and women, and dramatizes the struggle to create art in an alien social context, where art and women are seductive and threatening, demanding devotion and creating obligation. But the interplay between the two *personae* is more complex than in *Tarr*.

Lewis distinguishes the two male figures more sharply and emphasizes their differences by the use of two narrative styles. Percy Hardcaster, the elder man, is a dedicated Communist activist who has severed his working-class ties and prides himself on a cynical, unsentimental posture. He has contempt for all truth and idealism, and bases his actions on pragmatic considerations. We first meet him in a Spanish prison, where he reveals his isolation and strength of character. Though his first name suggests his attitudes are close to the author's (Hardcaster suggests Lewis's fondness for the 'carapace'), Lewis's tone is mocking when he narrates Percy's actions and conversations. As he lies wounded he vows to return to his mother in a suburb of Birmingham; secure in hospital, he resumes his contemptuous attitude to ordinary people, and affects to despise the nuns because their humane feelings keep the otherwise threadbare fabric of society together. Percy is honest enough to acknowledge to himself, and later to Jill, the uneven mixture of idealism and expediency in his political activity. The authorial tone is close to Percy's tone of voice, hard and impatient with cant, but it relaxes when the subject is Margot and Victor Stamp. The narrative comment on them is not used to underline their defects, but to define their feelings and ideas; it may be severe on their limitations, but the result is poignant rather than satiric.

In contrast to Percy, Victor is a young aspiring artist, dependent on the love of a woman and responsible for her, completely apolitical. They both lack faith in the future: Percy because experience has made him cynical, Victor because he does not believe in his own talents nor see the function they serve. There are still some traces of the Tarr-Kreisler opposition in these two: Percy is the cold, ruthless despiser of mankind, Victor the second-rate, doomed, would-be artist who needs a woman to love him. In *Tarr* the atmosphere is said to be hostile to the artist but is in fact merely bourgeois and stupid; in *Revenge for Love* Victor and Margot tragically cherish one another, surrounded by truly evil characters. Margot is supportive and self-sacrificial, not simply masochistic, like Bertha. Lewis uses her as the emotional and ideological centre of the novel, reflecting the other characters and articulating the theme. A suffering, asexual heroine, with a symbolic role to play in the artist's struggle to create art and meaning from experience, she is first an ally and finally a victim.

Tarr's idea that woman's love degrades the artist remains in Margot's assumption that her love spells doom for Victor. But the novel takes love seriously, and suggests that, like art, it demands loyalty and dedication. Margot's love encourages Victor to continue painting. The doom she intuits is the revenge for *art* as well. Lewis suggests that both love and art are instinctive and spiritual. Victor's loyalty to Margot is a 'rugged unrevolutionary principle', 'a pact of nature'. Their love is 'elemental': it opposes the Communists in the novel, who want to destroy society, and the capitalist dealers in arms and art, who reduce men to machines. Victor is not a thwarted genius, nor is Margot beautiful and brilliant: he is second-rate and she is a 'frail contraption' without money or brains. Victor's attempts to paint parallel Margot's faithful love; both love and art demand endless effort. Their commonplace qualities suggest that the power and interest of the novel lie not in the characters but in the ideas they represent. Through their destruction Lewis expresses his disgust with society and his pessimism about the two major political systems. The conclusion links all three protagonists: Percy becomes fond of them, tries to save them, is trapped by his own 'weakness' and sees their deaths as a tragic waste.

Lewis describes the setting of Victor and Margot's flat so

minutely and expresses the essentials of their characters so incisively that we feel he is writing about intensely felt experience. The clashing bedsprings, the wash in the kitchen sink, the strong tea with nothing to eat in the cramped flat, and the arrival of two letters (one announcing the return of unsold pictures, the other a bill for framing them), explain Victor's feelings about the futility of painting. He is nagged by a sense of passing time; he fears failure; he accuses Margot of wanting him to fail; she weeps. He feels he must create 'even if only in the void and in a blind spin, and to no useful purpose'. With no intellectual or artistic support, tricked by his own desire to paint, he 'returns to his vomit'. Like Kreisler he is a foreigner and an outsider; his Australian background emphasizes his remoteness from significant European culture. Like Tarr, Victor sees painting as a 'to be or not to be wager'; while painting that morning, 'he had been tossing red blocks with the Devil for his life'. He knows that he cannot win the game, since no one has any use for his paintings.

Margot is at the centre of Victor's paradoxical situation: she is at once a stimulus to art and a responsibility which forces him to earn money. She thinks her love is to blame for his misfortunes and that he is a marked man. Later Abershaw repeats this when he says it is 'a tragedy when a woman has too high an opinion of her husband', and the plot fulfils this prediction when her interference leads to their deaths. But she is also the chief vehicle of expression in the novel. Although Part Two is entitled 'Victor Stamp' we see him first through her anxious eyes, and most events are recorded through her suffering consciousness. Her inarticulate mind contrasts with the sophisticated comments of the narrator. After probing Margot's thoughts as she wakes up beside Victor, the narrator comments on the banality of her ideas: 'the Journey's End effect' of her fantasy suicide. But this detail of her inner life characterizes her capacity for emotional development. She rejects suicide, but finds pathetic comfort in fantasy. The cynical narrator's ironic tone dignifies, rather than diminishes, Margot's despair.

In contrast to the other characters, who express the fixed attitudes of automata, Margot is a detailed portrait of someone in the process of developing a greater understanding of her life.

She has dragged herself out of squalor and ignorance by her own efforts, and she acts with passionate commitment. In contrast to Gillian, she is nervous and insecure and lives in a 'painfully constructed pagoda of gentility': an image that suggests the fragile artificiality of her dress and accent. Lewis gets maximum ironic effect out of Margot's doll-like femininity, for he uses her as a powerful force of goodness, loyalty and truth which is opposed to nearly all the other characters. She is able to see through the Communists at O'Hara's party because she is of working-class origin herself. She weighs in her mind their revolutionary doctrine and their actual contempt for the poor. But, the narrator adds, these thoughts were 'transacted upon the plane of emotion, where words were all mixed up with images'. Margot is an ignorant woman, and thus says and thinks things which the narrator cannot.

The strength of her love gives her power and insight into the destructiveness and falsity of the people surrounding them. Her loyalty is strongly contrasted with Gillian's promiscuity. She hates Pete and Tristy's talk because she feels they destroy Victor's hope: 'everything they said bore upon the fact that in the modern world—that meant this tragic scene upon which she and Victor lived and suffered—there was no place for the artist, no place at all'. She observes Abershaw and O'Hara with Victor's forged signature behind the false wall and confronts them. Abershaw is 'an evil-looking shadow', a 'gutta-percha pretence', an automaton. At the party her sense of reality is most threatened, and she clings to Victor's arm for physical confirmation that they are themselves real. The phoniness and hypocrisy of the other characters are further underlined by two major scenes that follow: the discussion about political lying between Jill and Percy, and the scene at the forgery workshop.

Margot is a Dickensian heroine: like Little Dorrit, a child who must protect her helpless parent, the ultra-feminine Margot is forced to play a male role. Much emphasis is laid on her maternal protectiveness as she gets food for Victor and argues fiercely on his behalf. In Spain she feels the ground give way, as at the party, and her maternal passion turns to hysteria in the dwarf episode. The dwarf blubbers comically and pretends Margot is his mother. Margot's hysterical fear results in a fixed grimace which

makes her appear 'an evil madonna'. The dwarf's pretence corre-
sponds to a nightmare fantasy that she and Victor have produced
a baby, 'a crooked monstrosity'. This scene underlines Margot's
awareness and Victor's ignorance and passivity, as he observes
her cracking up under the strain of anxiety. It also suggests
(oddly, for Lewis) the injustice of her frustrated maternity.

Margot's reading of *Sesame and Lilies*, which immediately
follows, acts as a gloss on this curious scene. Ruskin, 'that high
priest of the natural order', discusses what woman's ideal role
ought to be. He argues that women are different from, not slaves
to, men. Their territory is the home and their function is to
provide wisdom and serenity for their menfolk, who go out into
the world. He adduces evidence from Shakespeare to assert the
noble and heroic capacities of women. Margot begins by quarrel-
ling with Ruskin's view of nature: 'the deep and sacred sensations
of natural scenery' seem now to be 'the malevolence of these
great blocks of awful matter'. She finds Ruskin's summary of the
heroic wisdom of women in literature depressing, because it con-
stitutes 'a sweeping belittlement of the male'. Ruskin says of
Shakespeare: 'The catastrophe . . . is caused always by the folly
or fault of a man; the redemption, if there be any, is by the
wisdom and virtue of a woman.' Lewis's plot follows this pattern,
as Victor becomes a puppet; and Margot strains every nerve to
'see', debating art and politics with Hardcaster: 'It was not easy
for her to play this part, and to come out as the opposite number
to the masterful male.'

She becomes Victor's good angel, battling against the forces of
evil. She is also his Muse, asserting 'My politics are art'; when
she intercepts him on the road, she recalls him to his true role in
life: 'It is all right for Percy Hardcaster . . . it's his business.
It isn't yours. You are an artist, Victor.' Though Margot aban-
dons Ruskin by the stream, she follows his pattern of wifely
devotion and wisdom. But the time is out of joint: Victor's work
has no social function and Margot has no home or children (she
is not even married). Victor becomes a mechanical man, driving
fast and bruising her 'in the savage onrush of the machine'.
Margot's consciousness is identified with the narrator as she calls
Victor a 'symbolic man', irrelevant to modern society.

The Revenge for Love pursues a completely different line of thought from *Tarr*. Lewis argues in *Tarr* that the family is an absurdity and women should be purely erotic objects; in *The Revenge for Love* he uses a noble heroine to demonstrate the breakdown of the old order and its tragic consequences for the artist. It is a powerful novel, with an elegant form and coherent pattern which make its political statement clear; but the relationship between Margot and Victor is not as fresh and true to Lewis's experience as the sexual relationships in *Tarr* and *Self Condemned*.

(iii)

Hester Harding, the heroine of Lewis's last novel, *Self Condemned*, begins as a satiric erotic figure, like Bertha. But she develops Margot's capacity for loyalty and self-sacrifice. René combines the analytical intelligence and superior attitude of Tarr and Hardcaster with Kreisler and Victor's poverty and failure. By concentrating on one man and woman who act out their conflict and articulate their pain, Lewis makes the theme more poignant. René Harding expresses the artist's conflict between his sensual and rational nature, his desire for ordinary life and his need for isolation. He also represents the dilemma of the artist-intellectual whose ability to see the absurdity of life, its illusions and conventions, robs him of the capacity to create. René's failure to resolve these conflicts leads to a tragic conclusion.

René is a Nietzschean protagonist, proud of his intellect and disgusted with ordinary life. He is sexually attracted to Hester, but intellectually aloof from her. He decides to go to Canada without consulting her, and makes up their quarrels by bedding her. Afterwards he feels mortified by his need and enjoyment of sex. Their sexual experience in London is not a bond, since René repudiates it as soon as the last spasm is over, and Hester uses it to get a new dress. This is a portrait of a marriage dominated by René's Tarr-like attitude—each partner is debased by the union. Hester resents her role as bird-brain while René believes she degrades his self-image; her attractiveness to other men makes his conflict even worse. She is 'an ill-conceived figure on the reverse side of a spendidly-designed coin', 'a sandwich-woman of his Achilles heel', 'a frightful reflection of himself, the image of his lubricity'. On the ship he observes her striking poses as she tries on clothes; to him she seems vain and silly, and their isolation intensifies his sense of degradation: 'Hester's obscene person must henceforth be his Muse, in succession to History. He was going to Canada in order to fornicate with Hester. What else!' Like Margot, Hester is an ironic Muse, for her love allows René the possibility of redemption, which he rejects.

Lewis explains Rene's conviction that sex is absurd and degrading by describing his feelings about parenthood. According to René, maternity is a bond, although exaggerated and sentimental, while paternity scarcely exists. All that remains of his father's influence on himself is his name; he dissociates himself firmly from the dull solicitor and says a final farewell to the old French lady. He believes that a husband who has deserted his young wife and infant has acted rightly, since he has refused 'to help her to perpetuate her unlovely self'. In his view only the mother is reproduced: thus René robs the sexual act, from a male point of view, of the dignity of a biological function. The scenes of parting from his mother and sisters relate René's repressed emotions to his intellectual drive. He approaches personal ties with the same analytic reductionism with which he writes history. Like Tarr, he deliberately divides his personality, suppresses the emotional side, and reduces his human relationships to the animal level. When he leaves England, only his relationship with Hester remains.

René is driven by intellectual passion to abandon his family, his job, his culture and his readers. He rejects his family's commonsensical response to his decision to leave, and says to Helen: 'the fact that Canada is four-fifths an authentic wilderness does not matter. It would be the same emptiness anywhere. The same ghastly void, next door to nothingness.' He retreats from Europe, which is about to plunge into war, because he sees its true horror with unendurable clarity. During his sojourn, a deliberately ascetic self-isolation, without the props of familiar culture, comforts and status, he searches for a coherent vision of life which will allow him to re-possess his soul after the unclean compromise of his life in London.

Hester's role in this scenario is crucial. She watches him 'as animals watch each other with sullen reserve in cages'. She continues to be, as Zarathustra says, the recreation of the warrior, a comfort René does not give up. But in 'The Room' she becomes more than a sexual partner, and accompanies him in his 'apprenticeship to death'. They are 'two inmates of this lethal chamber', an image which suggests the extermination camps. Their physical restrictions bring about a greater emotional interdependence. One of the novel's great achievements is the depiction of the ebb and flow of a long-term marriage. René, like Tarr, struggles between despising the world and craving recognition, while Hester dreams of nothing more than old friends and familiar surroundings. The details of poverty: Hester's lack of shoes, her anxiety over a few cents when shopping, contrast with her pride as she pins on René's decoration as they prepare to go out to dinner. Her loyalty and endurance, and René's barren life, lead to a deeper commitment to each other which transforms their relationship and enables René to acknowledge Hester's value.

But the fire destroys their intimacy, and René resolves never to be a victim of exile and penury again. He decides to re-enter the world, and solve his intellectual dilemmas without delay. He returns to his old problem of whether human life has any meaning, of whether it is possible 'to find anything of value intact and undiluted in the vortex of slush and nonsense: to discover any foothold (however small) in the phenomenal chaos, for the ambitious mind: enough that is uncontaminated to make it worthwhile to worry about life at all'. History is as futile as our daily lives. He grapples with 'the permanent instability of antinomy', the conflict between the higher and lower planes of being: between the mind's aspiration and the body's prison. For a solution he goes over to the party of Superman: if life is ridiculous, then we must breed a better race to deal with it. René loses the opportunity of integrating his new-found humility and emotional truth into his view of man's potentiality. Ironically, his evasive theorizing makes him more, not less, mechanical. He advocates 'the acceptance of a solution which formerly he would have refused. His life altogether was being mechanized upon a lower level—in everything expediency counted more with him'. His thinking has 'an insidious softening of the core' and his new book lacks integrity and belief.

Ostensibly, Hester kills herself rather than live in Canada with the new-old René, but her death also symbolizes the sacrifice of the affective capacity to the rational. After the fire, she wants to return to London more than ever and René tries to console her by his old methods—'amorous treatment, rigorously administered' —but she is not convinced. She refuses to live with him in his new incarnation as Superman, knowing instinctively that René's intellectual pride denies all she has to offer. Her death under a truck recalls Margot's bruising in the speeding car: they are both victims of the machine. As Victor allows himself to be a puppet, so René makes himself into a machine to try to escape the pain of grief and self-knowledge. His angry response to Hester's death is ironically irrational, the consequence of his repressed emotions.

The last pages of the novel delineate the consequences of René's rejection of all illusions. His 'furious analysis' disintegrates relationships and attitudes which are emotionally sustaining; once he has emptied his personality of illusion, a shell remains. He looks back at his career and realizes that in 1939 he had the chance to 'reflower or degenerate'. The loss of his family, his culture and his wife all damage his capacity to create, and turn him into an automaton. At the end of Lewis's winter's tale René becomes frozen, a statue that will not come to life.

Self Condemned is a retrospective novel which orders experience into a symbolic pattern of the artist's life. But the pattern reveals that Lewis returns to the ideas of *Tarr* rather than those of *The Revenge for Love*. In *Blast* 1 Lewis wrote boastfully that the artist finds material for art from within himself: 'he has to draw out of himself . . . that richness and fineness that is something more and different to the provender and contentment of the cow'. Tarr claims that he is the only begetter of his personality as well as of his work. Lewis's original conception of the artist depends on belief in his omniscient and omnipotent ego. René's life reveals the folly of founding one's sense of reality, of generating belief only in oneself. He discovers the hell that results from living for the sake of self-creation. The novel discredits Tarr's egotistic principles, but René's attempt has tragic dignity: he suffers a self-induced curtailment far worse than the lapse into 'mechanism' that he feared. Lewis shows how, if René is self condemned, Hester is also condemned by his attitudes and way of life. She is a Bertha re-examined and re-valued. Like Bertha, she is first cast as the villain because she is implicated in all that makes man mechanical: sex and domestic life. But Hester endures the strain of isolation with René, without his rewards of creativity, achievement and status. For a brief moment René rewards her for helping to make life bearable; when he goes back to intellectual arrogance and emotional aridity, life becomes finally unbearable for her. In contrast to Tarr's dictum that woman is suicide for the artist, the novel shows how that artist means suicide for the woman. *Self Condemned* carries Lewis's discussion of the relationship between the sexes beyond the dandy aesthetics of *Tarr* and the Victorian assumptions questioned in *The Revenge for Love*, to show how destructive the creative ego can be, how it tempts the artist to be inhuman.

17

Self Condemned

JEFFREY MEYERS

Some say the world will end in fire,
Some say in ice.
From what I've tasted of desire
I hold with those who favor fire.

But if it had to perish twice,
I think I know enough of hate
To say that for destruction ice
Is also great
And would suffice.

Robert Frost, 'Fire and Ice'

Lewis's greatest novel, which Eliot called 'a book of almost unbearable spiritual agony', was begun in Canada, where Lewis collected local newspaper clippings, lists of Canadian idioms and slang, and extensive material about the individual characters. Lewis showed Tambimuttu a *précis* of 'Château Rex' (as it was then called) just after the War, and wrote the book in the early fifties, after he became blind. In November 1952 he told Henry Regnery that his next work would be a novel called 'You are perhaps a fool, my son' (these words, spoken by Harding's mother, became the title of the second chapter), about the strange life of an *émigré* in Canada. And in February 1954, two months before the novel appeared, Marshall McLuhan, who observed that Lewis was the first writer to give serious treatment to any aspect of Canada, reported that Toronto had been alerted and begun to tremble. *Self Condemned*, which became Lewis's most successful book and sold 7000 copies in the first two years, took Toronto off the map.

Almost all of Lewis's previous novels had been compromised

by subjection to a preconceived theory. *Self Condemned*, by contrast, was not jagged and objective like *Tarr*, abstract and fantastic like *The Childermass*, external and mannered like *The Apes of God*, hard and mechanical like *Snooty Baronet*, didactic like *The Vulgar Streak*, ideological like *The Red Priest*. In *Self Condemned*, even more than in *The Revenge for Love*, Lewis abandoned theory and experiment, and returned to a realistic psychological novel that was analogous to his defiant and revealing self-portraits. Unlike *Tarr* and *The Revenge for Love*, where the characters who represent aspects of Lewis are split into Tarr and Kreisler, Stamp and Hardcaster, Lewis's intellect and emotions are concentrated and intensified in René Harding. It is difficult to agree with two of Lewis's best critics who have stated that *Self Condemned* does not accurately reflect the reality of Lewis's life in Toronto.[1] For Lewis's finest novel remains extraordinarily close to his personal experience, and gains enormous power by the self-lacerating exposure of his most intimate feelings and deepest suffering. Yet Lewis also maintained the requisite aesthetic distance, which allowed him to create a novel that transcended the barren and scarifying years in Toronto.

Though Lewis does not mention blindness in *Self Condemned*, the recurrent visual imagery makes it a central metaphor of the novel. For Harding, like Lewis, moves blindly out of England without ever clearly explaining why he left and emigrates to Canada without any realistic sense of what he will find there. Harding's analysis of the transition to the Canadian darkness applies with equal force to the terrible test of blindness which would either destroy or renew Lewis's courage and creative existence: 'Either the life he was now to enter was an empty interlude, an apprenticeship to death: or it was a breathing-space, a period of readjustment, preceding the acceptance of a much simpler type of existence for Hester and himself.' Harding's life in the hotel, like Lewis's isolation in his Notting Hill flat, 'stank of exile, penury and confinement'. Canada, with its bursting violent light, 'is no land for those with delicate eyes'; and Cedric Furber expresses his authority as well as his insensitivity by forcing Harding to face the glaring daylight till his eyes ache. Harding opposes the symbolic darkness of Canada with the same stoicism that Lewis summoned to face the functional darkness;

and while Lewis saw the 'Sea-Mists of the Winter' overwhelming his vision, Harding exclaims: 'I see a fiery mist wherever I direct my eyes. But the fire is not outside me, the fire is in my brain.' Lewis also makes poignant allusions to the tumour, 'a hot devouring something inside my skull', which caused blindness by pressing on his optic nerves and led to intense drowsiness. In Toronto: 'his personality had suffered profoundly. All freedom depended upon consciousness: but now, at times, he felt his brain clouding and blurring. His daily periods of semi-consciousness increased.'[2] These passages, like numerous others in the novel, achieve a profounder dimension of pathos and meaning by illuminating both Lewis's life and his art.

The opening section of the novel, an extensive prelude that occupies forty percent of the work, has been criticized for its slow-moving discursiveness. But like the static overtures to *Remembrance of Things Past* and *Joseph and His Brothers*, the prelude repays patience, admirably fulfils its function and grinds forward 'with the inevitability of a glacier'. The first part of the novel, which attempts to explain and justify Lewis's as well as Harding's reasons for leaving England in 1939, is emotionally but not intellectually convincing. For Harding, whose rational premises are mistaken, deliberately drives himself to ruin. As Lewis says of Vincent Penhale in *The Vulgar Streak*: 'This was a cell of his own making: full of cold, hard, sunlight, like a symbol of his mind.'

Harding's *Secret History of World War Two*, which led the *Times* to call him 'fascist-minded', is similar to Lewis's 'peace pamphlets' of the mid-thirties—*Left Wings Over Europe* and *Count Your Dead: They Are Alive!*—which anticipated and rather ineptly tried to prevent the coming war, stigmatized him as a Fascist sympathizer, encouraged his exile and made him abandon political writing. Harding's most impressive intellectual quality, like Lewis's, is a power of analysis so penetrating that nothing can withstand its intense and ultimately destructive scrutiny: 'The process of radical revaluation, the process which was responsible for the revolutionary character of his work, that analysis, turned inwards (upon, for instance, such things as the intimate structure of domestic life), this furious analysis began disintegrating many relationships and attitudes which only an exceptionally creative spirit, under very favourable conditions, can afford to dispense with.' Harding, like Lewis, is extremely idealistic but also 'carries a sceptic on his back'. He has repudiated the intellectual attitudes of his time and feels ostracized by his professional colleagues and rivals. He came to believe that history was not worth recording because it did not reveal man's passion for sanity, decency and morality but was, in fact, 'the bloody catalogue of their backslidings'. Perhaps the most forceful reason for abandoning his profession is Harding's confession: 'Through looking too hard at the material I was working on, I saw the maggots in it, I saw the rottenness, the fatal flaws; had to stop earning my living that way.'

The prelude is also a recapitulation of Lewis's pre-war life. Harding's French Catholic mother, with whom he shares an extraordinary sense of identity, recalls Lewis's paternal grandmother, Caroline Romaine, his Catholic mother, his own baptism in Montreal and his quest for the origins of his family that influenced the return to the land of his birth. Harding's visit to Rugby recalls Lewis's years at that public school when the young American boy consciously assumed the lifelong role of Outsider and chose the vocation of an artist.

Two of Lewis's friends also appear in the prelude. Harding's brother-in-law, Percy Lamport, who has rimless glasses and a light-brown thatch of hair, and is a wealthy collector of paintings, with a chauffeur and limousine, is based on Lewis's patron and friend, Sir Nicholas Waterhouse. Lamport alone recognizes and approves of Harding's self-destructive idealism, and generously offers to lend him £1000 to sustain him after the resignation. Harding's disciple 'Rotter' Parkinson, who has written a long essay on his Master's life and work, is modelled on Hugh Gordon Porteus, who wrote the first serious study of Lewis in 1932 and sometimes aroused Lewis's wrath. As Harding leaves Parkinson's flat after listening to him read his article: 'His critical frenzy had one of its regular spasms. He tore his best friend to pieces and himself as well; so much devotion was embarrassing; how could one really feel at ease with a parasite, and with what ridiculous assiduity he had encouraged this man to feed upon his brain. He went round there perhaps once a month to be milked, as it were.'[3] (The metaphor for their intellectual friendship ironically paraphrases Tarr's sensual relationship with Bertha: 'some such soothing milking process that nature wished him to have in place of passion'.)

Finally, the relationship of Harding and Hester, clearly based on Lewis's marriage, is solidly established in the prelude before being tested and destroyed in the Canadian crucible. Though Lewis wittily wrote in *The Art of Being Ruled*: 'Most people's favourite spot in "nature" is to be found in the body of another person', Harding (who has an abnormal sexual appetite) has an intellectual suspicion of the Yahooesque panting and grunting between the sheets. He sees Hester as an abstract woman and live pin-up, and never learns that she is a human being whose desires and needs are independent of his own. When he resists Hester's sensuality, the basis of their marriage, and she can no longer reach him on the physical level, their passionate solidarity begins to crumble and they start to watch each other with the sullen reserve of caged animals.

Like *Anna Karenina*, another novel of an outcast couple whose love cannot withstand the torments of almost universal opposition, the end of *Self Condemned* is foreshadowed in the beginning. The allusion to the suicide of Hyacinth Robinson in James's *The Princess Casamassima*, the moving reference to the anti-Nazi exiles—Ernst Toller and Stefan Zweig—who killed themselves after escaping to New York and Rio, the dangerous leap of Harding's sister from a moving train, Harding's fears that Hester might leave him, and Hester's threat: 'I would throw myself out of that window if I knew that my death would result in your returning to England, and that nothing else would do so'—all these dark warnings anticipate Hester's doom with the prophetic force of a classical tragedy.

Once Harding leaves England the novel follows actual events very closely. They refuse to sail on the *Athenia* and later hear that it has been torpedoed only one hundred miles from their own ship. War is announced while they are crossing the Atlantic, and to avoid submarines they zig-zag to the north, bound for Greenland. Though Lewis met Charles Abbott, who invited him to paint the Chancellor of Buffalo University, before leaving England, he appears aboard ship as the rather foolish and pompous Dr Lincoln Abbott, President of the University of Rome, in

Arkansas, and a great admirer of Harding's books. (Harding's disagreeable moustachioed London landlady is also called Mrs Abbott.)

Momaco, devoid of all character and charm, a living death from which no speck of civilized life could ever come, is a variant of Mimico, a suburb southwest of Toronto on Lake Ontario: 'The place was the grave of a great career: the barren spot where you ceased to think, to teach, or to write, and just rotted away.' The timorous academics at the University, who were anti-English, 'passionately held down their jobs and closed their ranks against the stranger of renown'. Harding, like Lewis, is cut off from all money in England, has to buy copies of his own books from second-hand dealers, becomes a columnist on the *Momaco Gazette-Herald* (i.e. *Saturday Night*), writes with a pad on his knee and drops the pages on the floor. He also receives a cascade of registered letters from 'someone in Vancouver' (David Kahma), who makes glittering promises of a university position and invites him to stay at his 'properties'.

Apartment 27A of the Blundell Hotel (their Notting Hill flat was 29A) was of course the Tudor Hotel, which also had an annex and a 'Beverage Room' (the Sahara Room) and became for Lewis the violent microcosm of the outside world. In that in-human void, nothing could be done 'except wait for the mail, which always brought discouraging news, or listen to the radio, which droned on in its senseless ritual, or write something which might never see the light'.[4] In *Blast 2* Lewis had explained why he could not create in such a deadening atmosphere: 'To produce the best pictures or books it is possible to make, a man requires all the peace and continuity that can be obtained in this troubled world.' Though Lewis seems to be exaggerating when he writes that a splinter of ice 'pierced a boy's eye and blinded him outside the Blundell Hotel', he reported to Nicholas Waterhouse in January 1943: 'The other day a man was killed [by an icicle], it shot down and pierced his skull.'[5] The cold penetrated the body like radium and temperatures often fell to 30 degrees below zero.

Lewis's Canadian patrons and friends also appear thinly disguised in his novels. In *The Vulgar Streak*, Lewis alludes to the meat magnate Stanley McLean when a letter from Vincent's well-married sister in Vancouver mentions a glamorous social event where she met Bob Brabazon, 'President of the Western Canada Canners Co.'. The wealthy book collector Cedric Furber —whose name is a variant of Cedric Foster, an American news broadcaster whom Lewis particularly disliked—is bearded like Lytton Strachey but based on the tall, affected homosexual Douglas Duncan. Like Duncan, Furber, 'a rich bachelor of forty, was very old-maidish and strict'. He was also saturnine, taciturn, superior and a barbarous snob. Though Furber generously gives Harding a monthly retainer to keep him from starvation, Harding (like Lewis) finds it difficult to feel gratitude. Duncan, like Sydney Schiff in *The Apes of God*, was pilloried for his callous kindness.[6] One of the few sympathetic Canadian characters, Professor Ian McKenzie, 'a smiling Scottish sophist of about forty-five with a faint and pleasing accent . . . a man of his own kind', was probably a composite of Marshall McLuhan, the painter Alex Jackson, and John Burgess, a chemist with strong philosophical and religious interests who offered Lewis 'some financial assistance as well as the pleasure of civilised conversation.'

'The Hotel, first and last, is the central feature of the book', Lewis told Michael Ayrton, who illustrated the fire on the dust jacket of the novel, 'and the death of the hotel gives you flames and ice, smoke, and ruin.' The fictional fire (foreshadowed when the continental crowds poured out of the train, 'like people making a frenzied exit from a building which was on fire', and on to the last boat out of Europe) was based on an actual conflagration that burned down the Tudor Hotel on 15 February 1943. The *Toronto Star* reported that Lewis had lost many manuscripts and in the novel Harding is unable to reach the furnace room where his papers are stored in a suitcase. In the Tudor fire Effie, the manager of the hotel and friend of Lewis, was asphyxiated by the smoke. In the Blundell fire, Mrs McAffie is also a sympathetic character: 'They developed an affection for this flying wraith, with the faintly rouged cheeks, who dashed, flew and darted everywhere, as though she desired to get rid of every remaining piece of flesh on her bones. She was tall and still enjoyed, in the manner of an afterglow, a vanished grace.' But in the novel 'Affie' is murdered by Mr Martin, the owner of the hotel, when she discovers him committing arson. Lewis named this arsonist-murderer, who was responsible for the deaths of fifteen people and was soon apprehended and hanged, after Paul Martin, the Windsor lawyer whom he quarrelled with in 1945 about payment for the portrait of Martin's wife, Eleanor. After the fire, the Lewises moved to the Selby Hotel just as the Hardings moved to the Laurenty.

Lewis's account of the fire, one of the most vivid scenes in the novel, was inspired by Dante's description of fire and ice in the frozen Lake of Cocytus, which holds the souls of traitors in the Tenth Circle of Hell:

> I turned and saw, stretched out before my face
> And 'neath my feet, a lake so bound with ice,
> It did not look like water but like glass. . . .
> Their heads were bowed toward the ice beneath,
> Their eyes attest their grief; their mouths proclaim
> The bitter airs that through the dungeon breathe. . . .
> Their eyes, which were but inly wet till then,
> Gushed at the lids; at once the fierce frost blocked
> The tears between and sealed them shut again.

The apocalyptic extinction of the hotel reinforces Harding's hellish suffering in that cursed place. At the very end of the novel, when he becomes 'a glacial shell of a man', he resembles the frozen cave of the burnt-out hotel:

The noise, the glare, the clouds of smoke, the roaring and crackling of the flames, this great traditional spectacle only appealed to him for a moment. But he could not help being amazed at the spectral monster which had been there for so long, and what it was turning into. It was a flaming spectre, a fiery iceberg. Its sides, where there were no flames, were now a solid mass of ice. The water of the hoses had turned to ice as it ran down the walls, and had created an icy armour many feet in thickness.[7]

Just as 'the destruction of the hotel by fire divided their life at Momaco into two dissimilar halves', so Lewis, four months after the fire, began to teach at Assumption College in Windsor. Lewis was invited to join the faculty by Father J. Stanley Murphy just as Harding was by Father Moody, a cordial and rubicund young priest whose eyes blazed with childish benevolence. Assumption (directed by the Order of St Basil) is the College of the Sacred Heart (directed by the Order of St Maurice) in *Self Condemned*, a tranquil retreat with a genial atmosphere: 'This training-centre for the priesthood was a well-disciplined community, whose life moved hither and thither in response to quiet orders, or to a settled routine. It was an idyllically peaceful place for the victim of dynamic excess to go.' The priests hope for Harding's conversion, as they had hoped for Lewis's.

Father O'Shea, the head of the Philosophy Department, is modelled on Father Edwin Garvey. O'Neill, the 'handsome, sheepishly devout as well as competent, harmlessly sly' secretary, is based on Father Murphy's assistant, Joseph O'Connor. And the Irish poet Padraic O'Flaherty is Joyce's friend Padraic Colum, whom Lewis met at Windsor in March 1944. Harding gives six Extension Lectures just as Lewis gave the twelve Heywood Broun lectures in Windsor during November and December 1943 on 'The Concept of Liberty in America'. And Harding receives convalescent pay from the University of Momaco while teaching at the College of the Sacred Heart just as Lewis was presumably paid by Assumption when Father Murphy took over his classes, and he moved to St Louis from February to July 1943 to lecture and paint portraits. Harding resolves this conflict of interest by returning his fee to the Registrar of the College; Lewis could not afford this magnanimous gesture, though it is possible that he did not collect his salary for the months he was away.

Though Lewis hated Canada much more than his wife, Froanna, did, he reversed their attitudes in the novel where Hester 'entertains the most vicious feelings' about Canada. Lewis's wartime portraits (*The Artist's Wife*, 1940; *Reading the Newspaper*, 1944; *Portrait*, 1944) make Froanna appear depressed and introspective, and reflect his own gloomy emotions. Hester's breakdown and suicide are based on Froanna's breakdown and attempted suicide, just after Lewis went blind, in the summer of 1951. As Lewis suppressed his intimate feelings and rarely showed affection, so Harding deadens and desensitizes himself and tries to ignore the 'Hesteria', ironically induced by the offer of a professorship at the University of Momaco, and her last desperate attempt to force him to return to England: 'Hester, whose face had been convulsing itself in a tragic mask, released, with a sort of howl, a torrent of tears ... an obstreperous cataract of grief.'

Lewis once deleted a moving passage from *Self Condemned* after Froanna had praised it; and when he asked her: 'What shall I do with Hester?' she replied: 'Bump her off'—and he did.[8] Margot Stamp in *The Revenge for Love*, who was willing to undergo slow destruction at her husband's side, had considered but rejected the suicide that Hester finally chose: 'The notion of death always— in spite of the fact that she saw it was quite impracticable for her —brought rest to her mind. For when she had first considered it —before she had realized the catch, from love's standpoint—it had deeply impressed her.' Like Vincent Penhale in *The Vulgar Streak*, Harding does not suspect the depth of his love for his wife or recognize the intensity of her suffering, until it is too late to help her. When Harding sees Hester on a slab in the morgue after she has thrown herself under a truck, her head, which had miraculously escaped destruction, seemed strangely detached from her body, as if to symbolize the separation of intellect and emotion in their marriage. Like the 'Dumb Ox' heroes of Hemingway, Hester represents the pathetic and 'passive little things to whom things are done'. Though Hester's death has a profound emotional effect on Harding—who retches, sobs and faints —he coldly condemns her suicide as a form of vengeance, an act of insane coercion, and refuses to be influenced by her sacrifice: 'My cold refusal to do what she wanted crazed her egoistic will. She was willing to die in order to force me off the path I had chosen. She probably thought, among other things, that her suicide would oblige me to give up my job at the University. She was acting vindictively.'[9]

When Harding resigned his position in England he had an intellectual crisis, saw the gulf between 'history' and reality, rejected the comfortable assumptions of society and the compromising restrictions of ordinary existence, and gave in to a wilful impulse to destroy himself. Though cynical about the possibilities of exile, and stricken with sorrow and regret, he never imagined that he would be struck down, humiliated, driven into the wilderness. When Harding recognized that his life in Momaco had become an unbearable self-exile, he tried to integrate himself within society. The hotel fire revived his hopes through its cleansing destruction, and was followed by professorships at Momaco and the Sacred Heart. But he was never able to live entirely by will and intellect, and never reconciled the opposition of the rational and emotional, the icy and fiery aspects of his character and marriage. Harding was more of a Tarr than a Kreisler—a hard, objective man who attempted to isolate himself behind a suitcase and blanket in the hotel room so he would not be distracted by his wife. When Hester killed herself, he realized that he could never fill the dark and chilling void left by her death because she had supplied his affective life and her suicide had left him emotionally empty. He accepts a job at a pretentious American university and ironically ends, as he began, a successful and disillusioned professor of history: the benefactor and victim of his penetrating power of analysis.

Self Condemned portrays the reality of Lewis's failure and poverty in Toronto as well as the consequences of being a permanent and professional Enemy. His isolation and humiliation led to the characterization of Harding as a tragic, self-destructive figure—intellectual, remote, humourless, egoistic—who denies human feelings in his futile attempt to avoid suffering. The experience of Toronto gave Lewis the deepest insights into his own nature and enabled him to anatomize his emotional limitations. But he does not give Harding this insight and humility, and projects through him the consequences of severing vital connections with other people and maintaining a hostile attitude toward the world. *Self Condemned* is an intensely revealing and self-lacerating novel that penetrates the hard external carapace, exposes through Harding Lewis's own emotional disabilities, and pays tribute while it atones for his impossibly demanding and potentially destructive relationship with his wife.

Like *Women in Love*, *Self Condemned* concerns the devastating psychological effect of war on civilian life. Like Trilling's *The Middle of the Journey* (1947) and Mann's *Doctor Faustus* (1948), it is a tragedy of intellectual defeat. Like Lowry's *Under the Volcano* (1947), it portrays the self-destructive resistance to love, depicted in a harsh landscape that reflects and intensifies a moribund marriage. Though Harding became a glacial shell of a man, indistinguishable from his academic colleagues, Lewis survived the torments of Toronto and, despite his blindness, transfigured the suffering into his most powerful and profound work of art.[10]

18

The Human Age in Retrospect

D. G. BRIDSON

I have already told the story of how *The Human Age* came to be written.[1] But as the account is now hard to find, it might be worth summarizing it briefly again.

In 1951, Harman Grisewood's enlightened direction of the Third Programme made it possible for me to undertake the adaptation and production of a dramatized version of *The Childermass* for the B.B.C. The script of my adaptation was submitted to Lewis for his approval, which was immediately forthcoming. I discussed the casting of the production with him, and blind as he then was, he attended the final rehearsals. Thanks largely to a brilliant performance in the role of the Bailiff by Sir Donald Wolfit, the broadcast proved a notable success—not least of all with Lewis himself. As he wrote me shortly afterwards:

> The Childermass is the book I set most store by, and it was for me an almost miraculous event for it suddenly to spring into concrete life, with live actors bestowing upon it an almost startling physical reality, and a very able and ingenious living composer playing the bailiff's barge across the mournful river and jazzing the appellants into a bacchic dance. Sitting at your rehearsals I could hardly believe my ears.[2]

Since he had lost his sight, indeed, Lewis had begun listening to radio with a new interest, and the radio play began to have a meaning for him as a dramatic medium in its own right. For it is worth remembering that the first of his major creative writings to be published, the earlier version of *Enemy of the Stars*, was essentially dramatic in structure.

The critical acclaim which greeted *The Childermass* on the air was such that I had no difficulty in persuading the B.B.C. to offer Lewis a commission to complete the trilogy of which it had been advertised as the first part over twenty years before. The fee they offered would make it possible for him (after completing *Self Condemned*, on which he was then at work) to devote himself to writing the two missing novels over the course of the next couple of years. This was something which it had never proved economically possible for him to do before, and he immediately agreed to the plan. The B.B.C. was to have the right to broadcast adaptations of the novels before publication: thereafter, copyright in both the original novels and the adaptations reverted to Lewis. And by the time the entire trilogy had been heard for the third time in a year, Lewis had been well rewarded for radio's first pre-publication broadcast of a major work of fiction.

Lewis decided that the trilogy was to go by the name of *The Human Age*, and the task of adapting the two new novels was to be done by the two of us in collaboration. But this work did not begin until both *Monstre Gai* and *Malign Fiesta* had been completed as novels. A set of the galley-proofs was then made over to me, and I sketched out what had to be done. Briefly, this was a matter of writing additional scenes which would be necessary to bridge the gaps left by cutting such a lengthy work. The extra scenes were written for me along the lines that I had indicated, and the whole was trimmed down to the four and a half hours of air-time agreed upon. As *The Childermass* itself had run for an hour and a half, this added up to six hours of broadcasting overall. Nonetheless, it was decided to broadcast all three parts, with special introductory talks recorded by Professor I. A. Richards, T. S. Eliot and Graham Hough, in the course of a single week. The marathon was repeated two months later, and yet again towards the end of the year.

So *The Human Age* first reached the listener in May 1955, the two new parts of the trilogy being published that October. Re-publication of *The Childermass*, now described as *The Human Age, Book One*, followed in November 1956. As it transpired, *The Human Age* was not the best title for the trilogy Lewis could have chosen; and a fourth part had already been projected which, had he lived to write it, would have changed the import —and also the title—of the entire work. For as Professor Hugh Kenner explained in the second edition[3] of *Malign Fiesta*, it was Lewis's intention to call the fourth part *The Trial of Man*, and the idea he had in mind would have altered his whole original concept.

As we have it, *The Human Age* is obviously incomplete: it ends with a cliff hanger. Even so, it was not until *Monstre Gai* and *Malign Fiesta* had been set up in galley-proofs that Lewis clearly saw what he intended to do next. In the original version of *Malign Fiesta*, Pullman, who is admiring a Japanese peony grown by Satterthwaite, is squashed flat by the giant foot of a hurrying mile-high member of Sammael's dark-angelic army. And this, be it noted from the galley-proofs, not simply in the radio adaptation: such was to have been the ending of the novel itself. In the novel as finally published, on the other hand, it is merely the peony which gets flattened—and Pullman himself is escorted off to Heaven by a couple of White Angels, who assure him—as Mrs Lovett does Toby in *Sweeney Todd*—that no harm will come to him. But as those who heard *Malign Fiesta* on the air may remember, the dramatic climax of the broadcast required a body—so a body had to be provided. Only Lewis and I knew that the pulped mass of blood and bones described so graphically by the Narrator was really the body of Satterthwaite's friend the gardener's boy—and not Pullman at all. This little matter would have been cleared up, of course, at the start of *The Trial of Man*, if ever that work had been heard on the air. Like Sherlock Holmes at the Falls of Reichenbach, in fact, Pullman merely *seemed* to be obliterated. Of such devices are sequels and good radio drama made!

But it was some four and a half hours of listening and some 566 pages of reading before that point was reached, and there are many earlier problems that Pullman's adventures pose for us. In *Monstre Gai* we leave the eerie, moonlike landscape of *The Childermass* and follow him through the gate of the mysterious city he had seen from the Camp across the river. But the city is a very different place from what *The Childermass* had led us to expect. There, its profile had been awesome and other-worldly, 'Above the walls appears, naissant, armorial, and unreal, a high-hatched outcropping of huddled balconies, black rufous brown vermilion and white; the upper stages of wicker towers; helmet-like hoods of tinted stucco; tamarisks; the smaragdine and olive of tropical vegetations; tinselled banners; gigantic grey sea-green and speckled cones, rising like truncated eggs from a system of profuse nests.'[4] This Arabian Nights' vision, whose buttresses are topped and 'finned like the biretta of a Roman priest', is a fitting backdrop to the Court of the Bailiff, ringed with volcanic cones and sheltering behind its ridge of nummulitic limestone. But to attain that city, and enter by the tunnel through its magnetized walls, is to leave all such mirages behind. For Third City, when we enter it with Pullman and Satterthwaite, is very much a city of today—where nothing is strange and everything is depressingly ordinary. It is a place of modern city blocks, of avenues and piazzas and subways, where the population is not one of angels, as Pullman had supposed, but of all-too human pensioned imbeciles, 'whose faces were like the silly saints in the iconography of a Swabian half-wit'.[5] For Third City most certainly is not Heaven, as Pullman quickly realizes. Third City, in fact, is but a stage on the journey to Heaven or somewhere else. And despite the welfare handouts upon which all of its citizens thrive, it is hardly the sort of stage in which Pullman would have chosen to spend much time.

It is easy enough to see in Lewis's description of Third City, as does Professor Hugh Kenner, a skit on 'Mr. Attlee's England between 1952 and 1954', where the architectural and other banalities sprang from 'its creative orgasm the Festival of Britain at Battersea'.[6] It was a place which may have had its comforts (the service appeared to be notably better than that obtainable on Rotting Hill) but it was utterly without excellence. Its luxuries were either farcical or corrupt: if the latter, they had to be paid for in ways that were—to put it kindly—demeaning and dishonest. Pullman was not surprised to find that the whole place was run by the Bailiff as an exercise in city-government modelled not upon Attlee's England, but on the political machines of modern America. Even so, it was not very long before Pullman found himself on the Bailiff's payroll: he was far more susceptible to comfortable graft than he cared to admit to the only honest friend he made in Third City, the clubman Mannock.

Lewis himself was never a clubman. Put up for membership of the Athenaeum, he had been irritated (but hardly surprised) to find himself blackballed: there were far too many sensibilities that he had offended in such smug and comfortable circles. And the sarcastic picture he has drawn of the Cadogan Club in Third City must have given him an amusing revenge. (It is far funnier than the picture he draws of the Savile Club in *The Revenge for Love*.) Indeed, the languors and nostalgia of clubland hold no more for Pullman than they did for Lewis himself. Which brings us round to the question of just how much—or how little— Pullman may be said to reflect Lewis's own attitudes.

There are two kinds of caricature in Lewis's satire. There are the portraits carefully drawn from life (perhaps most notably, the Finnian Shaws) and there are the composites in which traits and characteristics are drawn from many different sources. The composite characters are much more dangerously deceptive, insofar as they are likely to enrage everyone who recognizes this or that personal quirk in the overall portrayal. Not that the recording of characteristics or shortcomings is necessarily unkind: Lewis was a visual artist who drew what he saw. He was not in business, as artist or writer, to provide flattering likenesses: he chose rather to record distinctive variants, as did a biologist such as Darwin. But not all of his subjects were proud of their variations, and many felt they had been lampooned when they recognized aspects of themselves in any of his more amusing characters. (On the other hand, there were many eager contenders for the honour of having been the prototype of Daniel Boleyn.)

Nor was Lewis himself always quite sure who was uppermost in his mind when he was at work on some of his characters. I was much surprised, for instance, when he objected to my original casting of Ronald Simpson in the part, to be told that Pullman was actually a portrayal of James Joyce! What he meant to say, presumably, was that Joyce had supplied him with one or two of Pullman's characteristics. But to make the point entirely clear to the world, in the second edition of *The Childermass*, Pullman the onetime anglo-catholic becomes a *Roman Catholic*; and in *Monstre Gai* his early education is credited to the Jesuits! Even so, Pullman remains—like Lewis himself—an undoubted product of the English public school. Not quite 'top-drawer', Mannock decides from his shabby clothes: perhaps a schoolmaster, a rather unusual *gelehrter* who had spent some time (no doubt with an ironical bow towards myself!) 'within earshot of the Hallé Orchestra'. To put the matter beyond all doubt (except with Lewis's own supporters) Pullman is now described solemnly as 'the greatest writer' of his time—an authority, among other things, on the Patristic Age. But the dispassionate reader might still be excused for finding in him more of Lewis himself than of James Joyce—neat beard notwithstanding.

This is only partly due to Pullman's fondness for the sort of expensive living which Lewis himself enjoyed whenever he could afford it. Lewis himself would have much relished life in the Phanuel Hotel—with its impeccable cuisine in which his own fondness for good wines and iced *coupes* is reflected. But unlike Pullman, Lewis would never have compromised in order to enjoy it. Even so, Pullman's ideas on life in Third City have a strangely reminiscent ring to them:

> 'Let me compress what I have been saying in the following manner. We—the human kind—here consist of a horde of idiots. In addition to this degraded caricature of man, there are perhaps a few dozen—perhaps a few hundred—men of intelligence. This more intelligent, this more sensitive handful, they are all we need to consider. This knot of real living, thinking, men are all that counts, either as mortal or immortal. There are no intelligent immortals; intelligence is a compensation for our weakness, towered over—and tormented by— a number of huge, stupid immortals, who have no more intelligence than bulldogs, or police constables.'[7]

So might have written the author of The Art of Being Ruled— from the standpoint of genius—if he had found himself in Third City.

Like Lewis himself, in fact, Pullman is an élitist: he despises not only the vacuous idiocy of life in Third City, its masses of cretinous nonentities—he also has a poor opinion of the immortals among whom he finds himself. Still more is this true in the Matapolis of Malign Fiesta. (As Eliot remarked mildly in his broadcast introduction to Monstre Gai, 'I do not share his low opinion of the intelligence of Angels'.) But we are not to deduce from this that Lewis was using Pullman as anything more than an occasional vehicle for the expression of his own opinions. In the same way, he had used the Bailiff in The Childermass and was to use Sammael in *Malign Fiesta*. After all, so Milton had used Sammael—or Satan—in *Paradise Lost*.

As for the shape and tenor of the work, we should be wrong, of course, to regard *The Human Age* as a coherent trilogy, for that it clearly is not. *The Childermass* was a brilliant fragment torn out of the huge corpus once known as *The Man of the World*, which must have been much less coherent still. And it remains a brilliant fragment today. *Monstre Gai* and *Malign Fiesta* do not in any true sense continue the work which *The Childermass* had begun: they begin another work altogether, which *The Trial of Man* might or might not have completed. The characters of the Bailiff and Pullman have changed a great deal in the twenty-five year interim: perhaps only Satterthwaite remains what he has always been. But in the changed post-war world of Third City, Satters remains even more of a misfit than he was in the Camp: he is a figure from the realms of Greyfriars and St Jim's, translated into a world that has gone Comprehensive. It is hardly a world in which one would expect him to find his feet as quickly as he apparently does.

It is only in *Malign Fiesta*, however, that the idea behind the title of *The Human Age* begins to become clear. The Third City of *Monstre Gai* is indeed no more than a staging post on the journey. Reversing the order of the *Divina Commedia*, it is a sort of Purgatorio before we enter the Inferno. It is no more than a place of waiting, in which the mistakes of life on earth are being patched up by an attempt at the creation of a Welfare State. Nominally, the government of the city is in the hands of the Padishah and his company of White Angels (Padíshah was the pronunciation favoured by Lewis) but the governing class is frankly bored and disgusted by its office, and the inhabitants are left very much to themselves. Accordingly, wherever money is being doled out freely and women and liquor are in short supply, organized crime flourishes. The Bailiff is no longer concerned with the selection of entrants to the city as he had been in *The Childermass*: to all intents and purposes the complement of citizens has been made up—it is now the Bailiff's only function to organize and exploit them. This he does in much the way favoured by the late Al Capone: by pandering to their weaknesses. The process is interrupted somewhat by a threatened invasion of the forces of Lucifer (as Sammael is then called) who has designs upon the place for reasons which are not yet elaborated. The resultant blitz provides occasion for the best writing in the novel, and there are hints of atomic warfare on the way. (Even Heaven, we gather subsequently, is not proof against the threat of nuclear fission—much as in *Paradise Lost,* angels can provisionally be blown apart by gunpowder.) Finally, it is his assassination of Hyperides, the philosophic disputant of *The Childermass* who has emerged as a most unlikely Fascist agitator, which precipitates the Bailiff's withdrawal by space-flight to Matapolis—taking Pullman and Satterthwaite along with him as rather unwilling hostages.

So ends *Monstre Gai,* and with the trio's arrival in Matapolis we enter the new world of *Malign Fiesta.* This sinister place, beyond the star Canopus, proves to be the Bailiff's birthplace. It is there that Dis is situated, a politer name for the Inferno, a Punishment Centre where the Bailiff's father had been a respected torturer of the damned, and where his aged mother is still living. There at Matapolis, we are shortly introduced to Lucifer—known locally as the Lord Sammael—before whom even the Bailiff quails.

Sammael, it seems, is a stern judge. He has a hatred and contempt for sinners, and it is his task to punish them. This he does in accordance with the will of God—albeit reluctantly. But his reluctance merely reflects the fact that it is not in his nature to obey: punishment itself he has no qualms in dispensing. And reading *Malign Fiesta,* with its meticulous descriptions of the grisly punishments meted out, one can only wonder whether Lewis himself is not occasionally in secret sympathy with them.

In two instances, there might seem to be a reason for this. Lewis had suffered more than one desperate spell of bad health, and while he was writing *The Human Age* he was undoubtedly a sick man. Rightly or wrongly, I think, he blamed this upon the venereal infection he had contracted during World War I. (A poem was written about the woman responsible for this by Lynette Roberts during the fifties.) And there seems reason to suppose that this fact may well have been behind the appalling fate reserved by Sammael for the sinful Madame Carnot, whom he threw to the ghastly goat-men of Hell to be violated and eaten alive. The first version of this episode was so nauseating that Lewis's wife Froanna, who was typing the script, insisted on toning it down considerably. (The original draft was given to Michael Ayrton, and presumably still exists among his papers.) Sammael's excuse for the savagery of her punishment was that 'she broke the heart of her young husband Gabriel, and, it was believed, infected her third husband with the King's Evil . . . She was', he explains, 'as bad a woman as you could find anywhere.'[8] Despite this assurance, Pullman is still horrified at her terrible end—which proves yet again that deaths occur in Hell, this time for keeps.

There is only one other example of such sadistic thinking in Lewis's work, and it occurs in the same novel. It is his description of the punishment reserved for the German General Officer who is slowly grilled to death before Pullman's eyes in the Punishment Centre of Dis. It is surely significant that Lewis reserved this dreadful retribution for a member of the German military caste. He had fought against it in World War I, and had lived to see civilized Europe all but destroyed by it in World War II. He had himself been accused of acting as an apologist for Nazism in the thirties—unjustly, as I believe.[9] But the fact that he had seen that military caste nurtured and let loose upon the world again by Hitler (whom he had once been misguided enough to hail as a 'Man of Peace') must have been particularly bitter to him. For no one had suffered more than he for the mistake of identifying Nazism with the enlightened authoritarianism whose coming he had cheerfully predicted in *The Art of Being Ruled*. He had been made all too sadly aware that authoritarianism is not necessarily a panacea in itself—that there may be benevolent examples of it, but that there may also be criminally and disastrously bad. And if anything could be blamed for the trials that Lewis had suffered during World War II, it was certainly Hitler's brand of the latter. However barbarous the fate reserved by Sammael and his Dr Hachilah for the German General Officer whose sins during that war 'had startled everyone except the Germans',[10] one cannot help feeling that Lewis must have been of the opinion that it was well deserved.

One may wonder, reading *Malign Fiesta*, whether Sammael does not relish his role of executioner rather more than he suggests. But this he is at pains to deny while discussing his ghastly goat-men with Pullman:

'I really am much less of a brute than I appear. Those animals fill me with horror, they cause me such inexpressible disgust that it is as much as I can do to go near them. But that is physical and visible, nasal and visual; and the Women-Sinners disgust me even more. I realize that that is a little obsession. But what can you expect of an angel!' he laughed. 'The female of your species does really affect me as some people are affected by cats. If I could exterminate them I would. For the rest, I have never relished my job as executioner. As much as possible I have delegated it to others. On principle, I approve of punishing Man just for being Man: but I do not enjoy playing the *bourreau*. However, a century will see the end of all this. Christianity will not last much longer than that.'[11]

In the light of this confession, Sammael's final rejection of his office is perhaps less surprising than it might otherwise have been. For the climax of *Malign Fiesta*, and the fact which gives its title to the whole trilogy, is his decision to defy God, abolish Dis, and virtually destroy the caste of the angels by persuading them to mate with the sinners in Hell. By doing this, he aims to create a new species of *human* angels, or perhaps we should call them angelic mongrels. When this interbreeding has re-populated Hell —and later on, Heaven itself—the human age would have been achieved. God would have been defeated in his plans for the universe, and Sammael could confidently expect to inherit the whole.

This is indeed a bold project—calling for the co-operation of all the women sinners that Sammael can employ. But, as launched by the fiesta which it has been Pullman's task to organize for him, it remains in its first days when the book ends. Indeed, only four months after the fiesta has ended in an angelic orgy, Matapolis is invaded by the hosts of Heaven—expressly to put an end to any such programme. Pullman is removed to stand answerable to the Deity for his willingness to abet the infernal plans, and no Human Age seems likely to emerge in Hell or anywhere else except on earth, where it would seem to belong.

The question is, what was the thinking behind the idea of

The Human Age? What did it symbolize or imply? It might be argued that Lewis was simply concerned with telling a vivid and fantastic tale, and one which would give full play to his imaginative genius. If so, it would be the first time in his life that he had no ulterior message for which the tale provided a convenient vehicle. (The only possible exception to that which one can think of, perhaps, is *Snooty Baronet*—though there is much in that extravaganza which one can usefully ponder.) And it seems unlikely that Lewis of all writers would have devoted such time and trouble to devising a tale which had no underlying message at all.

We have to remember that Lewis intended *The Human Age* to be the last major offering to his public—the work which he had always hoped to write in one form or another. It was written when almost all that he had stood for in his lifetime seemed to have been proved wrong. He had forecast that government by the people was out of date—that it would be replaced by government placed firmly in the hands of the specialist. He had suggested that the many were there to be ruled—that only the few either wanted or were fitted to rule. He had seen authoritarian governments created—apparently along the lines that he had foretold. And with the exception of the Soviet government he had seen them overthrown by the democracies. The civilized world that he had admired for its best achievements had rejected his concept: the age of the so-called Common Man had been ushered in throughout Europe and America. India had been liberated: Africa was soon to be so. His old crony Ezra Pound, who questioned whether all this was a good thing, had been locked up in a madhouse. His other crony, Eliot, who gracefully accepted it all (with private reservations) had been honoured everywhere as the intellectual leader of his time. His rival, James Joyce, was deified and avidly studied at every academic institution in Anglosaxony. It must surely have seemed to Lewis that this was the time when he might be expected to change his ideas, and accept the world as he found it. If you can't beat them, the saying goes—then join them.

Yet it is hard to think of Lewis *joining* anything. He was not likely to become a member of the wedding between Common Man and Common Bureaucrat. To do so would be to turn his back upon all which had made him such a brilliantly *un*common man throughout his life. It would be to encourage the angels to join the masses—to accept an age of unremarkable humanity in which the ideals of the élite would be surrendered to expediency. If the artist could still be regarded as God, it would be to marry him off among his own apes. Such an idea, Lewis suggests, could only have occurred to Man's infernal enemy—and if pushed through successfully, it could only end in chaos.

Although he never said so to me while he was laying out the initial plan for The Human Age, I think some such idea may have been at the back of Lewis's mind. He would show the world what its general trend was really leading towards. As the supreme Anarchist, what would Satan-Sammael do to upset the wiser, authoritarian plans of Deity for an orderly universe? Would he not try to destroy all order—and the values of civilization—by intermixing the nobler ideals of the better with the lower aims and lack of ideals which he found in average mankind? Though Lewis's angels were unused to such intercourse (since the days of Lilith, at least) they might be supposed to retain the rudiments of sexual appetite. Let Pullman stimulate this by making use of the women available for punishment (or enjoyment) and Hell would become a different place. So, ultimately, would Heaven—when once the idea had been taken up by the good angels no less than the bad. (That even good angels were corruptible, the existence of fallen angels proved in itself.) And that such a corruption was already at work among his human contemporaries, Lewis was privately convinced. The Human Age merely reflected the human trend in a more memorable way.

Eliot may not have believed that angels were stupid, but that was merely a matter of personal opinion. Lewis believed that most of the ruling classes were stupid everywhere. And no one could have been more sublimely unconscious than his Padishah of what was going on in Third City—unless it was the British diplomat in Boston in 1776, or the British diplomat in Berlin in 1939. For as Pullman explained to Mannock, 'the wicked Bailiff could not exist without the stupid Padishah'.[12] George Washington could not have existed without King George III and his kind, or Hitler without the kind of Chamberlain and Daladier. In Eliot's Heaven, there would have been no revolt of the angels— yet Christian theology stoutly maintains that there once was.

But whatever the idea behind his plan for marrying off his angels, Lewis ended by realizing that it was not enough in itself. So a Human Age might be inaugurated—but then what? He saw that there must be a sequel in which the idea could be discussed, and the arguments behind it weighed in the balance between Devil and Deity. It was a pity, no doubt, that *The Trial of Man* was never written—though I still doubt whether it could ever have been successful. As Lewis once wrote to me 'God is a big problem', and to write up God as one more character in a novel, as Professor Kenner points out, is no easy task. To judge by the rejected opening chapter of *The Trial of Man* which he prints, Lewis was no longer the man to take the job on when it occurred to him. No Deity can devote himself for very long to the problems of one man, with some two thousand million others currently on the books—to say nothing of a backlog covering anything over five hundred thousand years. Lewis reported Lynette Roberts as believing 'that there could not possibly be a God because of the vast size, remoteness, and number of the stars'.[13] And however many of those stars have inhabitable planets, the concerns of even Pullman, 'the greatest writer of his time', on one of them would seem to be exaggerated—if they were considered by the Deity for some three hundred pages.

There are indeed many faults to be found in *The Human Age* as we have it—which is hardly surprising when we consider the almost superhuman task for a blind man sitting down to write it. Like the *Divina Commedia*, for instance, it is remarkably parochial in tone, finding room for only a handful of characters where we might logically expect to find an almost innumerable array. The concerns of Sammael in Matapolis are themselves parochial: one can hardly imagine him capable of handling anything larger than a local election. Nevertheless, the work is vividly memorable for its better things—of which the character of the Bailiff is easily the first. As Donald Wolfit complained to me, he is never again what he had been in *The Childermass*, but we can no longer think of him without his pooping Venus in Third City or his frightful mother in Matapolis. And if one forgets his role in the universe, and considers him merely as a fictional figure, Sammael himself is fine and impressive. In Lewis's concept, he may represent a satirical fling at democracy's plan for running its own affairs on a non-élitist basis, but we feel that we should know Sammael if ever we met him face to face.

Perhaps one day we shall meet him—ensconced in a leather arm-chair at the Cadogan Club or selecting an iced *coupe* from the trolley in the dining-room of the Phanuel Hotel. If someone rather like Pullman were his guest, I should not really be surprised.

Notes

1. Machine and Puppet: A Comparative View

1 Walter Michel, *Wyndham Lewis: Paintings and Drawings* (London, 1971), p. 97 (cited henceforth as Michel).
2 *Wyndham Lewis on Art*, ed. Walter Michel and C. J. Fox (London, 1969), p. 150 (cited henceforth as WLOA).
3 WLOA, p. 155.
4 WLOA, p. 269.
5 Michel, nos. 587, 596, 554, 589.
6 Michel, nos. 758, 770, 743.
7 Michel, nos. 642, 781.
8 Michel, nos. 566, 435, 436.
9 This character is called Margaret in the beginning of the book and Margot thereafter.
10 Michel, no. 875.
11 *The Revenge for Love* (London, 1937), II. 1.
12 Michel, nos. 646, 845.
13 *The Revenge for Love*, II. 1.
14 Michel, nos. 451, 449, 470 etc.
15 Quoted in Michel, p. 99.
16 Michel, nos. 531, 532.
17 Cf. Michel, no. 344, 'The Pole Jump' (1919); no. 403, 'Lovers with another Figure' (1920); no. 446, 'Abstract Figure Study' (1921). One may note that René's brother-in-law (*Self Condemned*, Chaps. 8, 9) is also a Tyro-figure: 'The Reverend Robert Kerridge was exhibiting proudly his fine *dental* Christianity to a fair-sized audience' (italics mine).
18 *Tarr* (London, 1918), VI. 5.
19 Michel, no. 358.
20 *The Revenge for Love*, V. 2.
21 Michel, no. 884.
22 WLOA, p. 88 ('The London Group').
23 *Self Condemned* (London, 1954), Chap. 16.
24 WLOA, p. 96 (from the 'Note' for the Catalogue of the 1915 Vorticist Exhibition).
25 WLOA, p. 59 ('A Review of Contemporary Art').
26 Michel, no. 524.
27 Michel, no. 893.
28 *Self Condemned*, Chap. 15.
29 *Tarr*, III. 2.
30 Michel, p. 26.
31 Michel, no. 123.
32 Michel, nos. 273, 309, 265.
33 Michel, no. 295.
34 Michel, no. 308.

35 Michel, nos. 125, 170, 1005, 969, 628. The 'Creation Myth' of the 1920s (Michel, no. 658) does not add weight to the argument, but does not detract from it either.
36 Michel, nos. 1011, 1037, 1036, 1048.
37 Michel, nos. 500, 334; I have already cited no. 566 ('Head of a Young Woman') in this general context.
38 Michel, P85, P96.
39 Michel, P28.
40 Michel, P30: see Michel's additional note.

2. Lewis's Letters and Autobiographies

1 *The Letters of Wyndham Lewis*, ed. W. K. Rose (London, 1963), p. 64.
2 *Blasting and Bombardiering* (London, 1967), p. 247.
3 Ibid., p. 1.
4 *Letters*, p. 9.
5 Ibid., p. 33.
6 'The Do-Nothing Mode', *Agenda*, 7–8 (Autumn-Winter 1969–70), 217.
7 Ibid.
8 *Rude Assignment* (London, 1950), p. 113.
9 *Letters*, p. 13.
10 Ibid., p. 14.
11 Ibid., p. 18.
12 Ibid., p. 27.
13 Ibid., p. 39.
14 Ibid., p. 45.
15 Ibid., p. 32.
16 Ibid., p. 33.
17 *Rude Assignment*, p. 109.
18 *Letters*, p. 40.
19 *Rude Assignment*, p. 125.
20 *Blasting and Bombardiering*, p. 36.
21 *Rude Assignment*, p. 124.
22 *Letters*, pp. 49–50.
23 Ibid., p. 50.
24 *Blasting and Bombardiering*, p. 35.
25 *Selected Letters of Ezra Pound*, ed. D. D. Paige (New York, 1971), p. 190.
26 *Letters*, p. 67.
27 *Blasting and Bombardiering*, p. 254.
28 Ibid., p. 58.
29 *Rude Assignment*, p. 122.
30 *Blasting and Bombardiering*, p. 252.
31 Ibid., p. 4.
32 *Letters*, p. 88.
33 *Blasting and Bombardiering*, pp. 152–3.
34 Ibid., p. 186.
35 Ibid., p. 8.
36 Ibid., p. 213.
37 Ibid., p. 215.
38 'Imaginary Letters' No. 1, (*Little Review*, 1917; this edition Glasgow, 1977), p. 5.

39 *Letters*, p. 117.
40 *Blasting and Bombardiering*, p. 104.
41 *Rude Assignment*, p. 53.
42 *Evening Standard*, 28 April 1927; reprinted in *Letters*, p. 168.
43 *Letters*, p. 246.
44 'The Mask of the Enemy', *Sewanee Review*, 80 (Winter 1972), 199.
45 *Letters*, p. 528.
46 'The Critic as Artist' in *The Artist as Critic: Critical Writings of Oscar Wilde*, ed. Richard Ellmann (London, 1970), p. 389.
47 'The Code of a Herdsman' (*Little Review*, 1917; this edition Glasgow, 1977), p. 4.
48 *Letters*, p. 142.
49 *Rude Assignment*, p. 136.
50 *Letters*, p. 239.
51 *Blasting and Bombardiering*, p. 48.
52 *Letters*, p. 238.
53 Ibid., p. 267.
54 Ibid., p. 277.
55 Ibid., p. 298.
56 Ibid., p. 331.
57 Ibid., p. 283.
58 Ibid., p. 303.
59 Ibid., p. 325.
60 Ibid., p. 383.
61 Ibid., p. 306.
62 Ibid., p. 427.
63 Ibid., p. 479.
64 Ibid., p. 384.
65 Ibid., p. 431.
66 Ibid., pp. 491-2.
67 Ibid., p. 551.
68 Ibid., p. 394.
69 Ibid., p. 559.
70 Ibid., p. 548.
71 Ibid., p. 10.
72 Ibid., p. 301.
73 'The Sea-Mists of the Winter', *The Listener*, 10 May 1951; rep. E. W. F. Tomlin, *Wyndham Lewis: An Anthology of his Prose* (London, 1969), pp. 393-7.
74 Ibid., p. 397.
75 *Letters*, p. 567.

3. The Philosophical Influences

1 'The Cornac and his Wife', *The Wild Body* (London, 1927), p. 161.
2 Herbert Read, *Reason and Romanticism* (London, 1926), p. 23.
3 Introduction to *Wyndham Lewis: An Anthology of his Prose* (London, 1969), p. 16, where I call it 'a kind of incandescent quality of vision'.
4 *Time and Western Man* (Boston, 1957), p. 391.
5 *The Lion and the Fox* (London, 1951), p. 36.
6 His true ideal was the art of the 'Classical Orient' as defined by René

Guénon (*Paleface*, p. 255); but Guénon's thesis was that such Classicism was originally the basis of civilization in general. Lewis was studying this great French scholar when his name was hardly known in England.

7 *Tarr* (London, 1928 rev. edition), Part VII, chap. 2.
8 *The Art of Being Ruled* (London, 1926), p. 386.
9 *Time and Western Man*, p. 322.
10 Ibid., p. 21.
11 *The Lion and the Fox*, p. 211.
12 *Time and Western Man*, p. 32.
13 *The Art of Being Ruled*, p. 199.
14 *Time and Western Man*, p. 362.
15 Ibid., p. 113.
16 Ibid., p. 112.
17 *The Art of Being Ruled*, p. 127.
18 Ibid., p. 404.
19 *Blasting and Bombardiering* (London, 1967), p. 113.
20 *Men Without Art* (London, 1934), p. 211.
21 *Paleface* (London, 1929), p. 255.
22 *Time and Western Man*, p. 371.
23 Ibid., p. 380.
24 *The Art of Being Ruled*, pp. 128–9.

4. Lewis and the Patriarchs

1 W. B. Yeats and T. Sturge Moore, *Their Correspondence, 1901–1937*, ed. Ursula Bridge (New York, 1953), p. 115.
2 See Lewis's *Rude Assignment* (London, 1950), p. 116. William Stirling showed Lewis's poem to William Rothenstein. See Rothenstein's *Men and Memories*, ed. Mary Lago (Columbia, 1978), pp. 134–5. Lago's note on Stirling is of interest: 'unemployed Scottish architect, poet, writer on aesthetic theory and the occult. His book, *The Canon: An Exposition of the Pagan Mystery Perpetuated in the Cabala as the Rule of All the Arts* (1897), proposes symbolism of the ground plans of early churches.'
3 *The Letters of Wyndham Lewis*, ed. W. K. Rose (London, 1963), pp. 25, 33.
4 See Donald Davie, 'Ezra Among the Edwardians', *Paideuma*, 5 (Spring-Summer 1976), 3–14.
5 'The Do-Nothing Mode', *Agenda*, 7–8 (Autumn-Winter 1969–70), 216–221.
6 *Rude Assignment*, p. 120.
7 Ibid., p. 119.
8 Quoted in Michael Holroyd, 'Damning and Blasting', *The Listener*, 6 July 1972, p. 9.
9 Lewis, 'History of the Largest Independent Society in England', *Wyndham Lewis on Art*, ed. Walter Michel and C. J. Fox (New York, 1969), p. 91.
10 *Letters*, p. 71.
11 *Rude Assignment*, p. 128.
12 *Wyndham Lewis on Art*, p. 409.
13 Quoted in Holroyd, op. cit., p. 10.
14 *The Demon of Progress in the Arts* (London, 1954), p. 3.
15 Richard Ellmann, *The Identity of Yeats* (New York, 1964), pp. 217–18.

16 *Yeats and Moore*, ed. Bridge, p. 117; *The Letters of W. B. Yeats*, ed. Allen Wade (London, 1954), p. 733.
17 *The Letters of Yeats*, p. 734.
18 Alfred North Whitehead, *Science and the Modern World* (New York, 1948), p. 76.
19 *Time and Western Man* (London, 1927), p. 176.
20 Ibid., p. 169.
21 Bertrand Russell, *Our Knowledge of the External World* (London, 1922), p. 111.
22 *Time and Western Man*, p. 209.
23 W. B. Yeats, *Essays and Introductions* (New York, 1961), p. 401.
24 Ibid., p. 405.
25 Ibid.
26 *The Letters of Yeats*, p. 739.
27 Yeats, *Essays*, p. 409.
28 *Time and Western Man*, p. 172.
29 Ibid., p. 116.
30 *Yeats and Moore*, pp. 122–3.
31 Ibid., p. 121.
32 Ibid., p. 119.
33 *Letters*, p. 293.
34 Ezra Pound, *The Cantos* (New York, 1969), p. 507.
35 Victor Cassidy, ed. 'The Sturge Moore Letters', *Lewisletter*, no. 7 (October 1977), p. 18.
36 'A Sicilian Idyll', in *The Poems of T. Sturge Moore*, iv (London, 1931), 168.
37 Ibid., pp. 175, 184–5.
38 'The Sturge Moore Letters', pp. 8, 14.
39 *Yeats and Moore*, p. 152.
40 Ibid., p. 119.
41 Ibid.
42 'The Sturge Moore Letters', pp. 21, 23.
43 *The Demon of Progress*, p. 32.
44 T. Sturge Moore, 'Gustave Flaubert', in *Art and Life* (London, 1910), pp. 116–17.
45 Yvor Winters, *Uncollected Essays and Reviews*, ed. Francis Murphy (Chicago, 1973), pp. 140, 145. Winters's high opinion of Moore's poetry is shared by few other critics, not even Frederick L. Gwynn, who has written *Sturge Moore and the Life of Art* (London, 1952). Lewis fixes on Moore's limitation even while praising him in *One-Way Song*. In Canto 29, Lewis writes of

> Moore, the sturgeon of the Hampstead Hill,
> Nations of Greeks and Hebrews drives at will
> Across a gothic landscape....

The archaic quality of Moore's biblical and mythological verse is contrasted with that of Yeats's verse:

> The greater Yeats,
> Turning his back on Ossian, relates
> The blasts of more contemporary fates.

Lewis seemed to prefer Moore's prose works, such as the study of Flaubert and the quasi-Platonic dialogue, *The Powers of the Air*.
46 'To Silence', *The Poems of T. Sturge Moore*, iv, 52.
47 *Self Condemned* (London, 1954), pp. 372–3.

23 *Hitler*, p. 65.
24 George Orwell, *Homage to Catalonia* (Boston, 1952), pp. 148–9.
25 Lionel Trilling, 'Introduction' to Orwell, *Homage to Catalonia*, p. xviii.
26 *Count Your Dead: They Are Alive! or A New War in the Making* (London, 1937), p. 196.
27 Ibid., p. 81.
28 As quoted in Kenner, op. cit., p. 80; source is not given.
29 *Left Wings Over Europe*, p. 164: 'that the industrious and ingenious Italian, rather than the lazy, stupid and predatory Ethiopian, should eventually control Abyssinia is surely not such a tragedy.'
30 *The Art of Being Ruled*, p. 381.
31 W. H. Auden, Contribution to *I Believe: The Personal Philosophies of Certain Eminent Men and Women of Our Time*, ed. Clifton Fadiman (New York, 1939), pp. 15–16.
32 *Poetry of the Thirties*, ed. Robin Skelton (Harmondsworth, 1964), p. 41.
33 *The Hitler Cult* (London, 1939), pp. 37, 40.
34 *The Jews, Are They Human?* (London, 1939), p. 8.
35 *Rude Assignment* (London, 1950), p. 209.
36 Kenner, op. cit., p. 85.
37 Martin Seymour-Smith, *Who's Who in Twentieth Century Literature* (New York, 1977), p. 211.

13. Lewis as Travel Writer

1 'The Cosmic Uniform of Peace', *Sewanee Review*, 53 (Autumn 1945), 519.
2 *Filibusters in Barbary* (London, 1932), p. 69.
3 John Holloway, 'Wyndham Lewis: The Massacre and the Innocents', *Hudson Review*, 10 (Summer 1957), 173.
4 *Filibusters in Barbary*, pp. vii–viii.
5 *Blasting and Bombardiering* (London, 1967), pp. 242, 244.
6 Irwin R. Blacker, ed., *The Portable Hakluyt's Voyages* (New York), p. 41.
7 *The Letters of Wyndham Lewis*, ed. W. K. Rose (London, 1963), p. 203.
8 Letter to Lewis from solicitors Soames, Edwards and Jones, 21 December 1933.
9 *Filibusters*, p. 123.
10 'Note of Proceedings before Mr Justice Acton', 23 February 1934, pp. 1–2. See also Bradford Morrow and Bernard Lafourcade, *A Bibliography of the Writings of Wyndham Lewis* (Santa Barbara, California, 1978), p. 67.
11 Some of these come to us through the men of Aeropostale, and Lewis retails them hilariously in his book.
12 *Filibusters*, pp. 23–4.
13 Ibid., p. 189.
14 Quoted in Alan Scham, *Lyautey in Morocco* (Berkeley, 1970), p. 29.
15 For a different analysis, see Gavin Maxwell, *Lords of the Atlas* (London, 1966), p. 154.
16 *Filibusters*, p. 77.
17 Ibid., p. 151.
18 *Lyautey in Morocco*, p. 6.
19 *Filibusters*, p. 15.

48 *Rude Assignment*, p. 181.
49 *Self Condemned*, p. 406.
50 'Response to Rimbaud's Later Manner', in *The Oxford Book of Modern Verse*, ed. W. B. Yeats (New York, 1936), p. 136.
51 *The Revenge for Love* (London, 1952), pp. 304–5.
52 'Nature', *The Poems of T. Sturge Moore*, iv, 58.

5. Lewis's Prose Style

1 *Enemy of the Stars* (London, 1932), pp. 15–16.
2 *Rude Assignment* (London, 1950), p. 128.
3 *Tarr* (London, 1918), I. 4.
4 *The Childermass* (London, 1956), p. 41.

6. The Taming of the Wild Body

1 *Rude Assignment* (London, 1950), p. 113.
2 William Pritchard, *Wyndham Lewis* (New York, 1968), p. 19.
3 *Rude Assignment*, p. 118.
4 This list was published for the first time in *Enemy News*, no. 10, May 1979.
5 See Bradford Morrow and Bernard Lafourcade, *A Bibliography of the Writings of Wyndham Lewis* (Santa Barbara, California, 1978).
6 This text is to be published for the first time by L'Age d'Homme (Lausanne) in a critical edition of *The Wild Body*.
7 'Anyway get your writing done, and then you can see' (from a letter sent to Brittany by the author's mother, dated 20 September 1908, Cornell University).
8 'The Vita of Wyndham Lewis', dated 1949 (Cornell University).
9 *Rude Assignment*, p. 117.
10 Hugh Kenner, *Wyndham Lewis* (Norfolk, Conn., 1954), pp. 12–13.
11 *Beginnings* (London, 1935), p. 100.
12 Hugh Kenner, *Wyndham Lewis*, pp. 1–4.
13 *L'Image Fascinante et le Surréel* (Paris, 1965), p. 267.
14 *Rude Assignment*, pp. 117–18.
15 Ibid., p. 117 and p. 118.
16 See for instance, Joyce Carol Oates's commentary in *The Hostile Sun* (Los Angeles, 1974), pp. 11–14.
17 *Rude Assignment*, p. 118.
18 Ibid.
19 *Finishing Touches* (London, 1964), p. 116.
20 We note: 'My mother's and father's principal way of spending their time at the period of my birth was the same as mine now: my mother painting pictures of the farmhouse where we lived, my father writing books inside it... For a person like myself to both write and paint is being bi-lingual' ('The Vita of Wyndham Lewis'). 'The "short story" was the crystallization of what I had to keep out of my consciousness while painting'; 'Beginning with pen and brush, the penman and the painter are apt to clash; but in my case this did not occur, when at a very early age these two personalities came on the scene' (*Beginnings*, p. 101 and p. 91).
21 *Sartre Par Lui-Même* (Paris, 1955), pp. 4–9.

22 Marthe Robert, *Roman des Origines et Origines du Roman* (Paris, 1972).
23 Hugh Kenner, *Wyndham Lewis*, pp. 88–92. Kenner speaks of 'a verbal impasto'.
24 *Rude Assignment*, p. 105.

8. *Enemy of the Stars*

1 Omar S. Pound and Philip Grover, *Wyndham Lewis: A Descriptive Bibliography* (Folkestone, 1978), pp. 32–3.
2 Wyndham Lewis, *Enemy of the Stars* (London, 1932), p. 5. All subsequent quotations from this work are from this edition.
3 *Enemy of the Stars*, p. 8. Some additional, minor variations not conveyed by the italics are the lack of initial capitals for 'Will' and 'Universe', the absence of parentheses around 'drinking heavy radiance', and a comma instead of a dash after 'blatant light'. As previously mentioned, the *Blast* text is in the present tense.
4 The 's' prefix of the name seems to be equivalent to the negating initial 's' in Italian. Hanp has previously accused Arghol of 'foxing' (p. 26) and on one occasion calls him 'Doctor Fox' (p. 28).

9. *Tarr*: A Nietzschean Novel

1 Ezra Pound, 'Tarr', *The Literary Essays of Ezra Pound*, ed. T. S. Eliot (New York, 1954), p. 425.
2 See Hugh Kenner, *Wyndham Lewis* (Norfolk, Conn., 1954), pp. 28–58; William Pritchard, *Wyndham Lewis* (New York, 1968), pp. 28–48; Timothy Materer, *Wyndham Lewis the Novelist* (Detroit, 1976), pp. 52–67.
3 Friedrich Nietzsche, *The Genealogy of Morals*, trans. Walter Kaufmann (New York, 1969), p. 95.
4 Ibid., pp. 121–5.
5 Ibid., pp. 143–5.
6 Nietzsche, *The Gay Science*, trans. Walter Kaufmann (New York, 1974), pp. 187–8.
7 Ibid., pp. 191–2.
8 Ibid., pp. 232–3.
9 Ibid., p. 117.
10 Ibid., pp. 267–9.
11 *Rude Assignment* (London, 1950), p. 120.
12 *Tarr*, Jubilee Reprint of 1918 edition (New York, 1973), p. 17.

10. A Reading of *The Childermass*

1 Dedication to Lord Carlow in a copy of the first edition of *The Revenge for Love* (1937), dated 1939, in the Carlow Collection, Poetry Room, Lockwood Memorial Library, University of Buffalo.
2 Northrop Frye, *Anatomy of Criticism* (Princeton, 1957), p. 309.
3 Hugh Kenner, *Wyndham Lewis* (Norfolk, Conn., 1954), p. 97.
4 *The Human Age*, Book One: *The Childermass* (London, 1956), p. 97. All references are to this edition, which is more accessible than the first

edition: *The Childermass: Section I* (London, 1928). The 1956 editi slightly revised. Lewis intended the 'infant-choruses' to be killed b gladiators (or haiduks) in a massacre of the innocents, but this pla not carried out. The title does not, therefore, describe the book' tents.
5 Fredric Jameson, 'Wyndham Lewis as Futurist', *Hudson Review*, 26 mer 1973), 325.
6 'Enemy of the Stars' (1914 version), *Collected Poems and Plays*, ed Munton (Manchester, 1979), p. 106.
7 *The Art of Being Ruled* (London, 1926), p. 129.
8 George Sorel, *The Illusions of Progress*, trans. J. and C. Stanley (Be 1969), p. 71.
9 'Essay on the Objective of Plastic Art in Our Time', *Tyro* 2 (1922), p
10 'Bestre', *Tyro* 2 (1922), p. 55.
11 'Essay on the Objective of Plastic Art in Our Time', p. 32.
12 Ibid., p. 26.
13 Dust-jacket description of *The Childermass*, written by Lewis for th edition. The original typescript is in the Wyndham Lewis Col Cornell University.

12. On Lewis's Politics

1 Hugh Kenner, *Wyndham Lewis* (Norfolk, Conn., 1954), p. 82.
2 Ibid., p. 83.
3 Ibid.
4 *Hitler* (London, 1931), p. 52.
5 Ibid., p. 34.
6 Ibid., p. 85.
7 Kenner, op. cit., p. 130.
8 Peter Dale, 'The Revenge For Love', *Agenda*, 7–8 (Autumn-Wint 70), 71.
9 Frank Swinnerton, *The Georgian Literary Scene: A Panorama* 1938), p. 476.
10 Kenner, op. cit., p. 132.
11 Marvin Mudrick, 'The Double-Artist and the Injured Party', *She* 4 (Summer-Autumn 1953), 59.
12 D. G. Bridson, *The Filibuster: A Study of the Political Ideas of W Lewis* (London, 1972), p. 108.
13 Ibid., p. 161.
14 Ibid., p. 103.
15 Ezra Pound, a private letter, quoted in 'On Wyndham Lewis', *She* 4 (Summer-Autumn, 1953), 17.
16 Kenner, op. cit., p. 49.
17 *The Art of Being Ruled* (London, 1926), p. 140.
18 Geoffrey Wagner, *Wyndham Lewis: A Portrait of the Artist* (New Haven, 1957), p. 72n.
19 *The Ideal Giant* (London: *The Little Review*, 1917), p. 36.
20 *The Art of Being Ruled*, p. 381.
21 *Left Wings Over Europe: Or, How to Make a War About Nothin* 1936), p. 294.
22 *Blasting and Bombardiering* (Berkeley, 1957), p. 108.

20 Ibid., p. 138.
21 *Rude Assignment* (London, 1950), p. 117.
22 G. W. Stonier, 'Air Raid', *New Statesman and Nation*, 4 (13 August 1932), 180.
23 *Filibusters*, p. 186.
24 Ibid., p. 163.
25 Ibid., p. 205.
26 Ibid., p. 95.
27 Lewis Jacobs, *The Rise of the American Film* (New York, 1969), p. 380. This book has a preface by Lewis's friend, Iris Barry.
28 *Collected Poems and Plays*, ed. Alan Munton (Manchester, 1979), p. 136. The quotation is from the play *The Ideal Giant*, first published in 1917.
29 Charles Olson, *Call Me Ishmael* (New York, 1947), p. 114. *Call Me Ishmael* bears rather the same relation to Olson's overall work as, in Lewis's case, did *The Lion and the Fox*, a copy of which Olson owned and annotated.
30 *Filibusters*, p. 229.
31 Ibid., p. 227.
32 Viva King, *The Weeping and the Laughter* (London, 1976), p. 88. The Orlebar portrait was done for Lewis's portfolio *Thirty Personalities and a Self-Portrait* (1932) and has been widely reproduced since.
33 *Filibusters*, p. 225. Saint-Exupéry's career is amply set out in Curtis Cate, *Antoine de Saint-Exupéry: His Life and Times* (London, 1970).
34 'What Are the Berbers?', *Bookman*, 85 (December 1933), 186.
35 See, for instance, Samir Amin, *The Maghreb in the Modern World: Algeria, Tunisia, Morocco* (Penguin Books, 1970), pp. 91–2, and Jamil M. Abun Nasr, *A History of the Maghrib* (Cambridge, 1971), p. 358.
36 'The Kasbahs of the Atlas', in *Wyndham Lewis on Art*, ed. Walter Michel and C. J. Fox (London, 1969), p. 261.
37 Ibid., p. 260.
38 *Filibusters*, p. 71.
39 Ibid., pp. 86–7.
40 Elias Canetti, *The Voices of Marrakesh* (London, 1978), p. 90.
41 Most of Lewis's Moroccan drawings are reproduced in Walter Michel, *Wyndham Lewis: Paintings and Drawings* (London, 1971). Misery was a subject congenial to George Orwell, and for his treatment of Morocco, in grim contrast to that of the ebullient Lewis, see 'Marrakech', in *England Your England and Other Essays* (London, 1953), pp. 143–50.
42 'Beginnings', in *Wyndham Lewis on Art*, p. 295.
43 Michel, *Wyndham Lewis*, pp. 112–13.
44 'Beginnings', *Wyndham Lewis on Art*, p. 291.

14. *Snooty Baronet*: Satire and Censorship

1 Julian Symons gives the figures in his article, 'The Thirties Novels', *Agenda*, 7–8 (Autumn-Winter 1969–70), 38. *Snooty Baronet* sold 2791 copies.
2 Hugh Kenner, *Wyndham Lewis* (Norfolk, Conn., 1954), pp. 107–13; William Pritchard, *Wyndham Lewis* (New York, 1968), pp. 108–15; Robert T. Chapman, *Wyndham Lewis: Fictions and Satires* (London, 1973), pp. 109–16; Timothy Materer, *Wyndham Lewis the Novelist* (Detroit, 1976), pp. 100–11.
3 Julian Symons is a notable exception. His article, 'The Thirties Novels',

describes Lewis's problems with Cassell. An excellent, unpublished Ph.D. thesis deals at length with Lewis's relations with Cassell: Linda Sandler, 'The Revenge for Love by Wyndham Lewis: Editorial, Genetic and Interpretive Studies', University of Toronto 1974. As the title indicates, the focus is on The Revenge for Love, but there is a discussion of Snooty Baronet.

4 These and other details are to be found in the correspondence between Lewis and the Flowers in the Lewis Collection at Cornell University.
5 Lewis to Newman Flower, n.d. [1932]. In this letter (typed copy), Lewis complains of Cassell's handling of Snooty Baronet after its publication, and outlines the history of his relation with the firm. Notes 31 and 32 refer to the same letter.
6 The Letters of Wyndham Lewis, ed. W. K. Rose (London, 1963), p. 203.
7 Ibid., p. 203.
8 Grayson to Lewis, n.d., Lewis Collection, Cornell.
9 Lewis to Grayson, Lewis Collection, Cornell.
10 Lewis Collection, Cornell.
11 Lewis Collection, Cornell.
12 Snooty Baronet (London, 1932), p. 58. All subsequent references in the text are to this edition.
13 Rupert Grayson, Stand Fast, The Holy Ghost (London, 1973).
14 Ibid., p. 133.
15 Lewis to Oswald Hickson, Collier and Co., 27 January 1938, Lewis Collection, Cornell.
16 Letters, p. 198.
17 Campbell to Lewis, n.d. [1932], Lewis Collection, Cornell.
18 Campbell to Lewis, n.d. [1929], Lewis Collection, Cornell.
19 Campbell to Lewis, n.d. [1932], Lewis Collection, Cornell. The letter is marked 'Received Dec. 2'. It is in this letter that Campbell says 'Snooty was grand'.
20 Roy Campbell, Taurine Provence (London, 1932), p. 50. Subsequent references in the text are to this edition.
21 Letters, p. 204.
22 Desmond Flower to Lewis, 25 February 1932 and 4 April 1932, Lewis Collection, Cornell.
23 Letters, p. 205.
24 Ibid., p. 206.
25 Ibid., p. 205.
26 Campbell published a volume of poetry called Mithraic Emblems in 1936. It opens with a short-sonnet sequence, 'Mithraic Frieze', which elaborates his Mithraic interests and symbols. Some of the poems in 'Mithraic Frieze' appeared in the New Statesman in 1933. In The Georgiad, Campbell mentions Lewis's attack on Lawrence (in Paleface), and uses Mithraic terms: 'Fit game for Lewis' toreadoring skill / And worthy such a Mithras, if you will' The Georgiad (London, 1931), p. 24.
27 Letters, p. 206n. See note 19.
28 Time and Western Man (London, 1927), p. 348.
29 No Quarter, p. 3, Lewis Collection, Cornell. All subsequent references in the text are to this typescript.
30 Lewis to Newman Flower, 13 April 1932, Lewis Collection, Cornell.
31 Lewis to Newman Flower, n.d. [1932], Lewis Collection, Cornell.
32 Ibid.

33 For a discussion of the delays, and of the alterations in the text, see Linda Sandler, op. cit.

34 Newman Flower wrote to Lewis on 25 May 1936 saying that although Lewis had been co-operating in taking certain things out of the book, it was still wrong for Cassell's. He asks if Lewis would agree to Cassell disposing of the book to another publisher (Lewis Collection, Cornell). Lewis did not agree (Lewis to Flower, 30 September 1936, Lewis Collection, Cornell).

15. Literary Criticism as Satire

1 *Time and Western Man* (London, 1927), p. 77.
2 Ibid., p. 78.
3 *Men Without Art* (London, 1934), p. 300.
4 Ibid., pp. 288–9.
5 Ibid., p. 303.
6 Ibid., p. 45.
7 Virginia Woolf, *A Writer's Diary*, ed. Leonard Woolf (New York, 1953), p. 221.
8 *Men Without Art*, pp. 159–60.

17. Self Condemned

1 T. S. Eliot, 'A Note on *Monstre Gai*', *Hudson Review*, 7 (1955), 524. See W. K. Rose's note in *Letters* (London, 1963), p. 263: The novel evokes 'the experience, not as it was but as it felt'; and Hugh Kenner's Introduction to *Self Condemned* (Chicago, 1965), p. xii: 'This is expressionist fiction, relieving the author's memory and gratifying his taste for fantasy, at the same time as it delineates René Harding's hell.'
2 *Self Condemned*, pp. 162, 211, 397.
3 *The Vulgar Streak* (New York, 1973), p. 217; and *Self Condemned*, pp. 105, 138, 401.
4 *The Art of Being Ruled* (London, 1926), p. 35; and *Self Condemned*, pp. 188, 341.
5 *Blast 2*, p. 42; and letter from Wyndham Lewis to Sir Nicholas Waterhouse, 13 January 1943, Cornell University.
6 Hugh MacDiarmid, *In Memoriam, James Joyce* (Glasgow, 1955), pp. 136, 141, paid tribute to Lewis by mentioning Furber and quoting from *The Wild Body* (New York, 1928), pp. 234–5:
> Mr. Furber, the Canadian dilettante,
> And all Yahoos and *intellectuels-flics*. . . .
> ('Larvae, hallucinated automata, bobbins,
> Savage robots, appropriate dummies,
> The fascinating imbecility of the creaking men-machines,
> Set in a pattern as circumscribed and complete
> As a theory of Euclid—essays in a new human mathematic.')
7 Letter from Wyndham Lewis to Michael Ayrton, 29 January 1954, in the possession of Elizabeth Ayrton; *Self Condemned*, pp. 203, 290; and Dante, *The Divine Comedy: Inferno*, trans. Dorothy Sayers (Harmondsworth,

1949), pp. 271–2. See the Dantean image on p. 185: 'Your face would be wet with tears which would freeze upon the face.'

8 *Self Condemned*, pp. 360, 379; and C. J. Fox's interview with Anne Wyndham Lewis, 25 June 1977. The Cornell manuscript contains a variant ending of *Self Condemned* in which the Hardings return to England and Hester, who cannot bear to see René treated so harshly by English society, commits suicide.

9 *The Revenge for Love* (Harmondsworth, 1972), p. 70; and *Self Condemned*, p. 391. The death of Hester is consistent with the violent deaths that conclude all of Lewis's fiction. In *Enemy of the Stars* Hanp stabs Arghol and leaps into a canal; in *Tarr* Kreisler kills Soltyk and hangs himself; in *The Apes of God* the decrepit Lady Fredigonde proposes marriage and then dies in the arms of Zagreus; in *Snooty Baronet* Kell-Imrie shoots Humph while in the Persian desert; in *The Roaring Queen* Donald Butterboy is found dead in bed, with bullet wounds in several parts of his body; in *The Revenge for Love* Victor and Margot fall over a cliff in a storm; in *The Vulgar Streak* Penhale hangs himself; and in *The Red Priest* Father Card accidentally kills his curate with a punch and (in a sardonic allusion to Canada) dies among the Eskimos.

10 For a thorough discussion of the Canadian background, see my book *The Enemy: A Biography of Wyndham Lewis* (London: Routledge, 1980).

18. The Human Age in Retrospect

1 In the Wyndham Lewis Special Issue of *Agenda*, 7–8 (Autumn-Winter 1969–70) and in *Prospero and Ariel, the rise and fall of radio: a personal recollection* by D. G. Bridson (London, 1971).

2 *The Letters of Wyndham Lewis*, ed. W. K. Rose (London, 1963), p. 540.

3 *Malign Fiesta* (London, 1966). With an appendix consisting of a rejected first chapter of *The Trial of Man* (wrongly called a synopsis) and an essay on *The Trial of Man* by Hugh Kenner.

4 *The Childermass: Section I* (London, 1928), p. 7.

5 *The Human Age, Book Two: Monstre Gai, Book Three: Malign Fiesta* (London, 1955), p. 17.

6 Ibid., p. 232.

7 Ibid., p. 166.

8 Ibid., p. 373.

9 See D. G. Bridson, *The Filibuster: A Study of the Political Ideas of Wyndham Lewis* (London, 1972).

10 *The Human Age*, p. 418.

11 Ibid., p. 377.

12 Ibid., p. 167.

13 *Letters*, p. 502.

Notes on Contributors

Douglas Geoffrey Bridson, after writing poetry and criticism, joined the staff of the B.B.C. in 1935, where he spent the next thirty-four years as a script-writer and producer. Among the eight hundred broadcasts he worked on were the dramatizations of *The Human Age*, *Tarr* and *The Revenge for Love* by Wyndham Lewis and a series of *Conversations* with Ezra Pound and other leading literary figures. He is the author of *Prospero and Ariel: The Rise and Fall of Radio*, *The Filibuster: A Study of the Political Ideas of Wyndham Lewis*, two books of poems and verse plays for radio, and *The Quest of Gilgamesh*.

William M. Chace, Associate Professor of English at Stanford University in California, is the author of *The Political Identities of Ezra Pound and T. S. Eliot* (1973) and *Lionel Trilling: Criticism and Politics* (1979). He edited *James Joyce: A Collection of Critical Essays* (1973), and has contributed essays to *American Quarterly*, *Mosaic*, *Novel*, *Contemporary Literature* and *The American Scholar*.

Robert Chapman teaches English at Nene College, Northampton. He is the author of several articles on twentieth-century literature and of *Wyndham Lewis: Fictions and Satires* (Vision Press, 1973). He co-edited (with C. J. Fox) *Unlucky for Pringle* (Vision Press, 1973).

Alistair Davies is a Lecturer in English in the School of English and American Studies at the University of Sussex. He is at present preparing a study of the work of Wyndham Lewis, with particular emphasis upon his relation to European ideas and literature.

Paul Edwards is a graduate of Jesus College, Cambridge, where he read English. In 1975 his M.A. dissertation on 'The Fiction of Wyndham Lewis from *Tarr* to *The Human Age*' won the Constance Naden Prize at the University of Birmingham. Since then he has worked on a Ph.D. thesis on Lewis's literary criticism at Royal Holloway College, London. He has contributed to the *Cambridge Review*, *PN Review* and *Enemy News*. He now teaches English as a second language as a member of an Industrial Language Unit in the West Midlands.

Wendy Stallard Flory received her B.A. from Bedford College, University of London and her Ph.D. from the University of Texas at Austin. She has taught at Rutgers University since 1970. Her critical work, A *Record of Struggle: Ezra Pound and The Cantos*, will be published in 1980 by Yale University Press.

C. J. Fox was editor, with Walter Michel, of *Wyndham Lewis on Art* (Thames and Hudson, 1971) and, with Robert T. Chapman, of a collection of short fiction by Lewis, *Unlucky for Pringle* (Vision Press, 1973). He also edited *Enemy Salvoes*, a selection of Lewis's literary criticism (Vision Press, 1976). He edits *Enemy News*, newsletter of the Wyndham Lewis Society, and has published articles on David Jones and Karl Kraus. A Canadian, he worked as a correspondent in London, Paris and Brussels for the Canadian Press news agency and now is a senior editor in London with Reuters.

John Holloway grew up in London, went to Oxford in 1938, served in the army during the Second World War, and subsequently taught Philosophy at Oxford, and English Literature at Oxford, Aberdeen, Athens (where he was seconded, 1961–3) and Cambridge, where he was, from 1954, successively Lecturer, Reader, and Professor of Modern English from 1972. He has published various critical works, has edited Shelley and Dickens, and (with his wife) nineteenth-century street ballads, and is the author of several volumes of verse of which the latest is *Planet of Winds* (1977).

Hugh Kenner, Professor of English at Johns Hopkins University, has written Introductions to *Self Condemned*, *Malign Fiesta*, *Wyndham Lewis: Paintings and Drawings* and the Morrow-Lafourcade bibliography as well as influential books on Lewis, Pound, Eliot, Joyce and Beckett. His major work is *The Pound Era*.

Bernard Lafourcade, a lecturer in English Literature at the University of Savoy in Chambéry, is co-author of *A Bibliography of the Writings of Wyndham Lewis*. Besides a number of articles on Lewis, he has translated *Cantleman's Spring-Mate* and *Tarr* (Paris, 1968, 1970), *The Revenge for Love*, *The Wild Body* and an anthology of Lewis's writings on French artists and writers (to be published by L'Age d'Homme, Lausanne).

Timothy Materer is Professor of English at the University of

Missouri-Colombia, where he teaches courses in modern English literature and science fiction. He received his Ph.D. in English and Humanities from Stanford University in 1968. He has written two books, *Wyndham Lewis the Novelist* (Wayne State University Press, 1976) and *Vortex: Pound, Eliot, and Lewis* (Cornell University Press, 1979), and is presently editing a *Pound/Lewis* volume for New Directions Books.

Jeffrey Meyers, who earned his doctorate at Berkeley, has taught in Japan, at UCLA and at Tufts University. In the early 1970s he was a professional writer in London and Málaga, and is now Professor of English at the University of Colorado. He has won fellowships from the American Council of Learned Societies, the Fulbright Program, the Huntington Library and the Guggenheim Foundation. He is the author of fourteen books on modern literature including several works on T. E. Lawrence and George Orwell, biographies of Katherine Mansfield and Wyndham Lewis, *Fiction and the Colonial Experience, Painting and the Novel, A Fever at the Core, Married to Genius* and *Homosexuality and Literature*. His books have been published in India, and translated into French, Italian and Danish.

Marshall McLuhan, who has taught at the University of Wisconsin, St Louis University and Assumption College, is now Professor of English and Director of the Centre for Culture and Technology at the University of Toronto. His books include: *Understanding Media, The Mechanical Bride, The Gutenberg Galaxy* and *Counterblast*.

Alan Munton is Senior Lecturer in English at the College of St Mark and St John, Plymouth, and was formerly lecturer in English at Reading University. He has edited Wyndham Lewis's *Collected Poems and Plays* (Carcanet Press and Persea Books, 1979), and wrote his Cambridge Ph.D. thesis on Lewis. 'The Politics of Wyndham Lewis' appeared in *Poetry Nation Review* (1976), and he has contributed a number of articles and reviews to the *Lewisletter* (now *Enemy News*). He edited the eightieth birthday tribute for Edgell Rickword in *Poetry Nation Review* (1979), and with Alan Young has compiled *Seven Writers of the English Left: A Bibliography of Literature and Politics 1916–1978* (Garland).

Valerie Parker received her B.A. from Cambridge University and M.A. from Tufts University. She has taught English literature in high school and college, and English as a Foreign Language to Italians and Vietnamese. She is the co-outhor of *George Orwell: An Annotated Bibliography of Criticism* (1977).

William H. Pritchard is the author of two books on Wyndham Lewis, of *Seeing Through Everything: English Writers, 1918–1940* and of the forthcoming *Lives of the Modern Poets*. He teaches English at Amherst College in Massachusetts, and is a member of the editorial board of *Hudson Review*.

Rowland Smith was born in Johannesburg and educated in South Africa and at Oxford. Since 1967 he has lived in Canada. He taught at the University of the Witwatersrand in Johannesburg, where he was assistant editor of *English Studies in Africa*, before moving to Nova Scotia. He is chairman of the English Department at Dalhousie University in Halifax, Nova Scotia and has been Director of the Centre for African Studies. In addition to many articles on modern literature, his publications include *Lyric and Polemic: The Literary Personality of Roy Campbell* (1972) and (ed.) *Exile and Tradition: Studies in African and Caribbean Literature* (1976).

E. W. F. Tomlin has written a number of books on philosophical and literary subjects, and he has contributed to such journals as *The Criterion*, *Scrutiny*, the *Times Literary Supplement*, *The Spectator*, *The Economist*, as well as to many foreign reviews. He has held professorships in the United States and in France. For public services he was awarded the C.B.E. in 1965, and he is a Fellow of the Royal Society of Literature. His essay *Wyndham Lewis* (1954, Longmans for the British Council) enjoyed a wide circulation, and his *Wyndham Lewis: An Anthology of his Prose* (1969, Methuen) was the first collection of its kind. He was a friend of Lewis for many years.

Index